Rhythm and Resistance

TEACHING POETRY FOR SOCIAL JUSTICE

EDITED BY LINDA CHRISTENSEN AND DYAN WATSON

A RETHINKING SCHOOLS PUBLICATION

Rhythm and Resistance:
Teaching Poetry for Social Justice

Edited by Linda Christensen and Dyan Watson

Rethinking Schools Ltd. is a nonprofit publisher and advocacy organization dedicated to sustaining and strengthening public education through social justice teaching and education activism. Our magazine, books, and other resources promote equity and racial justice in the classroom. We encourage grassroots efforts in our schools and communities to enhance the learning and well-being of our children, and to build broad democratic movements for social and environmental justice.

To request additional copies of this book and/or a catalog of other publications, or to subscribe to *Rethinking Schools* magazine, contact:

Rethinking Schools
6737 W. Washington St.
Suite 3249
Milwaukee, WI 53214
800-669-4192
www.rethinkingschools.org
© 2015 Rethinking Schools Ltd.

First Edition

Production editor: Elizabeth Barbian
Cover and book design: Nancy Zucker
Cover illustration: Erik Ruin
Proofreading: Lawrence Sanfilippo
Indexing: Marilyn Flaig
Business Manager: Mike Trokan
Director of Operations and Development: Valerie Warren

Library of Congress Control Number: 2015936783

Rhythm and Resistance
Teaching poetry for social justice

Most people understand creating a poetry book with the word rhythm in its title, but resistance? Some folks might think we mean students resisting poetry, but we don't. Students resist when poetry rustles in dusty tomes, when they are asked to bow before sacred texts, and memorize terms and spit them back on multiple-choice exams. But when students dive headlong into writing poetry, when they share the living, beating heart of their own words, when they hear the pulse of joy and rage from their classmates, they are hooked.

The opening chapters of *Rhythm and Resistance* demonstrate how poetry can build classroom community and develop students' confidence in their writing. In order for students to feel like they belong, they have to feel both visible and valued. As Alejandro, one of Linda's former students wrote, "It wasn't until we began to write poetry that I started to feel comfortable with writing. Poetry provided me the freedom to start in the middle of my thoughts and finish wherever I wanted. It was circular and allowed me to express myself. After I nervously read a poem in front of the whole school, I finally understood the power and influence of words. The compliments that I received from other students also challenged my definition of what I believed was the only way to get respect."

For us, the resistance in the title means defiance. We encourage teachers to resist making essays the pinnacle of all writing. Yes, essay writing is important and necessary and can be exciting, but the essay is only one genre of writing. Focusing almost exclusively on essay, as many districts encourage teachers to do, limits student ability to write with passion—and skill—across the genres. Even if the goal is to improve essay writing, we need to teach narrative and poetry. They provide the tools—story, sentence cadence, active verbs—that move students to write passionate persuasive/argumentative essays about issues in the world that trouble them.

We also encourage resistance to the narrowing of curriculum to serve the job market or college; we resist the focus of "drilling down" on facts and on what's testable. Certainly, students should leave school prepared to enter the real world—the real world where hunger and poverty exist alongside immense profits snuffing out opportunities for family-wage jobs, the real world where wars continue year after year, where governments promise glory to soldiers, but return broken humans. Part of an education for the "real world" must teach empathy, must call attention to policies and actions that harm society's most vulnerable.

Rhythm and Resistance encourages students to reflect on their own lives as well as the lives of others who people newspapers, literature, and history. We want them to cheer the triumph of Celie at the dinner scene in Alice Walker's *The Color Purple* or to care about Central American children as they brave "The Beast," or "The Death Train" as it is called by these migrants searching for parents and hope. Through poetry, young people can breathe life into the voices of those who usually don't find ways into classrooms or textbooks, including their own. This kind of education prepares them to meet the real world with a sense of humanity.

And by resistance, we also mean teaching students to talk back to injustice. When we open our classrooms for students to discuss contemporary issues, we encourage commitment to active engagement as citizens of the world by introducing them to poets like Martín Espada and Patricia Smith, Paul Flores and William Stafford, Katharine Johnson and Renée Watson, Lucille Clifton and Lawson Fusao Inada. We build a culture of conscience by offering students both a context and a vehicle for standing up and talking back when they witness injustice, encouraging them to add their voices to the choir of people who link arms and march in solidarity for a better world. Whether they recite their poetry on a stage framed by dusty blue curtains, as Alejandro did, or a makeshift bandstand at a protest in the park against budget cuts or police brutality, students need opportunities to voice their outrage, to spill their odes and hymns, sonnets and sonatas about the ways society needs to change.

As June Jordan wrote in *June Jordan's Poetry for the People: A Revolutionary Blueprint*:

> Poetry is a political action undertaken for the sake of information, the faith, the exorcism, and the lyrical invention, that telling the truth makes possible. Poetry means taking control of the language of your life. Good poems can interdict a suicide, rescue a love affair, and build a revolution in which speaking and listening to somebody becomes the first and last purpose to every social encounter. I would hope that folks throughout the U.S.A. would consider the creation of poems as a foundation for true community: a fearless democratic society.

Our title is an invitation—asking teachers to join in and resist along with us, to help build this "fearless democratic society" that our students deserve.

Why Poetry? Why Now?
by Linda Christensen

You ask, "Why a book on poetry? Why now?"

Because we stand at the brink of public
education's demise;
because funds from billionaires
control the mouths of bureaucrats,
who have sold students, teachers,
and their families for a pittance;

because curriculum slanted to serve the "job market"
carves away history and humanity,
poetry and narrative,
student lives and teacher art;

because teaching students to write an essay
without teaching them to write
narratives and poetry is like
teaching someone to swim
using only one arm;

because poets are truth tellers and lie breakers
wordsmiths and visionaries
who sling metaphors in classrooms,
in the narrow slices of school hallways,
on the bricks of public courtyards,
and cafés with blinking neon signs
without laying out a dime to corporations;

because new poets are rising up,
pressing poems against windows on Wall Street,
spilling odes down the spines of textbooks,
posting protest hymns on telephone poles,
bubbling lyrics on the pages of tests
designed to confine their imaginations;

because poems hover under the breath
of the boy in a baseball cap,
the girl with a ring in her nose,
the boy with his mom's name inked on his neck,
and the silent ones in the back:
she's the next Lucille Clifton
and he sounds like Roque Dalton, saying:

"poetry, like bread,
is for everyone."

Acknowledgements

We owe a debt to the many poets, teachers, and students whose work inspired ours—Daniel Beaty, Lucille Clifton, Kelly Norman Ellis, Martín Espada, Paul Flores, Myrlin Hepworth, Langston Hughes, George Ella Lyon, Patricia Smith, William Stafford, Kim Stafford, Renée Watson, and many more. Early on, the legacy of creating poetry with a political imagination captured our work in the schools, prompting us to marry literature and history with poetry in both our classrooms. The teachers at Jefferson High School, especially Dan Coffey, Pam Hooten, Andy Kulak, Dianne Leahy, Nyki Tews, and Amy Wright, offered insights, advice, and critique for many of the lessons included in this book.

We owe a huge debt to Kim Stafford, both for the generous gift of his father's work, but also for opening spaces like the Oregon Writing Project (OWP) and Northwest Writing Institute, which hosts poets and teachers together without making a distinction, allowing us to find a place in both worlds. Kim's continued support of the OWP for more than 30 years made this work possible.

Many of the essays in this book first appeared in *Rethinking Schools* and were improved by the magazine's rigorous editorial process. The staff and editors of Rethinking Schools—Wayne Au, Bill Bigelow, Melissa Bollow Tempel, Grace Cornell Gonzales, Helen Gym, Jesse Hagopian, Stan Karp, David Levine, Larry Miller, Bob Peterson, Adam Sanchez, Jody Sokolower, Kathy Xiong, and Moé Yonamine—have scrutinized every article, making all of us better writers and teachers in the process. But even more fundamentally, Rethinking Schools is a nest of possibility, a place where we return to fine-tune both our vision and critique of education.

The Oregon Writing Project not only nurtured many of the articles in this book, but nurtures teachers as well. Katharine Johnson and Mark Hansen, co-directors of the OWP, demonstrate daily what it takes to be social justice educators who raise writers in their own classrooms and in workshops with teachers across the Portland metropolitan area. Charles Sanderson, OWP coach, has been an inspiration as a poetry teacher; watching him nurture poets in his middle school classroom has bumped up our poetry moves.

For any book to hit the shelves, invisible hands make the impossible possible. This publication might not have ever made it past our imaginations if it hadn't been for Elizabeth Barbian, our production editor, who brought not only her capacity as an editor to the book, but also her knowledge as a writing teacher. She never let us get away with sloppy lessons, kept pushing us for the next draft. Because she is currently living in South Africa, the book was on a 24-hour clock. We rose each morning to new email, new tasks, new insights that kept us moving forward on a tight timeline.

Mike Trokan, Rethinking Schools' business manager, deserves credit for lining up funding and resources, as well as willpower. His push has been the wind at our back for many years. Although he officially retired, his knowledge about timelines, indexers, permissions, and publishers made this book possible. Tegan Dowling, office manager for Rethinking Schools, keeps all of our oars in the water. And Rachel Kenison, marketing director, brings a wicked sense of humor as well as keen eye for making our work visible.

Nancy Zucker brought both an artistic and poetic sensibility to the book, seeking artists whose visions matched the intention of the book. Throughout this writing, editing, visioning process, Nancy was a total partner in the work, putting up with us when we changed our minds, challenging us to see the book beyond the words. We also appreciate the watchful eye of Lawrence Sanfilippo, proofreader, who helped us through a tight manuscript deadline.

Finally, Linda writes:

Bill Bigelow, my husband, hiking partner, comrade, and best friend, first taught me what social justice education looked like when we co-taught Literature and U.S. History together at Jefferson High School, then he taught me to write about it. Our hikes in Forest Park, the Columbia Gorge, Point Reyes, and Sedona provide inspiration and insight for every article, poem, and story I have written. When I despair loudly and crankily that I cannot write another draft, his love and encouragement have kept me going. Anna Hereford, our daughter, has become my mentor, teaching me both patience and gardening. Through her photographs, Gretchen Hereford, our daughter, helps me see the beauty in the world—geese against the blue sky and forsythia just blooming. Xavier King Hertel, our grandson, delights me daily with his curiosity and imagination.

Dyan writes:

There is absolutely no way this book would have ever made it without Linda Christensen. I first met Linda when I was 14. My middle sister had Linda and Bill Bigelow as teachers and used to babysit for them. When I was 16, it was my turn—both to sit in their classroom and to babysit. In both places I grew. Linda, I love the way you love me and my family. Thank you for your support for nearly 30 years and for allowing me to join you on this amazing journey. This work would not be possible without the love, guidance, and nurture from my family: My mother, Carrie Watson, sisters Cheryl and Trisa, and my brother Roy. I am fortunate that the youngest sibling, Renée, was born last. It's as if my parents saved all their creative juices for her. Thank you Renée for the last-minute readings and advice, and for your passion for good writing and good teaching. I learn so much every time I attend your workshops or even hear you recount them. Last, this is for Nehemiah and Caleb. I want the best for you. I hope your teachers tune into your rhythms so that they and you can resist. ✳

Contents

CHAPTER ONE

Roots

Where we're from

SCOTT BAKAL

You Reading This, Be Ready
by William Stafford

Starting here, what do you want to remember?
How sunlight creeps along a shining floor?
What scent of old wood hovers, what softened
sound from outside fills the air?

Will you ever bring a better gift for the world
than the breathing respect that you carry
wherever you go right now? Are you waiting
for time to show you some better thoughts?

When you turn around, starting here, lift this
new glimpse that you found; carry into evening
all that you want from this day. This interval you spent
reading or hearing this, keep it for life—

What can anyone give you greater than now,
starting here, right in this room, when you turn around.

....

William Stafford, "You Reading This, Be Ready" from Ask Me: 100
Essential Poems. *Copyright © 1980, 2014 by William Stafford
and the Estate of William Stafford. Reprinted with the permission
of The Permissions Company Inc. on behalf of Graywolf Press,
Minneapolis, www.graywolfpress.org.*

Roots

Where we're from

In his famous poem "Like You," Salvadoran poet Roque Dalton wrote, "I believe the world is beautiful/and that poetry, like bread, is for everyone./And that my veins don't end in me/but in the unanimous blood/of those who struggle for life,/love,/little things,/landscape and bread,/the poetry of everyone."

Like Dalton, we believe that poetry is for everyone and that through poetry our students' lives—the "landscape and bread" of their homes, their ancestors, their struggles and joys—are invited into classrooms as subjects worthy of study.

In this chapter, "Roots: Where We're From," we hold a mirror up in class to reflect students' lives. When students write "Where I'm From" or "Raised by Women" poems, for example, they celebrate their roots, multiple heritages, customs, and languages that tie them to their families. When we teach Margaret Walker's "For My People," students' histories as members of a particular race, class, neighborhood, or even illness become part of our classroom anthology. Through poetry, we reclaim any part of our lives that society has degraded, humiliated, or shamed, and raise it up, share it, and sing praises to that "unanimous blood/of those who struggle."

These poems help create community in the classroom. As students share their poems during read-arounds, there is laughter, finger snapping, head nodding, as they discover their common bonds—from who raised them, to the songs they sing in church, to their family sayings. They also learn about other students' lives, cultures, and family traditions. To become a community, students must feel significant and cared about, and that happens with the genuine sharing of our lives.

These lessons also teach students that they are poets. The workshops in this chapter use some of the building blocks of poetry: lists, repeating lines, concrete images, stanzas. We encourage students to use their home languages, the details of their lives as the content of the poetry—from names of streets, parks, schools, buildings to the names of parents, grandparents, and all of the wisdom that vibrates in those city blocks or country roads.

Although students will ultimately learn the language of the academy about stanzas and line breaks, similes and metaphors, they will first learn that poetry can be playful, that it can use ordinary, everyday language, and sound just like their grandma or their aunts laughing together on the front porch, that it can be written in house slippers, that there is no right or wrong. As William Stafford, Oregon's poet laureate, wrote, "If I am to keep writing, I cannot bother to insist on high standards. . . . I am following a process that leads so wildly and originally into new territory that no judgment can at the moment be made about values, significance, and so on. . . . I am headlong to discover." ✳

Where I'm From

Inviting students' lives into the classroom

BY LINDA CHRISTENSEN

MEREDITH STERN

Over the years since this lesson was first printed, I have received poems from teachers in classrooms across the world, from elementary through graduate schools, sharing with me the lives of countless students from Sam Leach's gap-tooth 3rd graders in north Portland to Ron Baer's students who sling words like slam poets in Los Angeles.

Astra Cherry, one of my dear friends and colleagues from the National Writing Project, taught this poem to her children and siblings and built "Where I'm From" bags for each member of her family. Alma Flor Ada used this poem in her social justice literacy classes at the University of San Francisco, and her students created *Where I'm From* books to share with their students. Deborah Appleman, professor at Carleton College, taught the lesson through the Minnesota Prison Writing Workshop at a number of prisons in Minnesota. Beverly Tatum, currently president of Spelman College, used the poem to help students identify and share their cultural backgrounds when she was dean at Mount Holyoke College. Jana Potter, the youth program manager at Mercy Corps in Portland, Ore., created a dialogue between Portland, Palestinian, and Iraqi youth through the poem.

Why is this poem so popular? First, George Ella Lyon wrote an amazing poem. In the Oregon Writing Project, we talk about the "bones of the poem," the structure of the poem. Lyon's "Where I'm From" has good bones that help students organize their poems by standing on ground she tilled before us, so students of all ages can write about where they are from. This poem starts the year with a home run paper on the wall from every kid in the classroom. There are no rhyme schemes to follow. There are no fancy literary terms that too often separate students from the daily language of their lives. There are *just* the facts of their lives, and the beauty of those facts adds up to a literary show-and-tell about students' cultures.

In his essay "The Ground on Which I Stand," August Wilson wrote:

> Growing up in my mother's house at 1727 Bedford Ave. in Pittsburgh, Pa., I learned the language, the eating habits, the religious beliefs, the gestures, the notions of common sense, attitudes towards sex, concepts of beauty and justice, and the response to pleasure and pain, that my mother had learned from her mother, and which could trace back to the first African who set foot on the continent. It is this culture that stands solidly on these shores today as a testament to the resiliency of the African-American spirit.

And this is what each of our students learned in their homes: language, food, religion, the stories (sometimes) of their people. We hear this in the do-rags and prayer plants from Oretha Storey's poem, in the words of Lealonni Blake's strict dad, "sit yo' fass self down." We hear the pain and resiliency in Hend Abu Lamzy's poem about Palestine, "I am from a village I've never seen."

I still remember the teachers who brought my home and culture into school. I recall holding my father's hand as he read my story hanging on the display wall outside Mrs. Martin's 3rd-grade classroom on the night of Open House. I remember the sound of change jingling in Dad's pocket, his laughter as he called my mom over and read out loud the part where I'd named the cow "Lena" after my mother and the chicken "Walt" after my father. It was a moment of sweet joy for me when my two worlds of home and

I invite students to write about their lives, about the worlds from which they come.

school bumped together in a harmony of reading, writing, and laughter.

In my junior year of high school, I skipped most of my classes, but each afternoon I crawled back through the courtyard window of my English class. There were no mass assignments in Ms. Carr's class: She selected novels and volumes of poetry for each student to read. Instead of responding by correcting my errors, she wrote notes in the margins of my papers asking me questions about my home, my mother, my sister who'd run away, my father who'd died three years before.

These two events from my schooling capture part of what the editors of *Rethinking Our Classrooms: Teaching for Equity and Justice* (1994) meant when we encouraged teachers to make students feel "significant" in our classrooms:

> The ways we organize classroom life should seek to make children feel significant and cared about—by the teacher and by each other. Unless students feel emotionally and physically safe, they won't share real thoughts and feelings. Discussions will be tinny and dishonest. We need to design ac-

tivities where students learn to trust and care for each other. Classroom life should, to the greatest extent possible, prefigure the kind of democratic and just society we envision, and thus contribute to building that society. Together students and teachers can create a "community of conscience," as educators Asa Hilliard and George Pine call it.

Mrs. Martin and Ms. Carr made me feel significant and cared about because they invited my home into the classroom. They allowed me to bring the "ground on which I stand," as August Wilson wrote, into school. When I wrote and included details about my family, they listened. They made space for me and my people in the curriculum.

In my classrooms over the last 40 years, I've attempted to find ways to make students feel significant and cared about as well, to find space for their lives to become part of the curriculum. I do this by inviting them to write about their lives, about the worlds from which they come. Our sharing is one of the many ways

As critical teachers, we shouldn't overlook the necessity of connecting students around moments of joy.

we begin to build community together. It "prefigures" a world where students can hear the home language from Diovana's Pacific Islander heritage, Lurdes' Mexican family, Oretha's African American home, and my Norwegian roots, and celebrate without mockery the similarities as well as the differences.

Sometimes grounding lessons in students' lives can take a more critical role, by asking them to examine how they have been shaped or manipulated by the media, for example. But as critical teachers, we shouldn't overlook the necessity of connecting students around moments of joy as well.

George Ella Lyon's poem invites my students' families, homes, and neighborhoods into the classroom. Lyon's poem follows a repeating pattern, "I am from. . . ," that recalls details, evokes memories—and can prompt some excellent poetry. Her poem allows me to teach about the use of specifics in poetry, and

writing in general. But the lesson also brings the class together through the sharing of details from our lives and lots of laughter and talk about the "old ones" whose languages and traditions continue to permeate the ways we do things today.

Teaching Strategy

I am mindful that my students do not all live in single dwelling homes with picket fences and big backyards. Many live in apartments or the "projects." In recent times, students' living situations have become more vulnerable, so some of my students live in transitional housing, hotel rooms, and sometimes cars. Other students are in and out of foster homes. I ask students to think of a place they consider "home" for this exercise.

1. After students read the poem out loud together, I note that Lyon begins many of her lines with the phrase "I am from." I remind the class of William Stafford's advice to find a hook to "link the poem forward" through some kind of device like a repeating line, so the poem can develop a momentum. I suggest they might want to use the line "I am from" or create another phrase that will move the poem.

2. We go line by line through the poem. I ask students to notice the details Lyon remembers about her past. After we read, I ask students to write lists that match the ones in Lyon's poem and to share them out loud. We write each list, share each list, laugh, and add details. The idea is to fill the well so that when they move to write the poem, they have many details to choose from. This verbal sharing sparks memories and also gives us memories to share as we make our way through the lesson:

    *   Items found around their home: bobby pins or stacks of newspapers, grandma's false teeth in a jar by the bathroom sink, discount coupons for a Mercedes. (They don't have to tell the truth. Sometimes the exaggeration tells as much as the truth.)
    *   Items found in their yards, in the area surrounding their "home": broken rakes, dog bones, hoses coiled like green snakes. (I encourage them to think of metaphors as they make their lists.)

- Items found in their neighborhood: the corner grocery store, Mr. Tate's beat-up Ford Fairlane, the "home base" plum tree. I encourage them to be specific—include names of people, stores, streets. For example, I live on the corner of Fremont and Haight, around the block from More for Less Foods, across the street from the Living Gospel Church, and two blocks from Senn's Drive-Thru Dairy.
- Names of relatives, especially ones that link them to their past: Aunt Eva and Uncle Einar, the Christensen and Richert branches.
- Sayings that spill out and remind them of home: "If I've told you once. . ." "Who gave you the authority?" My students have great lines for this one that either pull me back to my childhood or make me want to steal their families' lines.
- Names of foods and dishes that recall family gatherings: lutefisk, tamales, black-eyed peas, chocolate mayonnaise cake, peach cobbler. Be prepared to get hungry.
- Names of places they keep their childhood memories: diaries, boxes, underwear drawers, inside the family Bible.

3. We share our lists out loud as we brainstorm. I encourage them to make their piece "sound like home," using the names and language of their home, their family, their neighborhood. The students who write vague nouns like "shoes" or "magazines" get more specific when they hear their classmates shout out "*Jet*," "Latinx," "pink tights crusted with rosin." Out of the chaos, the sounds, smells, and languages of my students' homes emerge in poetry.

4. Once they have their lists of specific words, phrases, and names, I ask students to highlight the pieces from their lists that most clearly show where they are from. The poet's job is to cherry-pick the best details, not use everything from their brainstorming. I encourage them to find some kind of link or phrase like "I am from" to weave the poem together, and to end the poem with a line or two that ties their present to their past, their family history. For example, in Lyon's poem, she ends with "Under my bed was a dress box/spilling old pictures . . . I am from those moments."

5. After students have written a draft, we "read around." (See p. 240 for a detailed description of this activity.) This is an opportunity for students to feel "significant and cared about," in the words of *Rethinking Our Classrooms*, as they share their poems. ✳

. . . .

Linda Christensen (lmc@lclark.edu) is director of the Oregon Writing Project at Lewis & Clark College in Portland, Ore. She is a Rethinking Schools editor and author of Reading, Writing, and Rising Up *and* Teaching for Joy and Justice.

Resource

Lyon, George Ella. "Where I'm From." *Where I'm From, Where Poems Come From*. Spring, TX: Absey and Co., 1999.

Where I'm From

by George Ella Lyon

I am from clothespins,
from Clorox and carbon-tetrachloride.
I am from the dirt under the back porch.
(Black, glistening
it tasted like beets.)
I am from the forsythia bush,
the Dutch elm
whose long gone limbs I remember
as if they were my own.

I am from fudge and eyeglasses,
from Imogene and Alafair.
I'm from the know-it-alls
and the pass-it-ons,
from perk up and pipe down.
I'm from He restoreth my soul
with a cottonball lamb
and ten verses I can say myself.

I'm from Artemus and Billie's Branch,
fried corn and strong coffee.
From the finger my grandfather lost
to the auger
the eye my father shut to keep his sight.
Under my bed was a dress box
spilling old pictures,
a sift of lost faces
to drift beneath my dreams.
I am from those moments—
snapped before I budded—
leaf-fall from the family tree.

Where I'm From
by Renée Watson

I'm made up of East Coast hip-hop and island
    tradition.
I'm from Baptist hymns and secular jigs.
Tambourine playin', late night stayin'
at the church house, or my friend's house, or their
    friend's house
(on the weekends).

Where I'm from there are corduroyed hand-me-downs
and family keepsakes.
Family pictures on the wall. Open Bible on the coffee
    table.

I'm from *that* side of town.
Where the media only comes for bloodshed. Blood
    wasted.
Never for blood restored, celebrated, or regenerated.

I'm from hopscotch and double Dutch.
Hide-n-go seek and Pac-Man.

I'm from curry goat, rice and peas and beef patties.
From turquoise blue water, white sand, and
    dreadlocks.
Reggae is in my blood.

Grew up in the Pacific Northwest. A place where rain
    falls
more than sun shines.
I'm from Douglas firs and pine trees,
where we walk under waterfalls,
drive up windy roads to Mt. Hood,
and escape to the beaches on the Oregon coast.

Where I'm from music takes away the blues.
I'm from Bob Marley. Mahalia Jackson. Aretha
    Franklin. James Brown.
I'm from Jackson 5 records and New Edition tapes.
I'm from rewinding tapes over and over and over
    again
so you can write down the lyrics and memorize them.

Where I'm from the whole neighborhood is your family
ladies sit on their porches looking out for you
shooing away boys like flies.

Callin' your momma to tell what you did
before you can get home and lie about it.

Where I'm from people ask my friend,
"Is that your hair?" and she says, "Yeah it's mine.
    I bought it!"

I'm from divorce being passed down to children like
    a family heirloom.
I'm from single mommas pushing strollers,
praying that their babies don't make the same
    mistakes as them.

I'm from a little goes a long way, from sun gonna
    shine after the rain.
I'm from persevering souls and hardworking hands.
From a people destined to make it to their
    promised land.
I'm from been there, done that, can and will do it
    again.
Now you, tell me—where you from?

. . . .

*Renée Watson (reneewatson.net) is an author, performer,
and educator. She teaches poetry at DreamYard in New
York City.*

I Am from Soul Food and Harriet Tubman

by Lealonni Blake

I am from get-togethers
and Bar-B-Ques
K-Mart special with matching shoes.
Baseball bats and BB guns,
a violent family is where I'm from.

I am from "get it girl"
and "shake it to the ground."
From a strict dad named Lumb
sayin' "sit yo' fass self down."

I am from the smell of soul food
cooking in Lelinna's kitchen.
From my Pampa's war stories
to my granny's cotton pickin'.

I am from Kunta Kinte's strength,
Harriet Tubman's escapes.
Phillis Wheatley's poems,
and Sojourner Truth's faith.

If you did family research,
and dug deep into my genes.
You'll find Sylvester and Ora, Geneva and Doc,
My African Kings and Queens.
That's where I'm from.

I Am from Swingsets and Jungle Gyms

by Debby Gordon

I am from jars for change collections,
cards from Grandma,
and chocolate milk.

I am from swingsets and jungle gyms
rusted metal mounted in dirt
used by many kids,
well broken in.

I am from the cherry tree,
and the pudgy faces climbing out on the branches
for a piece of juicy red fruit.

I am from tattletales,
keep-it-froms,
and "shut up and listen to me."
I am from Rice Crispy Treats,
and pretty rings,
from Melvin and Earline.

I'm from Will and Sharon's long branch,
chunky peanut butter and jelly,
from the house we lost to fire,
and surgeries we all have had.

I am from the old scrapbooks,
where pictures,
remind me of days that live only in the minds
of those of us who were there.

I am from the people who paved a way for me,
I am from the best that could be,
and I am the best I could be.

I Am from. . .
by Oretha Storey

I am from bobby pins, do-rags
and wide-toothed combs.
I am from tall grass, basketballs and
slimy slugs in front of my home.
I am from prayer plants that lift
their stems and rejoice every night.

I am from chocolate cakes and deviled
eggs that made afternoon snacks just right.
I am from older cousins and hand-me-downs
to "shut ups" and "sit downs."

I am from Genesis to Exodus
Leviticus too.
Church to church, pew to pew.

I am from a huge family tree,
that begins with dust and ends with me.

In the back of my mind there lies a dream
of good "soul food" and money trees.
In this dream I see me on top makin'
ham hocks, fried chicken
and smothered pork chops.
I am from family roots and blood
Oh, I forgot to mention love.

I Am from Pink Tights and Speak Your Mind
by Djamila Moore

I am from sweaty pink tights encrusted in rosin
bobby pins
Winnie-the-Pooh
and crystals.

I am from awapuhi ginger
sweet fields of sugarcane
green bananas.

I am from warm rain cascading over
taro leaf umbrellas.
Crouching beneath the shield of kalo.

I am from poke, Brie cheese, mango,
and raspberries,
from Marguritte
and Aunty Nani.

I am from speak your mind
it's OK to cry
and would you like it if someone did that to you?

I am from swimming with
the full moon,
Saturday at the Laundromat,
and Easter crepes.

I am from Moore and Cackley
from sardines and haupia.
From Mirana's lip Djavan split,
to the shrunken belly
my grandmother could not cure.

Seven diaries stashed among
Anne of Green Gables.
Dreams of promises
ending in tears.
Solidifying to salted pages.

I am from those moments of
magic
when life remains a
fairy tale.

Where I'm From
by Camila Calderon

I am from my pink baby blanket
from my *abuela*'s picture
and my stuffed bear Lucesita.

Yo soy del árbol sombroso
from quiet friends playing on the swings
and a gunshot in the night.

I am from my mom who comes from México and loves
    to dance
from my daddy who comes from México and plays
    soccer with us
and from my grandma who lives in México and who I
    miss.

I am from "Cami" "Pollito" and "Gordito."

I am from *posole con pollo*
ensalada y rábanos
y tacos dorados con pollo, tomates, crema y queso.

I am from my mom and daddy who are proud to be
from México
and my grandma who is from beautiful México.

I am from *el Día de los Muertos*
when my family eats special food
and we celebrate my grandpa's life.

I am Camila.
I am kind
respectful
and friendly.

I am from many places
I am Camila.

Where I'm From
by Roberto Alba

I am from a picture of my grandpa, my dad and me
a picture of my dog Nico
and dream catchers that remind me of my Native
    American heritage.

I am from the pear tree my family shares with our
    neighbors
the chimney swifts that come at night
and the gunshots that make me nervous.

I am from my mom and dad who care for and love me
my two older sisters who love me too
and my baby sister who slobbers on me.

I am from "¡*Adiós*!" and "Go to bed, Roberto!"

I am from my Native American grandma's meatloaf
and my *tía*'s green candy tamales.

I am from my mom who's proud to be Native American,
Mexican, and Italian
my dad who is Mexican American
and my grandma who is Mexican too.

I am from my sister's fun *quinceañera*
from wearing my fancy clothes and dancing slow
I am from getting blessed by the Eagle feather
the sound of drums
and dancing in circles.

I am Roberto
I have many different cultures
I like to help people
I am a peacemaker.

I am from many places
I am Roberto.

Name Poem

To say the name is to begin the story

BY LINDA CHRISTENSEN

URIAH BOYD, JEFFERSON HIGH SCHOOL / PHOTO BY JOANNA DARKE

"To say the name is to begin the story," according to the Swampy Cree Indians. In my language arts courses over the years, we begin our "story" together by saying our names—and by telling the history of how we came to have them. Because the first day of class lays a foundation for the nine months that follow, I want our year to begin with respect for the diverse cultural heritages and people represented not only at Jefferson High School, but in the world as well. Initially, I started the year with writing about our names because I was appalled that several weeks into the new school year, students still would not know each other's names. Telling about our names was my way of saying up front that the members of the class are part of the curriculum—their names, their stories, their histories, their lives count.

But I realized that I was missing an opportunity to frame the question of naming more broadly—and more politically. So this naming ritual has also become a way to say from the jump that naming is per-

The members of the class are part of the curriculum—their names, their stories, their histories, their lives count.

sonal, cultural, and political. In this case, to say the name is also to begin questioning whose story is told. I start class by asking students the name of the river connecting Oregon and Washington. When they say, "Columbia," I tell them that the first people here called it "Nch'i-Wana," the "Great River" or "Big River." I ask them to name the volcano that blew ash on Washington and Oregon in 1980; when they respond "Mount St. Helens," I tell them that the Cowlitz who lived here first named it "Loo-Wit."

Then we talk about how people who have the power to name also have the power to tell the story. I explain that in this class we will listen for whose voices get heard and whose have been silenced. I do this quickly without going into the linguistic decimation of Indigenous cultures because we will study that later in the year. This is the initial conversation—meant to say, "Whatever your name is, whoever you are, you are welcome. You don't need to change to belong here."

Students and I talk about how naming traditions differ depending on family, cultural group, nationality, or religious affiliation. We look at some of the naming traditions in Vietnam, Laos, Cambodia, and Mexico. I give examples from my family, where the first son was named using the first initial and the middle name of the father. My grandfather was William Meyer, my father was Walter Meyer, and my brother was William Meyer. My brother broke the tradition by naming his first son Steven Troy. I broke tradition by not taking my husband's name—and my mother and sister still addressed their letters to Linda Bigelow, not Linda Christensen, for many years.

We also speak—using student knowledge as well as mine—of how historically some groups of people were denied their names. Many people from Eastern Europe had their names shortened at Ellis Island be-

cause their last names were too long and too difficult for the officials to pronounce. When Africans were stolen from their homeland, their names and their history were stripped as well. I share the story that my friend Bakari Chavanu wrote about changing his name because he wanted a name that didn't begin in slavery (see p. 17).

In addition to Bakari's moving piece, I use an assortment of prompts to get students started writing. I've stumbled across name poems or stories over the years that I read to students as a way of priming the writing pump. One of my favorites is Marge Piercy's "If I had been called Sabrina or Ann, she said" (1985). Piercy fools around with her name, playing around with alternatives and poking fun at its dullness:

> Name
> like an oilcan, like a bedroom
> slipper, like a box of baking soda,
> useful, plain; impossible for foreigners,
> from French to Japanese, to pronounce.

Because my name is Linda Mae, I could identify with Piercy's dismal view of her name. I wanted a name like Cassandra, something fancy and long. My name sounded like a farm girl's, and I wanted to be sleek and citified.

I also love Sandra Cisneros' "My Name" from her book *The House on Mango Street* (1991). Cisneros' character Esperanza uses delicious details to describe her name: "In English my name means hope. In Spanish it means too many letters. It means sadness, it means waiting. It is like the number nine. A muddy color. It is the Mexican records my father plays on Sunday mornings when he is shaving, songs like sobbing."

Let me also say that I teach this poem quickly. I do this piece to set the tone for the year rather than teach poetic strategy. I want students to begin the year by sharing, by learning to be kind to each other. I also attempt to crack them open, to get them to be playful in their writing.

Teaching Strategy

I like to begin this activity with a combination of story and poem, humor and seriousness, so students can choose their own route to the assignment.

1. I pass out the name graphic organizer (see p. 18), so students can begin to collect ideas for their name piece when we begin reading models. I tell them, "We are going to look at the way different people wrote about their names. There is no one right way. I've written this poem in different ways over the years. Just begin collecting some thoughts and memories as we read the models."

2. Students read Chavanu's story, Piercy's poem, and Cisneros' piece about names. We discuss how differently each writer views his or her name. We pause to look at lines and point out specific details. For example, Piercy doesn't say she hates her name, she plays with it. "Name/like an oilcan, like a bedroom/slipper, like a box of baking soda,/useful, plain. . . ." We look at the metaphors in the Cisneros vignette. I ask students, "Whose name has a story?" I encourage them to share their histories, pull the stories out of them.

3. After reading Sandra Cisneros' piece, we look at how she plays with language and uses metaphors and similes. I ask students to write "My name sounds like." One year Isaiah noticed that she takes a "trip" in her name piece to talk about her grandmother's history. "In your piece, think about the side trip that you might include in your piece like Cisneros does in hers."

4. We read student samples from previous years. I find it helpful to save these from year to year as students often look up to their older schoolmates and find it amusing and powerful to see examples of their writing. The poem written by my student Mary Blalock is a great example of how students can mix personal history, songs, even religion into their poems. After we read her poem, I ask students if anyone has songs or rhymes that go along with their names.

   With each piece, I attempt to elicit stories and memories to create a classroom where students are comfortable talking. Another student, Sekou Crawford, wrote his name "poem" as a story about how his mother came to name him Sekou. Because it has dialogue and setting, it is a good model of how the assignment can be written as prose.

5. After saturating students in name poems and prose, I tell them, "Write about your names as a story or as a poem. You can tell the history of your name, the meaning of your name, memories or anecdotes connected to your names. You can choose to write about your feelings about your names or your nicknames. The only boundary on the assignment is that you must write something about your name, and it can't be an acrostic. Be playful. Be outrageous."

6. We start writing in class before the period ends, and I encourage students to talk with their parents—if they live with them—to find out the history behind their names. If a student has hit the mother lode and already has a piece written, I encourage her/him to share to give ideas to classmates. Students' homework is to finish the writing and bring their piece to class the following day. We share our work using the read-around method. (See the detailed description of read-arounds, which begins on p. 240.) ✳

....

Linda Christensen (lmc@lclark.edu) is director of the Oregon Writing Project at Lewis & Clark College in Portland, Ore. She is a Rethinking Schools editor and author of Reading, Writing, and Rising Up *and* Teaching for Joy and Justice.

I explain that in this class we will listen for whose voices get heard and whose have been silenced.

Linda Mae
by Linda Christensen

My name sounds like a country-western singer
wrangling cows and cowboy hearts
out on the range.

Linda Mae is my intimate name,
the name my family calls me when we're laughing,
when there's blackberry pie on the table,
and we spent the day swimming
at Grizzly Creek or Swimmer's Delight.

My name is full of pinochle on summer nights,
lit by stars and firelight.
My name sounds like the jukebox
at the Vista Del Mar
where Dad poured Jack Daniels
for fishermen
while Mom served clam burgers
and chicken fried steak.

Linda Mae is the lonely child
I became when my father died,
the Linda
who crawled beneath the overturned skiff
in the backyard,
and lit candles in the dark curve
of death.

Linda Mae is the name
Bill calls me when we're happy,
when we hike Tamanawas Falls
or watch salmon leap,
silver acrobats
climbing the white water
of the narrow Klickitat canyons.

Linda Mae sounds like home.

A Hand-Me-Down Name
by Mary Blalock

Mary
Mary was a hand-me-down
from Grandma.
I was
the "Little Mary"
on holiday packages.
Merry Christmas.
Mary, mother of God,
who is a strong woman
in a male-dominated religion.
Me,
a lone girl,
in a world of testosterone.
Because of her,
it means sorrow and grief—
I am very sad about this.
"How does your garden grow?" they often ask.
With colorful fruit like the pictures
I attempt to paint,
and beautiful flowers like the poems
I try to write.
They had
three little kids in a row,
and the middle one's me.
Mary, Mary, not always contrary.

My Name Means Something
by Sekou Crawford

I have a very unusual name. Not as unusual as I used to think because just last year I came face to face with another Sekou. He didn't look much like me, and we probably had very little in common, but when I stood in front of him and shook his hand, I felt we had some kind of secret bond. I could tell he felt the same way.

One day I asked my mom about my name, "How did you come to name me Sekou?"

"Well," she said, "I used to work with convicts, tutoring them, and one day as I walked across the prison courtyard, I heard someone yell, 'Hey, Sekou!' I thought to myself, 'Wow. What great name.' And I remembered it."

I didn't know how I felt being named after some inmate, but I've always been thankful for having it. I couldn't imagine hearing my name and wondering if they were talking to me or the other guy with the same name. I wouldn't like walking into a little gift shop and seeing my name carved onto a key chain. I've heard that somewhere in Northern Africa my name is quite common.

My name has a special meaning. Sekou Shaka, my first and middle name, together mean learned warrior. That's the way I'd like to see myself: Fighting the battle of life with the weapon of knowledge.

Bakari Chavanu's Story
by Bakari Chavanu

I changed my name to Bakari Chavanu six years ago and my mom still won't pronounce it. The mail she sends me is still addressed to Johnnie McCowan. I was named after my father. When I brought up the subject with her of changing my name, she said my father would turn over in his grave, and "besides," she said, "how could you be my son if you changed your name?"

I knew she was responding emotionally to what I decided to do. I knew and respected also that she was, of course, the giver of my life and my first identity, but how do I make her understand the larger picture? That the lives of people are more than their families and their birth names, that my identity was taken from me, from her, from my father, from my sister, from countless generations of my people enslaved for the benefit of others? How do I make her understand what it means for a kidnapped people to reclaim their identity? How do I help her understand the need for people of African descent to reclaim themselves?

History of name	Stories about name

Associations with name	Word play with name

Nicknames	Interior monologue about name

Weaving Poetry Through the Elementary Classroom

The beginning

BY BOB PETERSON

SHADRA STRICKLAND

"I liked poetry since 2nd grade when Ms. Stili had us memorize 'Honey I Love,' but it wasn't until 5th grade and this project that I realize I'm a poet too," wrote Juanita as she reflected on her bilingual poetry book that she made in my 5th-grade classroom.

I weave poetry into my classroom from the first day through our end-of-year ceremony when we tearfully send our students off to middle school.

I can't imagine an elementary classroom without poetry. It stirs children's imaginations and encourages wordplay. It brings dull topics alive and provokes thinking and talk about deep concepts like prejudice, segregation, and friendship. It's a pathway to writing for my most reluctant students. And it can work wonders helping students to improve their confidence and skills in speaking to an audience.

Poetry has made my three decades of teaching more powerful and joyful.

Over the years I've collected dozens of children's poetry books and have them stuffed into crates and bins in my classroom. Students demand to "borrow" them and take them home, and despite my pleading and best attempts at record keeping each year my pocketbook takes a hit as I resupply my collection of books. But it's worth it.

Gathering Stories

The first day of school I give each student a three-ring binder with eight dividers. We painstakingly write on the little white labels and cram them into the tiny plastic color sleeves on the dividers. On the first label we write "Songs" for the lyrics of the song of the week. The second label is "Poems." "By the time you're done with 5th grade you'll have a great collection of poetry," I explain. "I'm sure the poems we read will inspire you to make your own poetry book. And you'll get to choose a couple of your poems to recite in our 5th-grade poetry reading at Woodland Pattern, our neighborhood poetry book store."

My first writing assignment is a name poem. I do this to get to know my students, for them to know each other, and to start a pattern from day one that a key feature of many homework assignments is to talk to

Poetry provokes thinking and talk about deep concepts like prejudice, segregation, and friendship.

their parents, grandparents, and/or caregivers. It also sets the context for discussions about name-calling and the power of names and naming. Finally, the name poem is an assignment that all students are able to complete and be proud of as their name poem and photo are hung in the hallway outside the classroom.

Modifying Linda Christensen's ideas for introducing name poems (see p. 13), I tell my students that I'm fascinated with names and how many people in the past had their names forcibly changed upon arrival in the

United States. Slave owners stripped enslaved Africans of their names, while immigration officials changed the names of many immigrants. I read one or two sample name poems and then say, "Your homework tonight is to interview people in your family and find out as much information as you can about your name. Who thought it up? Did anyone in your family's past have their name changed? Are you named after someone else in your family? Are there any amusing stories that go along with your name or nickname?" I tell them, "The more information or stories you can collect, the more interesting and fun your name poem will be."

The second day of school I have a student check off the homework, so I know before afternoon writing workshop who hasn't turned it in. Given the nature of the assignment, I usually get a near-perfect return, but I want to make sure. During the morning I individually confer with anyone who hasn't turned it in and have them jot down at least a few ideas. If necessary, they dictate a few ideas about a nickname or when someone has made fun of their name to me.

Expanding Ideas

I start off writing workshop by returning children's homework assignments. I ask if anyone would like to share one new thing they found out about their name. Inevitably, these include relatives or famous people they were named after, funny or annoying nicknames, and little stories of who and how they were named. I list key words to give other students additional ideas for writing or to ask their families about.

I then choose one idea from a student to model how to take an idea and turn it into a poem. For example, if José says he was named after his uncle, I write, "My name is José. I was named after my uncle José." I say, "This is a correct statement and this is what many 5th-grade students might write. But let's ask José a few questions and see if we can make it more interesting."

I ask José, "Where is your uncle from? What does he do? Do you have a memory of him?" Using his responses I model by thinking out loud how to take basic ideas and put them into poetic form. I consult José while doing so, and make it clear this is but one suggestion for him to consider.

I put my hand on my chin feigning hard thinking, and say, "I don't need to say 'my name is José' because it's a name poem, so I'll just make the first line "José." I write "José" on a document camera. "I can change 'I was named after my uncle José' to just 'named after my uncle' and I don't have to repeat 'José' because if I was named after him then the reader will know his name is the same as mine." I write, "Named after my uncle" on the second line.

"Now José you mentioned several things about your uncle, what sticks in your mind the most?"

"He came from Mexico with my *tía*, and he liked to play soccer with me even when I could barely walk."

"Hmmm," I say, "I wonder if this captures what you were thinking" as I write: "José/named after my uncle/from Mexico/who played soccer with me/as soon as I could walk."

"Now José's not done with his poem. I want him to take his other ideas, like the nickname and maybe his last name and write more."

Many students will turn in their first draft by the end of the writing workshop. For those who don't, writing the draft becomes a homework assignment. During the first writing workshop, I circulate and help students individually. Usually while I am still helping a student just get started a different student will announce to the class, "I'm done—what do I do next?" forgetting that as part of the instructions I told them that upon completion they are to "read it twice to yourself to see if it makes sense and to see if you could add more detail, and then to share with another student who is also done and ask for more ideas."

Revising Drafts

On the third day—the second writing workshop session—I say, "Thank you all for working hard on your poems. I've learned a lot about you, but we have more work to do. Today we will start to revise our poems." Inevitably, a student raises her hand and says she put everything she knows about her name and there's nothing to add. I respond, "When I write—whether it's a poem, a story, a letter, or comments on your report cards—I always revise my first draft. In fact, good writers revise their work several times."

I emphasize that we are writing for a purpose and we want to make them the best we can be. "Your poem will be published three times," I tell my students.

"We'll put it with your photo on bright paper and hang it in the hallway for the entire school to see." I show a few examples from the previous year. (I make a point of making duplicates of student work each year.) "And you will include this name poem in two of your major projects this year—your autobiography and your bilingual poetry book."

Finally, I explain that I've chosen two students' poems to revise together as a class. I tell my students to pay close attention because they will work in partners or triads to help each other revise their own poems.

I have previously asked the two students for permission to project their poems. I have the student read the poem, or if they prefer, I read it. We answer three questions while peer editing: What do we like about the writing? What are some questions that we have about it? (to clarify and/or encourage more detail) and What are any other suggestions that you might have?

As a class we work through the two poems much in the way I did the first day with José's poem. By the end of our collective edit of the second poem, students are begging that we do theirs, too. I say, "We will do more as a whole class in the future, but now you'll work in pairs or groups of three using the three questions that I have printed up on this handout." Since this is their first experience with peer editing, I explain that "Sometimes I assign pairs for editing and sometimes I let students choose. Today, I let you choose." I do this to observe pre-established friendship patterns and to focus attention on the editing task versus potential complaints about who is working with whom. I circulate and help students without partners pair up, and, if necessary, bring two or three to the back table where I help direct their peer edit.

Over the next few days I make sure all the students complete a revised draft—sometimes working with them individually to encourage and revise.

The students' stories shine through their poems:

Jonah writes:

Some mornings
my mom calls me
"Gallo"
which means rooster.
She calls me that because
when I wake up
my hair sticks straight up.

Kiarra writes:

My big sister Nicole
named me at birth
Lion King was showing
at the theater
the little lion cub
had my name.

Knyiah writes:

My mom liked the name
Nyiah
but since her name started with a
K
she put the K in front
that's how I got my first name
Knyiah

On the weekend I type and print the poems. The students get a chance to "proofread" the final copy and often decide to make additional changes. I enlist a few student volunteers to stay in for lunch recess to help me mount the poems along with a photo of each student on brightly colored card stock. I laminate the poems and by the end of the second week the name poems and photos hang outside in the hallway on our "Poetry Wall" for the entire school to see. ✳

. . . .

Bob Peterson (bob.e.peterson@gmail.com) is a founding editor of Rethinking Schools. He taught 5th grade in Milwaukee Public Schools for many years and is currently the president of the Milwaukee Teachers' Education Association.

'Raised by Women'
Celebrating our homes

BY LINDA CHRISTENSEN

"WE WANT LAND, BREAD, HOUSING, EDUCATION, CLOTHING, JUSTICE AND PEACE."

— EXCERPT FROM BLACK PANTHER PARTY PLATFORM AND PROGRAM "WHAT WE WANT/ WHAT WE BELIEVE" 1966

MEREDITH STERN

When I first read "Raised by Women" by Kelly Norman Ellis, I knew the poem would be a hit with my students. I love Ellis' celebration of the women in her life, her use of home language, and the wit and wisdom of her rhythmic lines. And from reading student tributes to their mothers over the years, I knew most of my students would relate to the topic. "Raised by Women" also had qualities I look for in poems I use to build community and teach poetic traits: a repeating line that lays down a heartbeat for the students to follow, delicious details from the writer's life that could evoke delicious details from my students' lives, and a rhythm so alive, I want to dance when I read it.

Part of my job as a teacher is to awaken students to the joy and love that they may take for granted, so I use poetry and narrative prompts that help them "see" daily gifts, to celebrate their homes and heritages. Ellis' poetry provides a perfect example. As she wrote, "I was just lucky enough to have been born into a loving Black family. I want these poems to stand as witness to the beauty and abundance of that life: a Black Southern woman's life, a good life, a proud life, a life as rich and sweet as the pies I bake with Mississippi pecans. There are others like me, folks raised in the brown loving arms of family."

Part of my job as a teacher is to help students "see" daily gifts, to celebrate their homes and heritages.

I also use poetry to build relationships with students and between students. Ellis' smart and sassy poem helped launch our yearlong journey to establish relationships as the students and I learned about each other, but also their journey in developing their writing.

In each stanza of the poem, Ellis lists the kinds of women who raised her—from "chitterling eating" to "some PhD toten" kind of women. Ellis' poem follows a repeating but changing pattern. She writes that she was raised by women, sisters, and queens. She includes both description and dialogue in most stanzas:

> I was raised by
> Chitterling eating,
> Vegetarian cooking,
> Cornbread so good you want to lay
> down and die baking
> "Go on baby, get yo'self a plate"
> Kind of Women.

The full poem, as well as a video clip of Ellis reading the poem, can be found at the Coal Black Voices website, which was developed by Media Working Group to "honor contemporary African American culture and celebrate regional expressions of the African Diaspora through the works of the Affrilachian Poets."

Filling the Bucket with Delicious Details and Style

After reading "Raised by Women" twice, I asked students, "Who were you raised by?" Although Ellis discusses only women, I wanted to open other possibilities. I salted the pot by generating a few: mother, father, coaches, church. I also wanted them to reach out beyond the traditional, so I encouraged them to think about neighbors, neighborhoods, musicians, novelists, civil rights activists, the halls at Grant or Jefferson High School.

After students wrote their lists, we shared them out loud so they could "steal" more ideas from each other. I pushed students to get more specific as they shared. For example, when Melvin said, "Coaches," I asked which coaches raised him—all of them? What did his football coach say or do that helped raise him? When Alex said the men at the barbershop, I asked which men and what did they contribute. Because the best poetry—and writing in general—resides in specific details, I pushed students to move beyond their first response and get deeper.

I wanted them to see that they weren't limited by the original verb, raised, so I asked, "The verb is the workhorse of the sentence. Look at how it harnesses the rest of the stanza and moves it forward. Think about your verbs. What other verbs could you use besides raised?" We played around with alternatives: brought up, taught, educated, nurtured. This is the weightlifting function of teaching poetry. Instead of grammar worksheets, I teach students about the functions of language as we discuss how verbs work in the poem.

When we completed our initial brainstorming about the repeating line, we went back to the poem. I asked, "What kinds of specific details does Ellis include?" The first stanza was about food, the second stanza focused on hair, the third was about physical appearance—skin color and clothes—the fourth about choices, the fifth about music, the sixth about attitude, and the seventh about professions. Because I didn't want each poem to turn out the same, I said, "When you write your poem, you can use these as potential categories, but you can use other categories as well. What else could you list in your poem?" Students shouted out: cars, songs, languages. I encouraged them to create a list of categories like Ellis'—food, clothes, music—and to fill in each category with specific details.

After they brainstormed, we returned to the poem's form. "What do you notice about how Ellis developed the poem? Look at the lines. Where does it repeat? Does it repeat in the same way?" Kamaria noticed the repeating, but changing line. Damon talked about how Ellis' dialogue gives her poem flavor. Tanisha noted that she named specific people—Angela Davis and James Brown. Destiny pointed out that Ellis used home language rather than Standard English. As students noticed these details, I listed them on the board. "Take a look at this list—a repeating but changing line, dialogue, naming people, home language. When you write your poems, I want you to try to include some of these techniques. I know some of you speak another language at home. Experiment with using pieces of that language in your poems. Also, notice how Ellis catches a rhythm in her poem. See if you can create a heartbeat when you write."

The Read-Around and Collective Text: Structuring Response

Before students read their poems, we arranged the desks in a circle, so they could see and hear the reader. I asked students to pull out a piece of paper to take notes on what they learned about each classmate through their poem: "Who raised them? What's important to them? Who's important to them?" I discovered that students pay more attention during the read-around if I give them a specific task. For the most part, student poems were stellar, and even those that lacked the style and sassiness of their classmates' gave us a glimpse into their lives.

Students found their own ways into the poems by celebrating more than one person. Anaiah Rhodes, for example, wrote a stanza each for her mother and father, grandmother and grandfather, church folk, music, cousins, and track. Her classmates loved how she used language and details to capture each one in turn, but they especially loved how Anaiah wrote about her church:

I was taught by a tongue talkin'
Sanctified, holy ghost filled, fire baptized,
   shoutin'
"'Member to keep God first, Baby!"
Kinda church folk

Some aisle runnin', teary-eyed, joy jumpin',
Devil rebukin', seed sowin'
"How you doin', Baby?"
Type of church folk

Ellis' poem provided an opportunity for us to celebrate the brilliance and linguistic richness of my students' cultures. Destinee Sanders, who also chose to write about a variety of people in her family—mother, aunts, sisters, and *abuelita*—switched languages throughout her poem:

I was raised by *Mi Abuelita*,
Es mi abuela favorita,
Ella es mi corazón, mi amor, mi amiga
Mi noche, mi todos los días, mi siempre.
Yo amo a mi abuelita

[I was raised by My Grandma,
My favorite grandmother
She is my heart, my love, my friend
My night, my every day, my always.
I love my grandma]

Like Destinee, students shared information in the poem that helped us know their family and backgrounds. Jessica Chavez wrote about her "tortilla making/Grease usin'/cumbia dancin'" family. Adiana Wilmot wrote, "I was raised by that/curry goat and chicken cookin'/'Eat your vegetables, pickney,'/type of Jamaican woman." Kirk Allen wrote about his family—the Allens—rather than selecting out individuals:

I was raised by the gas, brake dipp'n,
Cadillac whip'n, Wood grain grip'n,
Old school, big body, pimp'n,
Ain't you bullshit'n Allens

I was raised by the show stopp'n,
Hater droppin',
Hat tilted to the side,
Look like a bad mutha,

Shut yo mouth Allens

In this and all class writing, I encouraged students to abandon the prompt and my suggestions and find their own passion and their own way into the assignment. Shona Curtis did that and forged her way to a poem about music instead of people:

I was raised by smooth jazz
Make you want to sit down and
Cry kind of music

Some move your feet and shake
Those hips feel like you dancin'
Down the streets of Argentina
Kind of music

When students wrote at the end of the assignment, many pointed to Shona's straying from the prompt as a strength in her poem. Details from poems brought shouts of laughter or nods as students recognized their own family in Destiny Spruill's description of her family's "Found Jesus/Church goin'/Your mouth can get you in trouble" and "Gumbo makin'/Hat wearin'/Mother of the church/Kinda grandmothers." They understood Ebony Ross' "I was raised to get the belt/If I was talking that lip." But it was Jessica's repeating line—"I wasn't raised by my daddy"—that brought the most affirmations from other students.

Framing Reflection: Milking the Learning

After students shared, I handed out note cards and asked them to look back over their notes and write about what they learned about each other and poetry through our lesson. Kayla Anderson wrote that she learned "that you can completely change a poem but still keep the meaning. Shona made her poem fun by using words like 'hip-hoppin', pop lockin', shake your dreads.'" She noted that many students used strong verbs and imagery. Shona pointed out that "when you say your poem with attitude it sounds better."

But it was students' revelations about each other that made me realize this poetry assignment is a keeper. Students wrote about how much they learned about each other in a short amount of time. "I learned that Adiana is from Jamaica, that Bree was raised by foster parents, and that a lot of us have been let down by our fathers." Destinee wrote:

I learned that I have something in common with every single person in this room. I realize that we have all been through a lot of the same things. I learned that most of us weren't raised by our dads. I learned that Shaquala loves soul food. I learned that although Bree is Latino like me, she was raised by different types of Latinos, and I can relate to that. . . . I learned that we're different . . . yet we're the same.

Out of the 30 students in the class, the majority were raised without fathers. This became a repeating "aha" for most of the class. Virginia Hankins, for example, wrote that she "learned a lot about my classmates that I would have never known. I was surprised that so many of us were raised without our fathers."

Knitting together poetry that teaches about our lives as well as the craft of writing builds the kind of caring, risk-taking community I hope to create. ✳

. . . .

Linda Christensen (lmc@lclark.edu) is director of the Oregon Writing Project at Lewis & Clark College in Portland, Ore. She is a Rethinking Schools editor and author of Reading, Writing, and Rising Up *and* Teaching for Joy and Justice.

Resource

Ellis, Kelly Norman. "Raised by Women." *Tougaloo Blues*. Chicago: Third World Press, 2003.

Raised by Women
by Kelly Norman Ellis

I was raised by
Chitterling eating
Vegetarian cooking
Cornbread so good you want to lay
down and die baking
"Go on baby, get yo'self a plate"
Kind of Women.

Some thick haired
Angela Davis afro styling
"Girl, lay back
and let me scratch yo head"
Sorta Women.

Some big legged
High yellow, mocha brown
Hip shaking
Miniskirt wearing
Hip huggers hugging
Daring debutantes
Groovin
"I know I look good"
Type of Women.

Some tea sipping
White glove wearing
Got married too soon
Divorced
in just the nick of time
"Better say yes ma'am to me"
Type of Sisters.

Some fingerpopping
Boogaloo dancing
Say it loud
I'm black and I'm proud
James Brown listening
"Go on girl shake that thing"
Kind of Sisters.

Some face slapping
Hands on hips
"Don't mess with me,
Pack your bags and
get the hell out of my house"
Sort of Women.

Some PhD toten
Poetry writing
Portrait painting
"I'll see you in court"
World traveling
Stand back, I'm creating
Type of Queens.

I was raised by
Women.

Raised

by Anaiah Rhodes

I was raised by a lovin'
Church goin', home cookin', belt whoppin',
Non-stop children bearin'
Money arguin',
"You're going to be something great one day"
Mom and Dad

I was raised by a Jesus lovin', behind tearin'
Bomb cookin', hair pressin', garage sale givin'
Grandma

A politic lovin', money givin', pipe puffin',
Fish fryin', Cadillac whippin', wine sippin',
"Study hard now!"
Grandpa

I was taught by a tongue talkin'
Sanctified, holy ghost filled, fire baptized, shoutin'
"'Member to keep God first, Baby!"
Kinda church folk

Some aisle runnin', teary-eyed, joy jumpin',
Devil rebukin', seed sowin'
"How you doin', Baby?"
Type of church folk

I was brought up with that hold on,
Wait on God, don't give up,
Weepin' may endure for the night,
But joy comes in the mornin'
What a friend we have in Jesus, music

By some double darin', house playin',
Fightin', scratchin', teasin', tauntin',
Crumb snatchin'
To football playin' and track runnin'
"I got cha back!"
Cousins

I was brought up by that race
Everybody on the block, barefoot, wind in my face,
win or lose, spirit of runnin'
To that sweatin', trainin', muscle tearin',
Shin splintin', intense burnin',
Heavy workout, deep breathin' crazy
Type of runnin'.

Raised.

Music
by Shona Curtis

I was raised by smooth jazz
Make you want to sit down and
Cry kind of music

Some move your feet and shake
Those hips feel like you dancin'
Down the streets of Argentina
Kind of music

Some hip-hop and you don't stop
Movin' to those beats feel the energy
Comin' out of the radio
Kind of music

Some hit right where you need it soul
Music make you think of the old days
When that was all we had
Kind of music

Some jump up and down slam to
The beat of the rock
Kind of music

Some poppin' pop grab your
Best friend and put on your
Favorite costume and dance
Kind of music

I was raised by music

Raised
by Elizabeth

I was raised by
swift hands, sturdy words, and strong minds.
"Do what I say,
not what I do.
Think for yourself,"
Kind of women.

I was raised by,
"He ain't no good.
We don't need him,
better off without him.
Never lower your standards.
You better demand respect."
Kind of women.

I was raised by
tears, doors slapping,
trying not to cry,
get outta my face.
"You don't need to see this, baby,"
Kind of women.

I was raised by
head bowing, god fearing,
holy ghost worshipping,
"Never forget your morals.
Praise the lord,"
Kind of faith.

I was raised with pride.
I was raised with pain.
I was raised with faith
I was raised with swift hands,
sturdy words, and a strong mind.

Me . . . I Was Raised By

by anonymous high school student

I was raised by
"Go on in there and watch yo' cartoons.
Come out here and pick them greens.
Go in the room. Stay out of grown folk conversations.
Come on in here so you can eat."
My grandma.

I was raised by
"Go outside and play. You getting on my nerves.
Be careful. Don't go in that street.
He betta not say nothing to my kids.
Get in there and clean that room.
Everything better be nice and neat."
My mom.

I was raised by
"Come upstairs. I wanna show you something.
Go into the bathroom and lay down.
Shhh. Don't tell nobody.
Everything is okay. Don't worry."
My cousin.

I was raised by
"I love you, Bria.
Be good. I'll talk to you later.
Tell Mom I called.
I'm so proud of you, Sis."
My brother.

I was raised by
"You don't have to worry about it no more.
You're okay. God will make you whole.
All you need to do is pray and forgive."
My aunt.

I was raised by
"I am fearfully and wonderfully made.
Love does not delight in evil, but rejoices with the
    truth.
And now these three remain: faith, hope, and love.
Therefore, there is now no condemnation for those
who are in Christ Jesus because
through him the law of the spirit who gives life has
    set
You free from the law of sin and death"
My faith.

I was raised by
I know you're capable. Believe in yourself. I believe in
    you.
Keep trying. Never give up.
Don't get distracted. Stay focused on you.
You're gonna go far and accomplish something big.
Hope.

I was raised by
Love.
I was raised by
Grace.
I was raised by
Faith.
I was raised by
Mom.
I was raised by
Lies.
I was raised by
Hurt.
I was raised by
Hope.

I Was Raised By

by Dylan Baron

I was raised by the sounds of basketballs
hitting the wooden gym floor,
by the smell of the leather
on the ball,
the pools of sweat
dropping down my face,
the sound of shoes
squeaking across the floor.

I was raised by that championship team,
that "you better make the shot"
kind of team.
I was raised by that "You better have some pride
when you put on those uniforms!"
that "Give it 100%" every day kind of team.

I was raised by pick-and-rolls
and alley oops,
by intense training
and drills.
I was raised by the game I love.

Teaching the 'I Am' Poem

BY BOB PETERSON

FRANK BIG BEAR

In my class study of Native Americans with 5th graders, I introduce Native American author and poet N. Scott Momaday's poem "The Delight Song of Tsoai-talee." I use the poem for several reasons: its simple yet powerful images, the sense of wonder about nature it engenders, and its format that lends it to being a useful model. It's also a beautiful and accessible example of what Momaday calls "Pan-Indian" cultural values.

I introduce Momaday and his poem during our class study of Native Americans by writing the author and title on the board for my students to copy into their "Poems We Studied" log. I tell the students that Momaday was born in 1934, during the Great Depression. Although he is Kiowa, he lived on Navajo, Apache, and Pueblo reservations in the Southwest when he was a child. His father was a great storyteller and told him many stories from the Kiowa oral tradition. His mother was a writer. *Tsoai-talee* is his Indian name; it means rock tree boy. In addition to writing beautiful poetry, Momaday is a novelist. He won the Pulitzer Prize for Fiction for his novel *House Made of Dawn*.

I then challenge them to see if they have enough willpower to close their eyes and listen for about a minute while I read Momaday's poem. (Something difficult for 10-year-old boys.) "As you listen to each line try to imagine it as a photo in your mind."

I am a feather in the bright sky.
I am the blue horse that runs in the plain.
I am the fish that rolls, shining, in the water.
I am the shadow that follows a child.
I am the evening light, the lustre of meadows. . . .

After the first reading, I ask students what they remember. I write down a few phrases they call out and then pass out the poem and a yellow highlighter, but insist they keep the cap on. I read the poem again asking them to read along silently. "Now I want you to read it to yourself and highlight your three favorite lines. When you have highlighted the lines, turn to a partner, share the lines you've chosen and tell them why you like those lines."

After they share, I project a copy of the poem on the board and ask for volunteers to tell us their favorite line and explain why. The responses and reasons vary. Some are memorable. "I like the 'angle of geese in the winter sky' because it's like geometry." And "I like 'the shadow that follows the child' because when the sun's out it's like you can't get rid of the shadow." As each student shares I ask how many others had it as one of their top three and we note the number next to the line.

As the students share, I say, "OK, based on what you liked and what you see in the poem, if you were going to tell someone they should write an "I am" poem patterned after N. Scott Momaday, what would you tell them?"

Hands go up. "Each line starts with 'I am.'" Most hands go down. The remaining ones offer a variety of suggestions. "It's about nature. It's about something that connects with you like math or your feet. It's about an animal doing something. It's happy like the person is happy to see nature." As the students give suggestions I write them on a tag board poster, so we have class record.

The students are eager to write. I emphasize that I will not accept a simple statement like "I am a tiger." I say, "Look at Momaday's poem. Never does he just say he's something—there is always an interesting description."

The students then begin to write. I circulate watching for examples of lines that are rich in language and imagery, but don't just copy Momaday's phrases. I ask students to pause and put their pencils down, as I read a student's line. I continue this to help students who are stuck and to motivate those who need a push to add more detail. Many students will finish during writing workshop. For others, completing the poem is one of their homework assignments.

During the next writing workshop I do a class edit with two or three of the students' drafts making sure I have a range of quality. The students then pair up to peer edit and write their second draft. In some cases, I sit with a group of students who might have special needs or didn't turn in their homework or were absent the previous day.

Their work is impressive:

Juan writes, "I am the strong apple tree in my backyard standing up to storm."

Hattie writes, "I am the sun in the sky burning the people below."

Francisco writes, "I am an Arctic wolf camouflaged in the snow waiting for victory."

Veronica writes, "I am the person that you love and care for."

José writes, "I am the sandy beach where the ocean waves are breaking the castles that the kids built."

Myra took the poem in a different direction, writing just about herself:

I am me
Myra Alejandra Tapia-Franco
The one and only
I am an 11-year-old female
quiet and sometimes shy
I am Mexican American
struggling through life
I am Native American

defending what's mine
I am American
Taking what I can
I am a person of dignity
Proud and respectful
I am a Catholic
With Jesus on my side
I am a friend
With ears to listen and advice to give
I am a student
Trying to succeed in life
This is who I am
Myra Alejandra Tapia-Franco

Osvaldo

One day several months after the class had written their "I Am" poems, I was teaching double-digit multiplication and division and problem-solving through a "sweatshop math project." While I was showing photos of child laborers Osvaldo raised his hand and said, "I know all about that. I used to do that when I was 5 years old."

"You did what?" I asked.

"I worked in the fields with *mi abuela*—my grandmother."

I thanked him for his comment and we talked some more. I asked him if he liked working in the fields—secretly hoping he'd confirm the problems with child labor that we'd been learning about.

"Yeah it was sort of fun, for a while," he said.

"Didn't you want to go to school instead?"

"No," he said, knowing full well I was hoping for a different answer. "The teachers are mean there. If you misbehaved in that school the teacher put biting ants down your back."

My only response was, "Oh, that's reason enough not to go to school or at least not to misbehave."

Later that day during writing time I asked Osvaldo to write a poem about this experience and eventually he came up to me with this poem:

A 5-Year-Old Boy, Based on the True Life of Osvaldo

I am a 5-year-old boy working to support my
    family
I am a boy walking for a mile just to get clean
    water out of the *pozo*

I am a boy carrying a sack full of *caña* more than
    a mile
I am a boy watching for snakes and scorpions
    while working
I am a boy carrying food for my farm animals
I am a boy working for hours in the sun
I am a boy working in pain in my back and arms
    and legs
I am a boy sleeping with pain and bruises on my
    fingers

I told him how much I like it and how his words painted a picture for me. I asked if he'd be willing to read it to everyone. As we finished writing workshop, I asked Osvaldo to come to the front. His classmates sat glued to his every word. Their applause sparked a wide grin from Osvaldo. The following morning Osvaldo brought in another poem handing it to me with a big smile on his face.

I am a 5-year-old boy living in the United States
I am a boy eating strange food
I am a boy going to school
I am a boy seeing for my first time a show
I am a boy having my first game station
I am a boy seeing other people like African
    Americans and Puerto Ricans
I am a boy living happily in my new home
I am a boy feeling sad for being far away from my
    grandma and grandpa

Osvaldo's status in the class rose over those few days. Although he had formally hung with other Spanish-dominant students in the class, others in the class started paying more attention to him. Osvaldo connected to the math project in a personal way. His classmates connected him to what we were studying. It seemed to increase the interest in the entire project. And it was all tied to Osvaldo's using the power of poetry. ✳
....

Bob Peterson (bob.e.peterson@gmail.com) is a founding editor of Rethinking Schools. He taught 5th grade in Milwaukee Public Schools for many years and is currently the president of the Milwaukee Teachers' Education Association.

Inner and Outer Worlds
Building community through art and poetry

BY ANN TRUAX

MAYA GONZALEZ

How does a teacher bring a complicated mix of personalities, backgrounds, ethnicities, abilities, and attitudes into a climate of mutual respect? No pat answer solves every classroom problem, but the key to building community is a deeper knowledge of each other beyond the facades, as well as recognition of commonalities within the group. Activities that promote sharing in a safe environment help bridge the gap between individuals. As the Rethinking Schools editors noted in the introduction to *Rethinking Our Classrooms*, "We need to design activities where students learn to trust and care for each other. Classroom life should, to the greatest extent possible, prefigure the kind of democratic and just society we envision and thus contribute to building that society."

During an intensive, five-week writing program, I faced the challenge of building community with a diverse group of 5th- and 6th-grade students. I met with students for five hours four days a week for five weeks as part of a partnership between Portland Public Schools and the Oregon Writing Project. Our students came from various schools in southeast Portland. Among the 22 students, there were two Latinx, five of Vietnamese descent, five African Americans, and 10 European Americans.

The task was to teach students to write effectively in five weeks, but I knew that I had to build a com-

I knew that I had to build a community before I could get students to take the kinds of risks needed to push their writing forward.

munity before I could get students to take the kinds of risks needed to push their writing forward. I had to move them beyond the safety of fill-in-the-blank worksheets that too often dominate the writing curriculum for struggling students.

The questions I faced included how to unleash students' stories, how to overcome resistance to writing, how to foster students' confidence as writers, and how to create an environment of mutual support and appreciation—all while teaching the craft of writing,

Self-Portraits: Art as the First Step in Writing

Instead of starting with writing, I opened my instruction with art. As an ESL teacher, I have discovered that images lead to talking and talking leads to writing. Art and conversation are time well spent because they build community, validate the individual, forge new links between students, and ultimately move students into writing. The combination of art and writing is dynamic. Creating art calms students, requires intense focus, and opens a channel for language learning. From the visible, concrete image, students—ELL as well as native English speakers—can discuss what they see, ask questions, formulate and expand ideas, learn new vocabulary, and think abstractly. For many students, talking about an image is an important precursor to writing. My first two lessons, "Self-Portraits, Inner and Outer Worlds" and "The Outside/Inside Poem," created a safe environment with multiple opportunities for students to talk to each other and share pieces of their personal histories.

I introduced students to a self-portrait by the artist Maya Christina Gonzalez. It is a brightly colored im-

age of a smiling woman dressed in purple and white polka dots with paintbrushes stuck in her hair. A red frame surrounds the self-portrait; two lines of words circle the frame. Gonzalez writes: "The words around the border are things I love, like polka dots and fire, and ways that I feel, like loud and hungry." Gonzalez's self-portrait is an invitation for students to create their own. I put her self-portrait on the document camera and asked students, "What do you notice in her portrait?" Students shared ideas with a partner, then the whole class. Nayisha commented, "She's wearing earrings shaped like hands with eyes on them." Steven said, "Maybe that's because she works with her hands and her eyes." Jenny pointed to what she thought were feathers painted at the bottom, but Julian thought it was a light or fire showing her energy. Then together we read the artist's narrative accompanying her self-portrait. She explained:

One night when I was 5 years old, I woke up and saw a light shining brightly in the corner of my room. Some people said it was an angel. Some people said it was a ghost. All I know is it made me feel really happy, like I was special. . . . In my painting I show the light shining from my heart.

After students read Gonzalez's narrative, I asked: "What do you notice about the artist's story? What symbols does she use in her painting? What do you think the symbols mean?" Students again shared responses with a partner first, and then with the whole group. I directed students to look at the words around the portrait. I asked, "What kind of words are on the inside line?" Steven immediately noticed they showed her feelings.

I pushed again to provoke more discussion. "What do these words tell us about her?"

Kendra responded, "Sometimes she has different feelings like loud and quiet and happy and sad."

Then I said: "Read the words on the outside line with a partner. What kind of words are they?" Students were quick to determine the words named things she likes: love, green, pencils, dogs, words.

When we finished discussing Gonzalez's self-portrait, I told students, "Now, you are going to create your own self-portraits combined with words." The students seemed eager to get going.

Word Lists

Before starting the self-portrait, students needed to create two word lists—one for the inner world and one for the outer world—using Gonzalez as a model. I gave a few "inside" examples of mood adjectives: sad, lonely, joyous, and so on. Then students added to the list of adjectives as I wrote their suggestions on the overhead. Jenny added, "Crazy." Jorge said, "Mysterious." I shared some of my feeling adjectives (adventurous, anxious, busy, creative, dorky, envious) to show that even the teacher has a mix of positive and negative feelings. Also, I hoped that sharing who I am added incrementally to the level of trust within the room. After the students created their own lists, they shared with a small group.

Then we started the second "outside" list consisting of nouns showing what students like or enjoy. Students again shared their lists, ranging from hoodies to puppies to hanging out to volleyball to go-karts to tank tops. Many students needed a few more minutes to add ideas ignited by their classmates. Conversations began loosening up as students discovered information about each other. We learned that Chris and Peter loved football, Nyasha lived in a big household with an extended family, Maira was an incurable Justin Bieber fan, Cristy wanted to learn to ice skate, John frequently went fishing with his father, Danny wanted to be a chef, Alicia lived with her grandfather, Lasandra's grandmother had recently died.

Personal Symbol

At this point, we returned to the model and discussed the artist's choice of symbols. I showed my students my self-portrait that incorporated two symbols: snow and wolves. I told the story about my symbols: "I love the energy that snow, the outdoors, and the fresh air give me. Recently, I was on a cross-country ski trip to Yellowstone in winter, where I saw wolves resting after a big meal of elk they had hunted down. I admire these animals for their independence, intelligence, and ability to work together. Now go back to your list of things you love and choose one or two to use as

your own personal symbol. Briefly sketch your own symbol or symbols, and then share the image and the story with your small group."

Jamil described his love of basketball and the times he spends with his older brother at the park playing basketball. John's symbol was a sturgeon; he told about going fishing on the Columbia River with his dad and uncle. Danny's symbols were a barbecue and a steak; he loves to barbecue for his family. This continual sharing slowly built students' confidence and comfort level; the groups became more animated, their laughter and noise level demonstrated that they connected. Jenny and Carla laughed and chatted like long-lost friends even though they had only just met.

The Self-Portrait

I gave students a black-and-white copy of a photo of themselves, which I had taken the day before. I told them to incorporate a personal symbol(s) into the photo. Some students decided to draw their symbols on the photo, and others drew theirs on a separate piece of paper, cut them out, and glued them on top of the photo. The variety of approaches and designs that sprang from this activity was impressive.

Once students completed the self-portraits, they selected a piece of light-colored construction paper (18" x 12" is a commonly available size) and glued their portraits onto this background. (The key is to choose construction paper at least two inches wider and taller than the self-portrait—enough space for the inside line of adjectives and the outside line of nouns.) The high level of concentration continued as students wrote their words around the portrait in the frame. Lasandra and Andre laughed with Maira about her obsession with Justin Bieber. Julian didn't like his photo, so he chose to draw his self-portrait instead, impressing his tablemates with his drawing skills.

Gallery Walk

In order to continue building community, language, and confidence, I hosted a gallery walk. I like to give students an opportunity to see and appreciate all the artwork as well as give positive feedback to the artists and make connections between students. I set up the gallery walk with the portraits displayed in the hall. I handed out multiple Post-it notes. To avoid the generic, meaningless statements like "I like it" or "It's great," I modeled specific appreciative statements: "I like how you put musical symbols around your self-portrait." "Playing basketball is important to me, too." "The flower you added to your hair really stands out." "Your self-portrait conveys so much energy and joy."

Each student stood in front of a different portrait, wrote the name of the artist on the Post-it, composed a specific, positive comment, signed the Post-it and handed it to me. At a signal, they moved one portrait to the right and repeated the process. I continued this process until their interest and focus began to wane. After I reviewed the comments, I handed them to the appropriate student artists, who were eager to read the responses.

The Poem

The self-portrait provided the perfect catalyst for the subsequent lesson: "The Outside/Inside Poem," which continued our community building, but moved us more squarely into writing. I like this poem because it springs from an immigrant culture, portrays a unique family, has a simple yet strong pattern, and paints a night at home with powerful imagery. I began by reading "The Outside/ Inside Poem" by Sarah Chan. As I read, I changed my voice to emphasize the distinction between the inside and the outside. Then, students did a choral reading of the poem—one half of the class read the outside lines, and the other half the inside lines. Choral reading is es-

When we construct a classroom around students' lives and cultures, we can raise academic expectations while we build a community.

pecially helpful for the English language learners in the classroom because they can practice the language without feeling self-conscious.

The Outside/Inside Poem
by Sarah Chan

Outside the night sneaks up with cat feet.
Inside my sisters listen to Chinese love songs
on the radio and sing along like movie stars.

Outside the snow rests on cars like thick rugs.
Inside my mother rubs circles in my brother's
    back
telling him stories of how she collected peanuts
from the riverbank after the spring floods in Lion
    Village.
Outside the stars climb into the cold winter sky.
Inside my father wraps our holiday presents,
newspaper and scotch tape crunching behind the
    door.
Outside the crescent moon hangs between the
    branches of a tree.
Inside I help my grandma make dumplings,
    pressing
my hands into the warm dough, shaping it into
    moon-smiles.
Outside the wind talks stories to the streets.
Inside my family stands at the window, holding
    hands,
listening to whispers. The night rubs against the
    glass,
trying to get in.

'Raise the Bones'

After the students became familiar with the poem, we "raised its bones," a term we use in the Oregon Writing Project to mean looking at a poem's skeleton. How did the writer build the poem? I want students to learn to "raise the bones" as they approach new pieces of writing, so they can see how writers approach different genres. After we read the poem together, students highlighted lines that resonated and then shared with a partner. When we returned to the whole group, a few students shared a favorite line, like "Outside the snow rests on cars like thick rugs." Peter noticed the comparison of the night to cat in the first and last lines. I was able to discuss how the poet used similes and metaphors in the context of the poem. We also looked at how Sarah Chan structured her poem, using repeating lines that begin outside or inside. Students noted the contrast between the coziness of the inside and the cold night outside. Inside the family was busy and interacting; outside it was lonely and dark.

To prepare students to write their own poems, I

had students experiment with writing metaphors. I referred them back to their self-portraits and directed them to take one of their nouns from the outside line. "Let's take Jamil's word 'basketball,'" I said as I wrote the phrase "Outside I am a basketball" on the document camera. "Notice how I extend the metaphor by adding a verb phrase, such as 'Outside I am a basketball pounding on the concrete.' Now let's look at Andre's lion. I might add, 'Outside I am a lion dreaming in the shade.' In my self-portrait I wrote, 'Outside I am a wolf.' I added the verb phrase 'loping across the snow.'" After the students wrote one or two metaphors and added verb phrases, a few students volunteered to read theirs aloud. Caitlyn wrote, "Outside I am snow dropping like leaves." Lasandra wrote, "I am a bubble trying to pop." An wrote, "Inside I am a pink shirt living in the closet."

Again, the movement between writing and sharing is an important piece of building a classroom community where students see each other more fully, but where they also learn with and from each other. The best moments are when students crowd together, sharing their lines, laughing or nodding at each other's wisdom.

Write the Poem

As we moved into writing the poem, I modeled my process first on a T-chart, listing inside pieces on one side and outside on the other. As students began their own writing, I reminded them, "Don't judge your ideas. Just let them flow and let one idea lead into the next." After the T-chart brainstorming session, they composed the poem in the Outside/Inside format, using some of the metaphors and verb phrases from their previous brainstorming.

When students finished the first draft, I handed out a poetry checklist I had created and asked them to highlight in one color all the specific details that created a clear image and in another color an example of a metaphor or simile. I asked for volunteers to share their poems on the document camera. Because of the sharing we had already done, many students were willing to place their poems in full view. I reminded them that we were looking for and appreciating specific details and figurative language. We were not judges or critics. I then gave students time to revise, followed by a final read-around.

Again, we only applauded students' efforts because a focus on individual strengths builds the confidence and cohesion of the entire community.

At a time when teachers are forced to do whatever it takes to improve test scores, we must pause to

I have discovered that images lead to talking and talking leads to writing.

remember that when we systematically construct a classroom around students' lives and cultures, we can raise academic expectations while we build a community. These two lessons serve many purposes: as an icebreaker, as a writing craft lesson, as a grammar lesson, and, most importantly, as a community builder. Students forged connections with peers; they laughed together; others listened to them; and they moved beyond stereotypes and shared their real selves in a safe, appreciative environment. They also revisited grammar and figurative language in the context of genuine writing and made revisions according to clear criteria. From this small opening lesson, our class took an important step toward building a community of writers and learners who support and inspire each other in an atmosphere of acceptance and respect. ✳

. . . .

Ann Truax retired from teaching ESL in Portland Public Schools and works as a writing coach with the Oregon Writing Project.

Resources

Selected art from *Just Like Me* © 1997 by Maya Christina Gonzalez.

Ada, Alma Flor, Violet J. Harris, and Lee Bennet Hopkins, eds. *A Chorus of Cultures Anthology: Developing Literacy Through Multicultural Poetry.* Des Moines, Iowa: Hampton Brown, 1994.

For My People

BY LINDA CHRISTENSEN

RICARDO LEVINS MORALES

"I don't understand how you could walk into that building day after day for 24 years," the older woman standing at the school copier told me. "I have to go in there once a week, and I fear for my life every time I walk up those stairs. All of those Black boys with their hoodlum clothes—sweatshirt hoods pulled up over their heads, baggy pants—I'm afraid they're going to knock me down the steps and steal my purse."

I look at her and remember Damon and Sekou, young Black men I taught at "that building"—Jefferson High School. I remember their brilliance, imagine their faces—one in graduate school, one at NASA. I think of Kanaan's huge heart, of Frank's humor. I think of Aaron Wheeler-Kay's poem written after we visited an art museum exhibit of Carrie Mae Weems' "I Went Looking for Africa" artwork. Using Weems' phrase as a starting point, Aaron wrote:

I Went Looking for Jefferson
and I found. . .
all the nations of the world
wrapped in baggy jeans
sweatshirts
braids.
Closed minds slowly opening
like doors under water.
Jefferson is our whetstone
the blade is our mind.

There was no blade to open the mind of the woman at the copy machine. I'd met her before, in countless other closed minds. Many people—teachers, parents, reporters, students from other schools—who sized up those of us who attended or worked at Jefferson based on stereotyped images and counted us out, usually without ever venturing inside to our classrooms. Their comments disrespected our school, our students, our community. And even when they weren't as blatant in their comments, their looks or their body language spoke bluntly.

Students, particularly students who don't fit the social norm because of their race, language, class, sexual orientation, weight, or ability to purchase the latest fashions, have plenty of reasons to share their anger and frustration—sometimes at inappropriate times and in inappropriate ways when they feel they've been disrespected. The classroom can be a safe place for students to not only talk back, but also to affirm their right to a place in the world. During the years I worked at Jefferson, I found it necessary to talk back to those disrespectful and untrue images that the media and popular opinion formed about my students, our school, and our community.

Teaching Strategy

I begin by reading Margaret Walker's powerful "For My People." Walker's poem teaches about the hardships that African Americans endured, but she also celebrates the triumphs of her people. She ends the poem with an exhortation, "Let a new earth rise. Let another world be born. . . . Let a beauty full of/healing and a strength of final clenching be the pulsing/in our spirits and our blood." It's the perfect poem to both examine our history and to talk back to the disrespect and disenfranchisement that many communities experience.

After we read the poem through the first time, I ask students what the poem is about. "Who are Margaret Walker's people? Go through each stanza and notice what she says about her people in each stanza. Write notes to yourself in the margins, what is she telling us? Underline words or phrases that help you understand what's happening." As a class we go through Walker's poem, examining the way she weaves the history of her people throughout the poem: their work, their play, their schooling, their triumphs and their problems. For example, we pause to talk about the stanza about playing:

> For my playmates in the clay and dust and sand
>   of Alabama
> backyards playing baptizing and preaching and
>   doctor
> and jail and soldier and school and mama and
>   cooking
> and playhouse and concert and store and hair and
> Miss Choomby and company;

Students point out that the kids play at being grown-ups—preachers, doctors, teachers. They also note that Walker names the place, Alabama, and describes the setting: clay and dust and sand. In the school stanza, I want students to see the change of tone, from playful to "bitter" and to think about the historical period of segregation and how that might help us understand this stanza. Ultimately, I push students to stand back from the poem to notice that Walker is examining the history of her people—creating a format that we can use to talk about our own people: What are our strengths? What misconceptions do people have about us? What hardships have we overcome?

Once we examine the content of the poem, I ask students, "What do you notice about the way Walker constructs her poem? What poetic features—like repetition or alliteration do you notice?" Most students pick out her repeating line "For my people. . ." and how she uses the phrase as an introduction to her theme for that stanza and follows it with a list. For example:

> For my people everywhere singing their slave songs
> repeatedly: their dirges and their ditties and their
>   blues
> and jubilees, praying their prayers nightly to an
> unknown god, bending their knees humbly to an
> unseen power;

I tell students to highlight the line because we want to use her poem as a model for their poems.

Walker's poem teaches the strength of using repetition and lists in poetry. If students don't notice her delicious language on their own, I point out the rhythm of the line—"their dirges and their ditties and their blues and jubilees"—as well as the repetition of sounds in each of the phrases: singing slave songs, dirges and ditties, and praying prayers. For beginning poets the format of a repeating line followed by a list as well as repeating sounds is a helpful link into the poem, but in my assignment, I don't require students to follow the format. The best poetry launches from models rather than religiously following a format.

Then I ask students to create a list of their "people." I tell them to think of all of the communities they belong to. I list mine on the board as a way to stimulate them to think beyond their immediate categories. My list includes: Jefferson, poor whites, working class, Norwegians, Germans, teachers, feminists, social activists, women, mothers, overweight people, environmentalists.

I often use Jefferson as a model because it's the one community we all share. We catalogue reasons to celebrate our school: its diverse student body, the many languages heard in the halls, the Jefferson dancers, *Rites of Passage* (Jefferson's literary magazine), the powerful student-created murals on the walls. Once we've brainstormed together, I ask students to share a few groups from their lists, so students who are stuck can get some ideas. Then I say, "Pick one of your communities and list what you can praise about it." After a few minutes, I encourage students to partner share and again I ask a few students to share out.

Once they have their praise in place, I say, "This time I want you to think about any common misconceptions people have about any of your people. What are some of those misconceptions?" This category sometimes stumps students. Hearing how their classmates approach this topic can prompt new insights. "It's important that we 'talk back' to those judgments that people have made about our groups. In the same way Margaret Walker talked back by showing her people standing up against the injustices they endured: 'For my people standing staring trying to fashion a better way/from confusion, from hypocrisy and misunderstanding,/trying to fashion a world that will hold all the people, . . .'"

In this, as in any assignment, some students might immediately get an idea, while others need more time to figure out who their "people" are, or what they want to say about them. This is a time when I circle the room, noticing whose writing is flowing and whose writing is stuck. I often conference with students who look stumped.

My student Cang Dao was stuck initially. We discussed how kids made fun of his newcomer English, but we also talked about how he can speak more languages than most of the student body. He embedded pieces of that talk in his poem:

People don't know how I feel
"You can't talk like us."
The words hurt me more than
It hurts them to say.
I'm getting an attitude.
Too many jokes,
I can't accept it.
What's wrong about me
That may not be accepted by them?
Is it the way I look or
The way I talk?
How many languages can you speak?
I speak four.
Is there something from
Me that you want?
My beautiful brown eyes or
My lovely skin?
Don't get jealous.

Cang's poem, "Race," talks back to those who have put him down, but his poem also celebrates some of the attributes he shares with his people.

Sophia Farrier takes the opening lines from Walker and uses them to describe her pain in her poem "This is for. . ." She writes:

This is for the people who believed I was nothing,
that I would never be special in anyone's mind.
This is for the people who said they were my
    friends,
but always put me down. . .
This is for the people who took my self-esteem
    away,
for those who never cared,
who ignored me because I wasn't "fashionable."

At the end of her poem, she attempts to find strength in herself. She changes the line from "This is for the people" to "This is for me. . .":

This is for me because I didn't believe in myself.
For me because I tried too hard to be who I
    wasn't and
couldn't be. . .
And this is for my blood that rushes thick and thin
that sometimes stands tall,
but sometimes cowers away.

Lori Ann Durbin, a senior in my Writing for Publication class, was a transplanted self-described cowgirl who ended up at Jefferson High School. Her poem celebrates that heritage:

Country Folk
For my folk, two-steppin', shit-kickin' pioneers.
Blue-collar, redneck, bowlegged horsemen. . .
This is my song to you.
Moonshiners, horse ranchers, hillbilly roots,
wild women, bare feet, it's nothin' or it's boots,
twangy sweet fiddle, songs about our lives,
maybe sappy to everyone else, but that's how we
    survive.
Fishin', singin', ridin' bareback in the field,
tight cowboy butts and Wranglers.
I love the way they feel.
Tailgate parties, couples in the barn, hay in our
    hair.
It's not just music.
It's a way of life.

Justin Morris, another senior, took stereotypes about Black people and used them in his celebration. His poem demonstrates an in-your-face love for all aspects of his heritage. One night I was at a local copy store making huge posters of these poems to hang around the school. Several African American men from the community were copying on a machine close to my oversize machine. They laughed when they read Justin's poem and took one of the copies to hang in their office.

For My People
This is for my people
who are "colored"
who are proud.

For my people
who cause white women to clutch their purses
who white men look down on
who drank from different fountains
who fought prejudice.
For my people
with kinky afros
and Jheri curls.
For my people
with big lips
and wide noses.
For my people
with black power
fingertips drenched with barbecue sauce.
For the people
with pink hearts
and brown/black skins.
For my people:
Stay strong.

The woman who feared for her life each time she walked Jefferson's halls "confessed" her racism—which is perhaps the first step toward change. I want her to read my students' poems. I want her to see beyond the baggy pants and sweatshirts to the whetstone that sharpened their minds. I hope that by reading their words, she'll see the "pink hearts" inside the "brown/black" skin, she'll hear the intelligence that ricochets off Jefferson's walls, and know she doesn't have to be afraid. ✳

. . . .

Linda Christensen (lmc@lclark.edu) is director of the Oregon Writing Project at Lewis & Clark College in Portland, Ore. She is a Rethinking Schools editor and author of Reading, Writing, and Rising Up *and* Teaching for Joy and Justice.

Resources

Walker, Margaret. "For My People." *This Is My Century: New and Collected Poems.* Athens: University of Georgia Press, 1989.

"For My People" by Margaret Walker is available in the Poetry Foundation's Poetry magazine (www.poetryfoundation.org/poetrymagazine/poem/11053).

For My People
by Debby Gordan

For my people on Kerby and Commercial,
Alberta and Killingsworth,
sitting in their cars and porches
drinking their Kool-Aid
and listening to their music.

For my people, stuck between lies
and hate
in front of discrimination
and behind set minds.

For my people who send their children
to Jefferson to learn a better way of life,
For my people, whose children
are pushed aside by society and forgotten.

For my people who live
and struggle.

. . . .

Country Folk
by Lori Ann Durbin

For my folk, two-steppin', shit-kickin' pioneers.
Blue-collar, redneck, bowlegged horsemen. . .
This is my song to you.
Moonshiners, horse ranchers, hillbilly roots,
wild women, bare feet, it's nothin' or it's boots,
twangy sweet fiddle, songs about our lives,
maybe sappy to everyone else, but that's how we
survive.
Fishin', singin', ridin' bareback in the field,
tight cowboy butts and Wranglers.
I love the way they feel.
Tailgate parties, couples in the barn, hay in our hair.
It's not just music.
It's a way of life.

For My People
by Justin Morris

This is for my people
who are "colored"
who are proud.

For my people
who cause white women to clutch their purses
who white men look down on
who drank from different fountains
who fought prejudice.

For my people
with kinky afros
and Jheri curls.

For my people
with big lips
and wide noses.

For my people
with black power
fingertips drenched with barbecue sauce.

For the people
with pink hearts
and brown/black skins.
For my people:
Stay strong.

A Pure Medley

by Adeline Nieto

In a class on culturally responsive teaching at Ithaca College, my professor, Jeff Claus, asked us to create poems of introduction. He was modeling how to use two of Linda Christensen's poetry lessons: "Where I'm From: Inviting Students' Lives into the Classroom" and "For My People." This is a poem I wrote in response.

This is not about the debated clash of civilizations
But about the vibrant, continuous bleeding of cultures
This is for the Americanized, assimilated immigrants' children
The evolving, eclectic generation
Who never purposely left behind an identity
Who never purposely decided to plow forward and
Who never purposely stopped reflecting back
This is for those who inhale the desire to recount histories
And exhale the desire to discount them
This is not for my grandparents, or even for my mother or for my father, Jorge
This is for my sister and for my brother, George
Who eat *lumpia* and *kare-kare*, and *pollo saltado* and *arepa* in the same week
Who say *Ay naku po* and *Ay ay ay*, and Tita and Tía
Who tan and freckle, drawing constellations on exposed flesh
Attempting to connect fleeting shooting stars
Who sit side by side and are mistaken for
Not brother and sister, or even cousins
But friends
This is for those of us who are the artifacts of a marriage
Of two humans who originated on opposite sides of the world
Who choose to remember roots for the sake of diversity
And to forget them for the joyous sake of simplicity
This is for those of us who long for strong family reunions
That flower from our branch on the cactus
Delicately settled atop spines
For those who have never witnessed their mother's relatives and their father's relatives
Relate
And who consequently forfeited world peace at a young age
This is for the ones who pump tangoing mixed blood
Of entities not quite white and not quite black
Not quite indigenous and not quite invasive
For the dancers who mirror twisting kaleidoscopes
Morphing into beautiful, seemingly graceful patterns of colorful beads
For the chameleons in this world occupying myriad bodies of land
Inquisitive to live beyond, and therefore leave, the familiar
This is for my journeys to a motherland and to my imperialist forefather
That only resulted in more exclusion and confusion
This is for fighting against being commodified and exotified
For overcoming triple the stereotypes
Triple the ignorant remarks

And triple the caricatures
This is for educating schoolmates that Filipino is spelled with an F
And café owners that Colombia is spelled with an O
This is for the understanding that a half or a quarter of an ethnicity
More often eliminates me from the group rather than adding me in
This is for the ability to choose which facet to identify with
Only after I analyze which would be most convenient
For calculating a witty response to "Where are you from?"
And for becoming so *damn* confused when
Offering a literal response to the philosophical question "What are you?"
This is for those of us who have inevitably become accepting of all walks of life
After our own walk in life
For those whose half-life, and even quarter-life, crisis
Never quite leaves shore because the identity crisis is still out at bay
Running the length of the marathon
This is for those of us who have the knowledge of nomads
Thumb tacking trails of tears and visited validations
Learning to hate
The borders and unforgiving definitions
Society stresses to create and uphold
To construct contrasts to outshine the shadowed
And the ethnocentricism and xenophobia
That scares and scars
Learning to love
The transcendence and ambiguity
That comes with linked journeys and linked fates
With shared middles and shared tenses
And the self-discovery and self-acceptance
Initiating genuine engagement
Yet this is primarily for those of us who
While we may have sacrificed world peace
Still find the energy to nurture inner peace
Because we know that with deep-rooted discoveries
We may extrapolate our findings and our amends
From a sample of self to a population of plenty

. . . .

Adeline Nieto teaches 6th grade in New York City.

Talking Back to the World
Turning poetic lines into visual poetry

BY RENÉE WATSON

ROXANNA BIKADOROFF

I am not a visual artist. At best, I can draw a heart. But it stops there. Even my stick figures could use improvement. So when my middle school students asked me if they could do an art project, I quickly made an excuse. "We don't have time. It's not a part of the unit."

It was partly true. I had planned out a four-week poetry unit on exploring identity. Besides teaching students the basics—What is a stanza? Why do poets break lines?—I also had to find the best poems to spark my students' interests and get them motivated to talk and write about who they are, where they are from.

At the start of our after-school program, the teachers decided our goals would include teaching students how to connect poetry to their living histories and how to use poetry as a means to talk back to the world. My 90-minute lesson plans were bursting with free writes, reading and critiquing poems, writing poems, revising poems, performing poems—there was no room for art. Especially not the simplistic assignment I have done in times past: "Choose an image from your poem and illustrate it." If students were going to make illustrations, I wanted these to have meaning and tie into our unit.

It wasn't until our fourth lesson that I thought of a way to incorporate art into our poetry class. Students had written poems about what raised them (see Linda Christensen's "'Raised by Women': Celebrating Our Homes," p. 23), and they had written a response to the free-write question "If people could see the true me, what would they see?" We spent two sessions writing about and discussing our roots. I learned that my Bronx students carried in them the turquoise blue water of Jamaica, the sweet mangos of the Dominican Republic, and the steaming hot *café con leche* of Puerto Rico. They were raised by video games and praying grandmothers, by leftovers that taste better on the second day and empty pockets, with not even lint or change. In "Ode to My Skin Tone," Richard wrote:

> I am Sunset Beige, the color of the beach
> the color of Spanish tongues

Rozalyn gave homage to her heritage, acknowledging in her poem that sometimes, because of her light skin, she can hide her ethnicity:

> No longer will I deny Puerto Rico
> I will wear the bright colors of
> PR with pride

They took great risks. I modeled the risk-taking by sharing with them how I wish I knew more about my Jamaican heritage, how I grew up a Black girl in Oregon and what it was like attending a predominantly white middle school. I introduced my East Coast students to the Northwest through my poem "Where I'm From":

> I'm from. . .
> A place where rain falls
> more than sun shines.
> I'm from Douglas firs and pine trees,
> where we walk under waterfalls,
> drive up windy roads to Mt. Hood,
> and escape to the beaches on the Oregon coast.

Just a few stanzas later, students saw a glimpse of my Northeast Portland neighborhood:

> Where I'm from the whole neighborhood is your
>   family
> ladies sit on their porches looking out for you
> shooing away boys like flies.
> Callin' your momma to tell what you did
> before you can get home and lie about it.

As a writer in the schools it is important for me to share my work with students and to let them see me create alongside them. In one of our lessons, the writing prompt "If your skin tone could speak, what would it say?" led me to share how that when I was young, I felt uncomfortable in my skin: "I am dark-skinned with brown eyes, and my mother is very light-skinned with green eyes. When we went places together, just the two of us, I felt out of place."

'How Do You Want to Introduce Yourself to the World?'

My class is made up of Latinx and Back students who range across light and dark shades of brown. They are middle school students who are questioning their self-worth, learning from society who is and isn't beautiful. They live in the Bronx and they are aware that there is a stigma attached to their neighborhood. I tell them: "Your journal is the place where you can respond to the many voices speaking to you. What do you want to say about your community? Your family? How do you want to introduce yourself to the world?"

Page after page, my students wrote poems that spoke directly to the stereotypes they are judged by. Khaiya wrote:

> I am a black girl, yes
> But not a typical one
> I am a girl full of dreams
> I am not parentless
> I was born into a family of caring

It was during our class sharing that I realized I wanted to do something with these poems. Something more than type them and hang them on the bare white classroom wall. These poems were about seeing a student for who she or he really is. For looking past the clothes, hearing past the accent, and listening—really listening.

What if I could really look at Kaheem and see lyrics of the gospel hymns that his grandmother sings to him? What if every time I looked in Leticia's eyes I saw the words *strength* and *beauty*? I decided to close the unit by having students create self-portraits using the strongest lines from their poems.

Poetry Lines Become Visual Self-Portraits

When students came into the room, they were greeted with a question on the board: "Who am I and how can I recreate myself?"

I asked students to comb through their journals and select three or more of the very best lines and phrases from each of their poems: "Narrow it down to the heart of your piece. What are the most important phrases in the poem? Copy them to a new sheet of paper."

I walked around the room and checked in with students who seemed stuck. Because most of them had shared their poems in previous read-arounds, I had a sense of the powerful lines they had written and reminded them of the feedback their peers had given them. "When you read that poem to the class, we all really liked your last stanza. What about getting phrases from there?"

After about 15 minutes, students had "greatest hits lists" of their own words. I then asked students to write one-word responses to the following prompts: List two places you've lived in, visited, or want to go to. List two types of music you enjoy listening to. List three words that have special meaning to you. For the last prompt, I gave a few examples. "For instance, the word 'rebirth' is the definition of my name, so that word means something to me. I also like the word 'faith' because I have had to rely on my faith to get me through hard times."

I allowed time for student volunteers to share one phrase or line of poetry, and a few shared their favorite place or meaningful word. Two of Malek's favorite words were "vibrant" and "heroic."

Once a few students shared, I wrote the word "Self-Portrait" on the board and asked the class to come up with a definition. I then explained the activity. "Today, you are going to make a self-portrait. Except, instead of drawing your features, you are going to use words." I passed my example around, using lines from my "Where I'm From" poem since students were familiar with that piece. The template I used was the outline of a blank face. "What do you notice about my

ears?" I asked.

"They have the words 'gospel' and 'jazz' written on them."

"What do you notice about my forehead?"

"Lines from your poem are written across the forehead."

I continued asking questions as my self-portrait made its way around the class. "Are all the words the same size? What do you notice about the angle of the words?"

Cory noticed that some words were bigger than others and that I used multiple colors. Layah pointed out that I wrote in a circular direction, except for the placement of my eyes, nose, and lips.

I told the class: "This is your chance to show people who you really are. To show them all the things that have shaped you."

Khaiya raised her hand. "So it's like we're focusing on our soul—not the physical parts?"

"Exactly."

Before giving them the art supplies and template, I challenged students to be thoughtful about the placement of their words. "What words should be your eyes?

My students wrote poems that spoke directly to the stereotypes they are judged by.

What lines should be written around the side of your face? Your forehead? Which lines should be your hair?"

I wrote the instructions on the board, giving students a step-by-step checklist:

- Create your eyes using two of your meaningful words.
- Create your eyebrows using the two places you wrote down.
- Create your nose using your initials.
- Create your mouth using your third meaningful word.
- Write your favorite music along your ears.
- Fill in the face with lines and phrases from your poem.

"This is a checklist for those of you who want structure or need help getting started," I told the class. "If you want to switch the placement of the words, that's fine."

Students got to work, using the thin-tipped markers I passed out. While they worked I played music that reinforced many of the themes we had talked about in the past few weeks (including "Little Things" and "I Am Not My Hair" by India Arie, "Comin' from Where I'm From" by Anthony Hamilton, and "Doo Wop [That Thing]" by Lauryn Hill).

During work time, I listened in on my students as they talked to each other. "Where do you think I should put this line?" Rozalyn asked Khaiya.

"Under your mouth," Khaiya suggested.

I read the line "My tongue travels through the portal of time and speaks the language of my ancestors."

Malek listed his favorite childhood songs along the top of his head. Leticia's hair was full of memories of her and her cousin.

When students finished, they cut out the face and came to me to select their background paper. I had a stack of patterned card stock that we used for mounting the faces. Students glued their cutout face on the paper and traced around the face with a black marker, to make it stand out against the background color.

Self-Portraits to Share

At the end of class, students stood up and shared their self-portraits. I asked students to listen closely to the person who was sharing. "Try to find one thing you have in common and one new thing you didn't know." Even my quiet students volunteered to share. And our after-school classroom, made up of students from different schools, different backgrounds, became a community. "I go to church, too!" a student said.

"I remember that cartoon!"

"My family eats curried goat, too."

And yet, with all the similarities, no one's face looked the same, no two portraits were alike.

I later went through the self-portraits, re-reading lines and taking in who my students were. I learned a lot about them, not only because of what they included in the portrait, but also because of what they left out, and where they placed certain words. Each time I looked at these works of art, I noticed something different—a new word or phrase stood out that made me want to know more.

I realized that I wanted to know more about *all* my students—even the ones I taught in other programs at other schools. I modified this activity and used it in poetry residencies with both elementary and high school students. Instead of having a whole unit's worth of poems to choose from, sometimes students just had one—an "I Am Poem" or a "Neighborhood Poem." Any writing that is autobiographical has worked well and has given students the power to mine the beauty and strength that is within them.

A few weeks after my first attempt at bringing visual art into the classroom, my middle school students had an open mic for the community. Parents, teachers, and family members came together to celebrate the powerful words of our young people.

My students were so proud to see their self-portraits showcased. Parents surveyed the wall and saw inside the souls of their children. One parent stared at the wall and smiled, pointing to her daughter's line that read "I dream of traveling to London." She looked at me and said, "I didn't even know that."

Together we stood at the wall learning and relearning the young people we thought we knew. Together we saw them again, for the first time. ✳

. . . .

Renée Watson (reneewatson.net) is an author, performer, and educator. Her children's books have received several honors, including an NAACP Image Award nomination. She teaches poetry at DreamYard in New York City. Student names have been changed.

CHAPTER TWO

Celebrations

Lift every voice and sing

MEREDITH STERN

Gurl

by Mary Blalock

From Adam's rib
it's prophesied
I came,
but that's his story.

I'm walking on my own
down these streets
with a stop sign on every corner,
taking my time.
I've got no place to go 'cept forward.

Down these highways without a road map,
down these sidewalks,
where the cracks want to break my mother's back,
where the city is crowded.

I'm walking on my own.

I'm not on a Stairmaster,
and I won't wait for an elevator.
I'm taking the fire escape
to the top floor.

If I want to,
I'll walk all around the world,
taking the long way
or the shortcuts,
'cross the countries and through the oceans.
I won't be swimming.
I'll walk
on my own.

Celebrations

Lift every voice and sing

On Feb. 12, 1900, as part of Lincoln's birthday celebration, a choir of 500 children first performed James Weldon Johnson's poem/song "Lift Every Voice and Sing" at the segregated Stanton School, where Johnson served as principal. Often called the "Black National Anthem," the poem is a song of joy and hope in the midst of despair, signifying gratitude for the changes that have occurred for African Americans, yet mindful that the struggle for justice and equality is not over yet.

Our Celebrations chapter seeks the same balance. In the 1900s African Americans faced lynchings, Jim Crow laws, and the failure of Reconstruction. In contemporary times, students face school shootings, war, climate chaos, mean-spirited immigration policies, the defunding of public schools, and more.

And yet, despite the recurring waves of pain and despair—and our need to help students make sense of the world—we also want our students to experience joy. Sometimes this delight comes when we pause to remind ourselves of the beauty of the world as Langston Hughes does in "Daybreak in Alabama."

> When I get to be a composer
> I'm gonna write me some music about
> Daybreak in Alabama
> And I'm gonna put the purtiest songs in it
> Rising out of the ground like a swamp mist
> And falling out of heaven like soft dew.
> I'm gonna put some tall tall trees in it
> And the scent of pine needles
> And the smell of red clay after rain

For student Francis Ram, joy is the smell of Indian curry on his mother's stove; for Jenelle Yarbrough, joy is Grandma's Kool-Aid on the front porch on a hot summer day. In Elizabeth Schlessman-Barbian's "Aquí y Allá," Juliana celebrates raindrops "that dance on the floor." We believe critical educators should engage students in critique, but we should also lift up and celebrate what is right and beautiful and true in the world.

Sometimes we need to teach students to recognize and celebrate all of the ways *they* are beautiful—from their language, to their too-big or too-little hips and lips to their hair that refuses to be tamed, and from the color of their skin to the size of their thighs. In this chapter, teachers help their students reclaim the pieces of their bodies, languages, and cultures that society has tarnished and tainted—as Katharine Johnson's 1st- and 2nd-grade students do when they celebrate all of the colors of their skin.

These poetic celebrations of student lives illuminate the brilliance that each child brings to class; they encourage the kind of resiliency young people need to hone to survive in a world wracked by pain. ✳

. . . .

Hughes, Langston. "Daybreak in Alabama," in Rampersad, Arnold (Ed.), The Collected Poems of Langston Hughes. *New York: Alfred A. Knopf, 1994. Available at www.poemhunter.com/poem/daybreak-in-alabama.*

Praise Poems

Celebrating and back talking

BY LINDA CHRISTENSEN

BEC YOUNG

As I try to equip students to shake off the media and social expectations of how to look, sound, and live in the world, I find it necessary to balance the critical stance we strive for in class with times of laughter and playfulness. I want to create more opportunities for joy. But even in those moments of joy, of community building, I want students to think critically about the world.

We read poets who found it necessary to praise themselves as a way to talk back to the dominant European American standards of beauty and culture. For example, Lucille Clifton and Maya Angelou praise big women—rejecting the norm of beauty that holds thinness as the standard. Mari Evans' poem "Who Can Be Born Black" and Dudley Randall's "Blackberry Sweet" both sing the beauty of blackness. I found many of the poems I use in *In Search of Color Everywhere: A Collection of African-American Poetry*, edited by E. Ethelbert Miller. We read poems by Langston Hughes, Renée Watson, and others who celebrate African American culture and beauty.

We also read Lawson Fusao Inada's "On Being Asian American," Naomi Shihab Nye's poem "Blood" about being Palestinian, and poet Bao Phi, who praises the Vietnamese who survived wars. (See Resources.)

Writing praise poems gives us a positive way to look at ourselves, but these poems also speak against the negative portrayals of race, language, gender, sexual orientation, and size that Jefferson students too often see associated with their neighborhood and their school. This is a poetry assignment I return to again and again as my students and I explore thematic units throughout the year. I encourage students to praise themselves, their "people," their school, their neighborhood—as they praise what society too often denounces.

Of course, this is awkward. Most students have been taught that bragging is not acceptable. That's why I frame the idea socially and historically. When Clifton writes in her poem "homage to my hips" that "these hips are big hips/they don't like to be held back./these hips have never been enslaved. . . . these hips are mighty hips/these hips are magic hips," she critiques the way women have been judged as well as the treatment of African Americans.

As we talk about standards of beauty and materialism in the "Unlearning the Myths" unit (*Reading, Writing, and Rising Up*), students gain permission to criticize commercially produced images. In writing about themselves, students learn to praise their own attributes that often have been overlooked or held in contempt by society. Some students love the opportunity to describe the beauty that the world has overlooked. Curtina Barr wrote:

The mirror told me,
Yo' skin the color of coffee
after the cream's been poured in.
Yo' body's just the right size—
not too plump,/not too thin.

Damon wrote a praise poem about his backside. Marcus wrote about his luscious lips. In my classroom, students across races need to find room to praise, whether their physical qualities have been overlooked or held up as the ideal. Aaron Wheeler-Kay wrote about his eyes in a poem called "I Got the Blues": "Blue eyes/Yes, Ma'am./Blue./Like the ocean—/No, blue like new jeans./Stiff and comfy."

And Mary Blalock refuted the image of women as frail and needy in her poem "Gurl."

From Adam's rib
it's prophesied
I came,
but that's his story.

I'm walking on my own
down these streets
with a stop sign on every corner,
taking my time.
I've got no place to go 'cept forward.

In the essay "Black Like Me" (see p. 202), my former student Renée Watson, author and poet extraordinaire, tells about an incident in her middle school science class, where a teacher used Renée's race as a weapon against her. Years later, Renée wrote a beautiful praise poem that both celebrates her skin and her culture and talks back to her teacher:

black like collard greens & salted meat
    simmering on a stove.
black like hot water cornbread & iron skillets,
    like juke joints & fish frys
black like soul train lines & the electric slide at
    weddings and birthdays
black like vaseline on ashy knees, like beads
    decorating braids
black like cotton fields & soul-cried spirituals.

my skin is black

After spending nearly 40 years in the classroom, I know that many students walk around with wounds inflicted by a society that tells them they aren't smart enough, good-looking enough, thin enough, rich enough, light or dark enough, linguistically correct enough. Through the praise poem and classroom talk, students can begin to dismantle those wounds.

As students read aloud, the poems bring kinship and often a great deal of laughter to our classroom community. When Marcus returned two years after he graduated, we still laughed about his "luscious lips."

Teaching Strategy

1. We begin by reading Maya Angelou's "Phenomenal Woman," Lucille Clifton's "homage to my hips," and others. I ask the students to talk about what the poets are praising and why they might feel it necessary to praise themselves. If I am teaching this during a unit on the Harlem Renaissance, I talk about the history of the movement and historical times as well.

2. I ask students to think of something about themselves, their bodies, homes, community, school, culture, or language that deserves praise, but that may not often receive praise. I ask a few students to share their ideas so they can help shake loose some ideas for classmates who are stuck.

3. As I select the poems—whether they are models to help us praise ourselves in the "Unlearning the Myths" unit, praise our homes and cultures in the immigration unit, praise our language in the "Politics of Language" unit, or praise our school or neighborhood after negative media coverage—I look for poems that provide a pattern or hook. Clifton's "what the mirror said," for example, is a great opening for students. They can look in the mirror

I encourage students to praise themselves, their "people," their school, their neighborhood—as they praise what society too often denounces.

and pay homage to themselves as Curtina Barr did, or they can praise their heritage as Chetan Patel did in his poem "Tiger Eyes." It helps if students have several ideas of how to begin their poems. I try to use models from both professional and student writers.

4. I spend a couple of days reading and discussing poems because I want students to notice what stereotype or misinformation the poet is talking back to. For example, Renée Watson celebrates her Black roots, and she also talks back to her science teacher's derogatory remarks. Chetan Patel tells the story of his people in "Tiger Eyes."

5. Sometimes students get stuck in this—and other—assignments. Some have difficulty praising themselves. I understand this problem because I haven't been able to write a decent praise poem about myself either, so I allow students to find their own passion in the assignment while reminding them to remember the intent of the poem: Praise something that may not traditionally be valued in our society.

6. I usually turn the lights off and ask students to find a space where they can write quietly. Some like to sit on the floor, others on the windowsill, some turn their desks to the wall. This allows them time to get prepared. Then I tell students that when I turn the lights back on they must begin writing in silence. I also tell them, "If you get stuck, go back to the models. Which ones speak to you? How can you lift off this poem to create your own? Is there a repeating line? Is there an image? Is there a list? Don't overthink it, let the writing flow. When you get stuck, just drop down a line and start a new stanza."

I love the book *We Make The Road While Walking*, a conversation between Myles Horton and Paulo Freire, because it is the perfect metaphor for our classrooms. Every step, every lesson is part of the road we make in our yearlong journey with our students. There is no one lesson that helps undo the harm our society has nested into our students' consciousness through messages about who counts and who doesn't, who is beautiful and who isn't, which language is "standard" and which language is inferior, what measures success or failure. We make new paths into student consciousness by helping them imagine a place where "everyone is equidistant from perfection," as my student Uriah Boyd wrote in an essay:

I like to think that there still exist times and places where the color of one's skin is completely irrelevant to the way that they are treated. There are places where nobody needs saving, nobody feels mistreated, and everyone is equidistant from perfection. Ideally, everyone would live in this type of place. Ignorance would be replaced with understanding. Fear with curiosity, timidity with unashamed interest. But realistically, as history has taught us, these places are often near impossible to find. ✳

. . . .

Linda Christensen (lmc@lclark.edu) is director of the Oregon Writing Project at Lewis & Clark College in Portland, Ore. She is a Rethinking Schools editor and author of Reading, Writing, and Rising Up *and* Teaching for Joy and Justice.

Resources

Angelou, Maya. "Ain't That Bad" and "Phenomenal Woman," in *And Still I Rise*. New York: Random House, 1978.

Clifton, Lucille. "homage to my hips" and "what the mirror said," in *Good Woman: Poems and a Memoir 1969–1980*. (American Poets Continuum Series, Vol. 14.) Rochester, NY: BOA Editions, 1989. Available at www.poetryfoundation.org/poem/179615 and www.afropoets.net/lucilleclifton15.html

Inada, Lawson Fusao. "On Being Asian American," in Chin, Frank (Ed.), *Aiiieeeee!: An Anthology of Asian-American Writers*. New York: Mentor, 1991.

Miller, E. Ethelbert (Ed.). *In Search of Color Everywhere: A Collection of African-American Poetry*. New York: Stewart, Tabori, & Chang, 1994.

Nye, Naomi Shihab. "Blood," in Blum, Joshua, Holman, Bob, and Pellington, Mark (Eds.), *The United States of Poetry*. New York: Harry N. Abrams Inc., 1996.

Phi, Bao. "You Bring Out the Vietnamese in Me." www.youtube.com/watch?v=qqGDfFkaMaM

What the Mirror Said—

In admiration of Lucille Clifton's poetry
by Curtina Barr

The mirror told me,
Yo' skin the color of coffee
after the cream's been poured in.
Yo' body's just the right size—
not too plump,
not too thin.
Yo' lips like cotton candy
sweet and soft.
Yo' sho' done good.
Yo' like a city,
strong and tall,
though deep in yo' eyes
I can still see yo' pain,
yo' smile and laugh.
Keep doin' yo' thang.

. . . .

I Got the Blues

by Aaron Wheeler-Kay

Blue eyes
Yes, Ma'am.
Blue.
Like the ocean—
No, blue like new jeans.
Stiff and comfy—
No, blue like hard times.
Yeah.
Blue like cold steel and oil.
Blue like the caress of jazz at a funeral.
The azure ice cubes in my head
Melt hearts.
Yes, blue like lightning in a desert storm.
Blue like twin sapphires blazing in a jeweler's
palm.
Blue like my baby.
Like my baby blues.
Blue like cold lips in winter,
Indigo stains
In an optical vein.
I got the blues
And they got a tale
To tell.

Tiger Eyes

by Chetan Patel

I look into a mirror
and watch the history inside of me
flood out.
I see the *Kshatriya* warrior,
sword in hand,
the *Sudra* laborer,
working hard at his feet.
I see the stories passed
under the Banyan tree
and the cleansing Ganges,
slicing down the Himalayas.
I see the village Panchayat,
the Lok Sabha,
the House of People.
I see the deep-fried samosas,
full of carrots and peas,
wrapped in flour,
ready to eat.
I see the river flooding
in the monsoons,
the locusts lying
in the fields of Jammu.
I see the tiger eyes
waiting in the high grass,
for me to come back
and relive the past.

Just Thick
by Bree Levine-DeSpain

Just thick
Thick like North Carolina sweet grained
Sun-kissed cornbread thick,
Melt in your mouth, smothered
With butter and honey thick.

Thick
Thick like homemade pancake batter
Smooth to the touch
Yet creamy and delectable
To the tongue.

Thick
Thick like caramel sauce
Mouthwatering, sweet, and sticky
To the touch.

Thick
Thick thighs
Thick hips
Just thick.

Good ol' Southern style, eat what tastes good
"You wanna go to Popeyes?"
"Naw, I'll have a milkshake!"
Cornbread, pancakes, caramel sauce.
I'm thick.

Black
by Anaiah Rhodes

Black is beautiful
Black is bold
Like the peppa in the salt shaker
Black words on white paper

Black is harmony
Like the notes in a symphony
The hymns my mama hums to me

Black is love
Courage in hard times
To tell it like it is

Black on the ledger
Makes the money flow
Black is success

Black magic
Elegant and classy
The feeling before the curtain pulls back
Black entourage

Black is the heartbeat
Of the soul
Like still waters
Riches untold
Black is beautiful

Odes
Celebrating the ordinary

BY LINDA CHRISTENSEN

RICARDO LEVINS MORALES

Over winter break I had breakfast with one of my former students, a poet and teacher; we discussed the box of grief that we held in our chests these days. The box is overflowing: the back-to-back deaths of Black boys/men at the hands of white police officers, the lack of justice over these deaths, the poisoning of our rivers, the removal of our mountaintops, the destruction of our schools through corporate takeovers. And on a more personal level: the death of a beloved aunt, a treasured friend, and the demise of a longtime colleague into dementia. Our talk turned toward the need to pause once in a while to remind students of the beauty that exists alongside the tragedies. The world can be a hard and scary place, especially for young people who don't have the long miles of age to see that the world can get better. So from time to time we need to take class time to ponder moments of joy; we need to stop and remind ourselves of the beauty and solidarity that surrounds us.

So every quarter, my classroom stops the grinding wheels of our curricular units to celebrate the ordinary, the common daily events we take pleasure in: the way the sun hits the water tower one morning in December, illuminating its dusty green metal to the color of the first growth on trees in spring; the smell of soup on the stove or vegetables roasting in the oven; the walk with a friend. To coax joy back into the classroom, especially when students feel down about the ways of the world, I use odes, a traditional poetic form, to help students re-see the beauty in the world outside of the shopping center.

The appreciation of the ordinary is an ongoing theme in my class, an attempt to counter the barrage of advertisements that assail our students daily with the message that they must buy, buy, buy to be happy. The ode is one more way I attempt to chip away at our consumer society. Odes give students an opportunity to appreciate the nuances and wonders of their homes, their cultures, their languages, the food on the stove, the natural world. I want students to re-see and appreciate what is in their lives instead of falling into the advertising trap of longing for what they don't have.

Instead of imitating the classical Greek odes, we follow in the footsteps of Chilean Pablo Neruda, who makes the "ordinary extraordinary" in his poetry as he celebrates the beauty in daily life: onions, tuna, socks, a woman gardening. Neruda's odes push students to use concrete details and imagery in their pieces. I use *Selected Odes of Pablo Neruda*, which has the original Spanish as well as the English translation. I also use Gary Soto's *Neighborhood Odes* with younger students.

Teaching Strategy

1. Students read Neruda's poem "Ode to My Socks" in both languages. This validates students who speak Spanish, locating writing in the broader linguistic world. I encourage students who speak more than one language to write in their home languages.

2. After we read the poem, I ask students to re-read it on their own and highlight all of the ways Neruda describes the socks. Students notice how the comparisons to fish and to birds make the socks come to life: "two woolen/fish,/two long sharks/ of lapis blue/shot/with a golden thread,/two mammoth blackbirds." We also point out the lines that compare the socks to "woven fire" that glow on his feet. The socks become magical, special, elevated, which is the point of odes. In fact, later in the poem Neruda writes that he resists the temptation to save them "as learned men collect sacred texts." I have noticed over the years the more time I spend examining the imagery in Neruda's—or Soto's—poems, the more students attempt daring, outrageous imagery on their own.

I want students to re-see and appreciate what is in their lives instead of falling into the advertising trap of longing for what they don't have.

3. To give students more ideas about how to enter the poem, we read over my previous students' models. As students read each model, we point out what's working, what "moves," or poetic devices the writers use in their pieces.

4. I tell students how Francis Ram just sat staring at his computer in room C-23 at Jefferson High School until he thought about his mother's cooking. Then he wrote furiously. His "Indian Kitchen" provides students with a great model because he lists the dishes that his mother cooks, the ingredients, and the smells—"curries and soups." He uses strong verbs: "The scent of spicy peppers/punctures the clouds of steam./The curry presses against my tongue."

5. After students are saturated in models I ask them to make a list of objects they might praise—a gift,

an everyday object, something that has meaning for them even though it might not seem important to anyone else. We also look at categories: aspects of their cultural traditions to praise—food, dance, music, language. Then I ask them to list hobbies they can write about: soccer, dance, music, etc. The idea in brainstorming is to be as inclusive as possible, so that students, who are frozen, like Francis Ram, can find a topic.

6. As students create these lists, we pause to share, so that students who are stuck can gather more ideas from their classmates. Sometimes students just need time to contemplate. I have come to appreciate that some writers are sprinters and others are long-distance runners who may need a little more time to move into their writing journey.

7. I turn off the lights and ask students to take a few deep breaths and close their eyes. They object to this at first. They fear that someone might look at them. It takes patience to get this strategy to work, but it's worth it because it teaches students how to slow down and get centered before they write. Then I ask students to think about what they are going to praise. I do this part slowly. There's a tendency to rush because the class is silent, but it takes a while to get a visual image. I ask students to remember what the object looks like, smells like, sounds like, what else it reminds them of, how they came to get it. I find the guided visualization helps students remember more details.

8. After the visualization I say, "When I turn the lights on, I want you to write in silence. Write as quickly as you can. Make mistakes, they create great poetry. When you are stuck, move down a line and start again."

9. With classes of younger students, I sometimes begin by asking them to write a paragraph describing the object. They can use these details as they condense the lines and move words into stanzas.

Students have written odes to the Spanish language, their skin, their weight, lesbians, a mother's hands, animal cookies, a grandfather's hat, coffee, Jefferson High School, the color red, writing, and more.

The ode is a form students frequently return to in their writing.

I don't want to exaggerate the importance of this lesson. It is a small tool in my fight against consumerism, cynicism, and despair. But I do believe that if I want my students to imagine a more just society, I must spend time teaching them how to find what's good as well as to find what's wrong. My classroom provides a small space to undermine a social system that daily damages my students with belittling messages. I hope to help students not only construct a critique, but also to build a community that can appreciate the ordinary, laugh, and share joy. ✳

. . . .

Linda Christensen (lmc@lclark.edu) is director of the Oregon Writing Project at Lewis & Clark College in Portland, Ore. She is a Rethinking Schools editor and author of Reading, Writing, and Rising Up *and* Teaching for Joy and Justice.

Resources

Neruda, Pablo. "Ode to My Socks," in *Selected Odes of Pablo Neruda* (translated by Margaret Sayers Peden). Berkeley, CA: University of California Press, 1990.

Soto, Gary. "Ode to La Tortilla," in *Neighborhood Odes*. New York: Scholastic, 1994.

The Beast
by Tim McGarry

Sold for a hundred bucks
backseat stained with my vomit
roaches and clips
stashed in the back of the glove compartment.
Biggest goddamn car on the block.
Power everything!
Steering, windows, brakes.
The ultimate cruising car.
The lowrider's drool
when this mother rolls by.
"Wow, man!"
"You see that_____Chevy?"
"If I had that, I could get laid every night!"

Sold for a hundred bucks
to a guy needing spare parts
never once thinking
of its former glory—
cruising Hollywood Boulevard on a weirdo watch,
tilted up at a drive-in movie
with a big bucket of greasy fried chicken
and two six packs
nestled in the backseat.
Earned its nickname when it rolled
over and totaled the boss's Triumph
and received only a bent muffler pipe.

The kind of car
you expect to see wrapped
around a telephone pole
or rolled into a brick wall
by someone overwhelmed by its awesome power
not rotting
in a car heap
in the LA sun
sold for spare parts.

Kool-Aid
by Jenelle Yarbrough

You soothed me on hot summer days
and relaxed me on humid summer nights.
I remember blue skies and green grass
when we used to rest in Grammy's yard.

I always knew we were her favorites.
Don't worry.
I believe you.
I know you're really made with 1/3 less sugar,
but Grammy still thinks you're sweet.
I think Grammy admires your nationality.
You know, Grammy doesn't know too many
    foreigners.
She adores your red native color,
the fact you come from somewhere Tropical
and have an ethnic name like Punch.
And that scent you wear,
Grammy loves it.
She says it smells fruity, but yet subtle.
And she'll swear when she kisses you,
you taste like Sweet Tarts.
I agree with Grammy.
'Cause in our eyes, Kool-Aid is the one.

Indian Kitchen
by Francis Ram

The sounds and smells
have been with me since birth.
Curries and soups.
Chicken to eggplant.
Cabbage to potatoes.
My mom stirring,
a new and better smell
with every stroke.
A whole herbal garden rising
up from the pot.
Curry on the stove and
rice or roti on the other.
The splashing, sizzling sounds of
fresh vegetables as they hit the
bottom of the steaming pan.
The smell of curry powder.
The scent of spicy peppers
punctures the clouds of steam.
The curry presses against my tongue
a hundred different flavors jump
toward me at once.
The last bite leaves me wanting more.

Dragon Dance
by Loi Nguyen

Tung . . . tung . . . tung
Dragon dance, dragon dance
head and tail
legs and feet
moving
Tung . . . tung . . . tung
Dragon dance, dragon dance
drums play loud
head jump up
tail run down
open the mouth
cut down again
bite sweet treat
Tung . . . tung . . . tung
Dragon luck
Dragon strong
like a young man's
big shoulders
Tung . . . tung . . . tung
Dragon dance, dragon dance

Jefferson
by Dawn Adams

You see her rough exterior,
tough as nails.
You put her problems under a microscope,
like any celebrity,
magnifying them far beyond the reality of their
    severity.
You see what the media shows you:
The police at her door,
the babies at her feet
and the fire in her belly.

But I see her grace and beauty
as she dances sleekly across the stage.
I see her passion and force
as she projects her words out over the murmuring
    crowd,
hushing the audience with her speech.
And I see her influence and persuasion
as she cries, or laughs, or screams,
or whispers in her dramatic performance.
If you look closely, you can see it too.

I see her pride and confidence
when she raises her eyes to the flag
and "Lift Every Voice and Sing,"
resounds from her lips.
I see her commitment and determination
as she flexes her muscles
to rise above anyone who challenges her mastery in
    competition.
I see her compassion and heart
as she fills up a page with words
that stir my soul.
I see the intensity and the desire
she possesses as she strives
to maximize the education and opportunity
that so many people try to take from her.
It shines through her graduates, her students,
her faculty,
and aspiring Jeffersonians
who long to be a part of her legacy.
Do you see what I see?

Matzo Balls
by Sarah LePage

Grandma's hands,
wise, soft, and old,
mold the Matzo meal
between the curves of each palm.
She transforms our heritage
into perfect little spheres.
Like a magician
she shapes our culture
as our people do.
This is her triumph.
She lays the bowl aside
revealing her tired hands,
each wrinkle a time
she sacrificed something for our family.

Aquí y Allá
Exploring our lives through poetry—here and there

BY ELIZABETH SCHLESSMAN-BARBIAN

SCOT BAKAL

Allá en las montañas,
para entrar no necesitas
papeles, estás libre.

There in the mountains,
to enter you don't need papers,
you are free.

Adriana's steady gaze accompanies her sharing of her poem during our *Aquí/Allá* (here/there) poetry unit. Her words are met with silence and sighs, nods and bright eyes. She gets it, I think. In this verse of her poem, Adriana suddenly pushes beyond a contrast of the smells of pine and the cars of the city streets. She voices her critique of the world through her poem, contrasting two important places in her life—the city and the mountains.

The opportunity and space to find our voices—to see, name, analyze, question, and understand the world—is an invitation I work to create again and again in our 5th-grade dual language classroom about 30 minutes south of Portland, Ore. Labels and statistics define our school as 80 percent Latinx, 70 percent English language learners, and more than 90 percent free and reduced lunch. My students spend 50 percent of their academic day in Spanish and the other half in English. Cultures, however, are not so easily equalized. The dominant culture—one in which much of my own identity was formed—can too easily shutter and silence the multifaceted, complex cultures of students' lives. My daily challenge is to pull up the details and experiences of students' lives so they become the curriculum and conversation content of our classroom.

Our *Aquí/Allá* poetry unit did just that. It surfaced the layers and parts of lives often overpowered by a common classroom curriculum. It created spaces where students could analyze and name the details of their lives.

In the past few years, the bilingual poetry and stories of Salvadoran writer Jorge Argueta have been an invaluable resource in my classroom. I've used poems from *Talking with Mother Earth* for homework and class analysis during a study of ecosystems, the story *Xochitl and the Flowers* to lead into persuasive writing, and *Bean Soup* to teach personification, similes, and beautiful poetic language. As I scanned books for a poem that would raise the level of vivid imagery in my students' narrative writing, I returned to this trusted source. Argueta's poem "Wonders of the City/Las maravillas de la ciudad," from his book *A Movie in My Pillow/Una película en mi almohada*, has the potential to pull the everyday details of students' lives into a place of power. It is a tightly packed representation of the tension of bridging cultures and places, something most of my students negotiate on a daily basis.

"Wonders of the City" has a simple and accessible structure, particularly for language learners, a category that fits all of my students at one time or another during our 50/50 day. The introductory stanza hints at the irony of the poem: "Here in the city there are/wonders everywhere." The second stanza surprises the reader with a puzzling observation: "Here mangoes/come in cans." As the reader wonders why someone would eat a mango from a can, the third stanza calmly counters, "In El Salvador/they grew on trees." The repetitive contrast pattern and concrete details are simple windows to the profound dissonance of longing for one place while living in another.

Breaking Down a Model, Building Up a Draft

After reading the poem out loud a few times and discussing the meaning, we read the poem again, this time as writers. I prefaced this reading with our usual writers' questions: "What do you observe or notice about the writing?"

"The author is contrasting two places."

"There is repetition, a pattern—here, there."

One Spanish language learner, Ben, surprised me by noticing the parallel language structure: "When the author talks about 'here,' he writes in present tense. When he talks about 'there,' he uses past tense."

> My daily challenge is to pull up the details and experiences of students' lives so they become the curriculum and conversation content of our classroom.

When the responses to the open-ended question began to dwindle, I probed for more. "What does Jorge Argueta do to show the contrast? What details does he choose to compare?"

"He contrasts food." Students had a harder time naming the author's content choices. I pointed out the use of everyday details, like the comparison of the packaged wonders of the city with mangoes and chickens in a more natural environment.

We ended our discussion of the poem's meaning with the questions: "What do you notice about the author's attitude toward the two places?" "What feelings does Jorge Argueta convey in the poem?" "Does he seem to like one place more than the other?"

Students noticed the irony: "He likes El Salvador more." We talked about how the culture that is labeled by the world as "more advanced" and full of technological wonders is often missing the richness and connections to the natural world that are an integral part of Indigenous cultures.

After discussing the poem's irony, I asked students to think about contrasts in their own lives, suggesting possibilities that would open the assignment to all: home/Grandma's house, the United States/another country, school/nature, Oregon/another state. Miguel's eyes lit up when he received an affirmative answer to his question "Can I contrast life in school and video games?"

As students shared some of their ideas, I tried to push them to critique and value.

Once students had chosen their topics, they began using a two-column *Aquí/Allá* list to generate ideas for their poems. We looked back at the poem to notice how the author contrasted mangoes in both countries, how he compared mango to mango, and not mango to melon. I shared my own list of ideas comparing school with nature. Although I too wanted to write a poem contrasting two countries, I knew that many of my students had lived their whole lives in our community.

There is nothing "mini" about a brainstorming session in my classroom. I find that the more ideas we share during the prewrite stage of the writing process, the more excited, confident, and successful my students are as they begin their writing. We shared lists once students had a few ideas down. "Here in the United States we celebrate Halloween; there in Mexico they celebrate Day of the Dead," read Juliana. Although validating the observation (especially since we were listing ideas on Oct. 29), I realized that our challenge to show, not tell, had followed us across genres.

"How might you show the reader how people are celebrating Halloween or Day of the Dead so that the reader can see the difference? What do you see on Halloween? What do people do to celebrate *el Día de los muertos*?" I asked. Students eagerly shared their experiences of families gathering to honor ancestors and loved ones. Ana Maria suggested, "Maybe you could say, 'Here we knock on doors in our costumes/There families gather at the cemetery.'"

As students shared some of their ideas, I tried to push them to critique and value. I tried to explicitly value the *allá*: "I wish more people here celebrated Day of the Dead. What a powerful way to remember loved ones."

Students continued to share ideas: "The money is different," said Carlos. "You play different games." "The stores are different," Mayra observed. "Here I need to speak two languages to be understood, and there only Spanish." "In Florida it is hot, and in Oregon it is rainy."

I responded with questions that would generate word pictures: "What does the money look like? How could you show the reader the difference in appearance or value?" "How are the toys different? Where and what do children play?" "How do people dress or what do they do that might show us the difference in weather?" "What do you see and hear in the market?" As students headed off to write their drafts, I reminded them to write with vivid images instead of generalities.

Some days during writing workshop you can hear pencils scratch and thoughts flow directly from the brain to the page. Not on our first *Aquí/Allá* drafting day. The clamor of questions and conversations continued as pencils carved thoughts in the white spaces between blue lines. "Alejandra! What do you call the toys the kids play with in Mexico?" asked David. "Which toys?" "The ones that you spin, the ones. . . ." "Oh, yeah," I heard Roberto murmur from across the room.

Noticing, Naming, and Applying

At the end of the initial drafting session, we gathered in a circle on the floor. Students read a few of their favorite lines or their entire poem to the class. This in-progress read-around motivates students by providing an immediate audience, allows them to borrow and adapt ideas from others, and helps me develop revision mini-lessons. We all work together to notice and name what students are already doing so that others can try the technique in their own writing.

The bulk of my teaching about writing happens once students have a working draft that can be revised. Although all the students had easily applied the "here/there" structure to their poems, most students were struggling to show details instead of telling them. Their energy until this point had been focused on identifying the contrasts instead of crafting an image.

The next day began with a series of revision invitations that I listed on the board as I introduced them. "When Erica writes, '*Aquí dicen* trick-or-treat,' she inserts dialogue in her poem. You might try the same technique in your own writing today."

Next, I used a student poem as a revision possibility. "Dalia uses personification in her poem when she says, 'Over there in Mexico there is brilliant yellow lightning/that cuts the sky like a cake.' Go back and find a place where you might add personification."

Later, as I conferenced with individuals, I noticed David's "*Aquí dicen* hello, goodbye/ *Allá dicen hola, adiós*." He also wrote that children play with "wooden tops that dance."

Eva revised her lines about *paletas*:

Aquí venden
paletas dulces y sabrosas
"ay, que ricas, que deliciosas"

Allá en México
hay paletas picosas
con chile
color fuego ardiente
"ay, ay, ay, me pica me pica
quiero agua"

Here they sell
sweet and tasty *paletas*
"oh, how yummy, how delicious"

There in Mexico
there are spicy *paletas* with chile
burning fire color
"oh, oh, oh, it's hot, it's hot
give me water"

Fernando moved from "They are different" to:

Aquí los zapatos son famosos
por la marca y cómo se mira

Allá no les importa mucho
de cómo se mira
nomás les importan
si duran y están baratos

Here shoes are famous
for the brand and look

There it doesn't matter a lot
what they look like
it only matters
if they last and are cheap

Luis used a subtle form of personification:

Aquí hay trabajos de sudando
y de dolor de pie a cabeza

Here there are jobs of sweating
and ache from foot to head

Toward the end of our work on the poems, students met in small response groups. They shared their poems with one another, writing down favorite lines and images, describing cultural contrasts, trying to name what they noticed. In one group we paused to think about how much more sense it makes to play with a top or a ball than it does to buy a $200 video game system. In another we marveled over the personal relationships and interactions involved in buying tomatoes and onions in the market.

Students read their favorite lines from others' poems during a whole-group share. As I passed from one group to the next, Alex exclaimed: "Wow, you should read Juliana's poem. It is really good":

Aquí cuando llueve
sólo caen gotitas pequeñas
que bailan en el piso

Allá los truenos caen
y casi te desmayas del miedo
los relámpagos caen
pueden romper a la mitad un árbol

Here when it rains
only tiny drops fall
that dance on the floor

There the thunder falls
and you almost faint from fear
lightning falls
it can break a tree in half

Taking It Beyond Our Walls

Alex wasn't the only one who thought our poetry was "really good." When I shared our poems with Catherine Celestino, a 2nd-grade teacher whose class my students knew as "reading buddies," she responded with an invitation: "Could your 5th graders teach the poem to my 2nd graders?"

The plan to teach our reading buddies to write *Aquí/Allá* poems blasted fresh energy and relevance into our work. "When I plan a lesson for you, I always think about the goal of expressing our lives and views through the writing of a poem, as well as the skills I want to teach you in your writing. What are our goals as we teach our reading buddies?" I asked.

Students broke into groups of three or four to create a list of the important skills they had learned while writing their poems. We shared ideas with the whole group and then, together, determined which were most important. We decided that the prewriting and revision goal would be to use a list with commas, sensory details, and similes. The students defined the most important editing goals as taking out unnecessary words and deciding where to use line breaks.

"Who doesn't have a partner? Raise your hand." As we entered Mrs. Celestino's 2nd-grade classroom, students formed pairs and settled into work.

"What does your grandma's house look like? What kinds of things do you find there?" I heard Adriana ask her partner.

I saw students develop new strategies to scaffold learning: "We've decided that I will write one line for my partner and he will write the next." "I'm writing down whatever she tells me on this paper, and then my partner is copying the words onto hers." Jessica, Michelle, and Alex were dividing the *Aquí/Allá* columns horizontally and adding categories: food, names, toys, activities.

"*Aquí* we speak Spanish, *allá* we speak another language," I heard 2nd grader Alma explain to Mayra. Most students who had compared the United States and Mexico focused on the English in the here and the Spanish in the there.

"Can you teach us some words in your other language?" I asked in Spanish as I lowered myself to the rug to join the conversation. Alma smiled with the confidence of an expert as she told me the words for tortilla and water. Mayra and I repeated the new words, practicing and trying to learn the sounds. I moved across the room, and Mayra helped Alma move from oral idea to a new line in her poem: "Here we say *tortilla* and *agua*, in Mexico we say '*sheck*' and '*nda*,'" she wrote.

When we returned to the room after our first teaching session, I heard about successes and frustrations. "My partner picked Mexico and she can't remember what Mexico is like." We talked about the importance of picking a place you know and remember well, and brainstormed some possible local choices. "My partner just sits there." "We've already written a whole page!"

Stepping Back and Learning Forward

I feel fortunate each time we shake to the surface parts of students' home lives, traditions, languages, and cultures, as well as their views of the world around them. I can't completely know and understand the *allá* of every student's life, but I can join Jorge Argueta in his critique of the "wonders" of *aquí*. I can create space for students to name the details and cultures of their lives in the classroom curriculum. I can help students question the *aquí* and value the *allá*. Next year I will ask even more questions, probe for more details, and leave more spaces for talking and sharing and critiquing the contrasts of our lives.

Students often follow me as we head out to the playground, eager to share a thought or experience that they weren't comfortable enough to share in class. We head out to midmorning recess after drawing and labeling detailed diagrams of crickets during a study of ecosystems. Andrea hesitates for a moment as some of her classmates sprint off, eager to join the game of tag or secure the best swing.

"We eat crickets at home. You know, they are really good with a little bit of lime and salt," she tells me, staring off in the distance as she stands at my side. "Really?" I ask, turning to face her. "What do they taste like? How do you catch them?" Andrea continues to talk, and, as we line up to head back to the classroom, we share her cricket connection with the class.

How can I continue to open spaces so that rich moments of linguistic and cultural revelation are not chance conversations on the peripheries of the playground and hallway, but a central core of the classroom curriculum? How can I help students bridge the conflicting cultures of their lives? ✳

. . . .

Elizabeth Barbian (formerly Schlessman) taught 4th and 5th grade in a Spanish dual language immersion classroom in Woodburn, Ore., for five years. She is a teacher-consultant with the Oregon Writing Project.

Notes

"Wonders of the City/Las maravillas de la ciudad" by Jorge Argueta is reprinted from *A Movie in My Pillow/ Una película en mi almohada*. Permission arranged with Children's Book Press, an imprint of Lee & Low Books Inc.

All conversations and student work in this article were originally in Spanish. Student work was translated by the author.

The words "sheck" and "nda" come from the Oaxaca Amuzgo language, spoken in the village of San Pedro Amuzgos in Oaxaca, Mexico. The spelling of the words is taken directly from 2nd-grade student work.

Resources

Argueta, Jorge. *Bean Soup/Sopa de frijoles.* Toronto: Groundwood Books, 2009.

Argueta, Jorge. *Talking with Mother Earth/Hablando con madre tierra.* Toronto: Groundwood Books, 2006.

Argueta, Jorge. *Xochitl and the Flowers/Xochitl, la niña de las flores.* San Francisco: Children's Book Press, 2003.

Wonders of the City
by Jorge Argueta

Here in the city there are
wonders everywhere

Here mangoes
come in cans

In El Salvador
they grew on trees

Here chickens come
in plastic bags

Over there
they slept beside me

. . . .

Las maravillas de la ciudad
by Jorge Argueta

Aquí en esta ciudad
todo es maravilloso

Aquí los mangos
vienen enlatados

En El Salvador
crecían en árboles

Aquí las gallinas vienen
en bolsas de plástico

Allá se dormían
junto a mí

Aquí, Allá, México, Woodburn
by Ana

Aquí en las escuelas
los niños se ponen
cualquier ropa
solamente que no sea
tan pequeña
o camisas de tirantes

Allá en México
se ponen una falda,
un chaleco color de una nube de tormenta,
una camisa y medias
color de una nube blanca y esponjada

Aquí en Woodburn hay
lavadoras y secadoras
hacen un ruido feo y ruidoso
chuk, chuk, chuk

Allá las personas
lavan a mano
tienden la ropa
afuera para que
se seque colgada con pinzas

Aquí venden
paletas dulces y sabrosas
"ay, que ricas, que deliciosas"

Allá en México
hay paletas picosas
con chile
color fuego ardiente
"ay, ay, ay, me pica, me pica,
quiero agua"

Here, There, Mexico, Woodburn
by Ana

Here in schools
children wear
any kind of clothing
as long as it isn't
too small or
a tank top

There in Mexico
children wear a skirt
a storm cloud color vest
puffy cloud color
shirt and socks

Here in Woodburn there are
washers and dryers
that make an ugly and loud noise
chuk, chuk, chuk

There people
wash by hand
they hang the clothing
outside so that
it can dry hanging on clothespins

Here they sell
sweet and flavorful *paletas*
"ah, how delicious"

There in Mexico
there are spicy *paletas*
with chile
burning fire color
"ah, ah, ah, it's hot, it's hot
give me water"

The Age Poem
Building a community of trust

BY LINDA CHRISTENSEN

SAID BELLOUMI/CORBIS SYGMA

uilding a community that might contribute to June Jordan's "fearless democratic society" is no small accomplishment in most classrooms. Over the years I've learned that poetry helps move students to listen and care about each other while they build literacy skills.

Too often community building happens in the opening days of the school year. Teachers and students engage in a series of games designed to foster group skills and bonding, but in my experience, these activities drop off after the first week—as if community is established with one or two activities. In addition, these opening strategies are frequently divorced from the content area. Creating a community of learners is not at odds with building literacy skills in a language arts classroom. We don't need to put aside words to develop a classroom where students can share their lives.

The age poem is a great community-building activity. Students get to talk about childhood memories—big wheel bikes, story time at the library, and freeze tag—that connect them and allow them to acknowledge their common bonds. This activity also brings in their family

We don't need to put aside words to develop a classroom where students can share their lives.

stories, languages, and customs that shape their lives. The structured approach to the age poem gives students lots of choice—from the age they choose to the details about their lives that they want to reveal.

I start this activity by using Garrett Hongo's poem "What For" from *Yellow Light*. Hongo's poem is rich with details; it tells stories, names foods, and uses his grandparents' language.

> At six I lived for spells:
> how a few Hawaiian words could call
> up the rain, could hymn like the sea

In later stanzas, he evokes his grandfather, "I lived for stories about the war/my grandfather told over *hana* cards," and his grandmother, "I lived for songs my grandmother sang/stirring curry into a thick stew." Hongo's use of verbs and imagery provides a strong model for student writing. His repeating line "I lived for" helps students see how to pull the poem forward with a linking line.

More recently, I have added the first stanza of Gary Soto's poem "Black Hair" to show students how another poet opened an age poem:

> At eight I was brilliant with my body.
> In July, that ring of heat
> We all jumped through, I sat in the bleachers
> Of Romain Playground, in the lengthening
> Shade that rose from our dirty feet.
> The game before us was more than baseball.
> It was a figure—Hector Moreno.
> Quick and hard with turned muscles,
> His crouch the one I assumed before an altar
> Of worn baseball cards, in my room.

The age poem teaches students some basic facts about poetry—the power of specifics and repeating lines. It teaches them to collect "evidence" prior to writing, to sort their details, and then to select the best ones. They learn to shape their poem through the use of a repeating line, followed by a list of specific details.

Teaching Strategy

1. After reading Hongo's and Soto's opening lines and several student poems, I ask students what the poets valued, what was important enough for them to include in a poem. For example, in Bea Clark's poem, Bea remembers the details of her kindergarten world—the brown readers and tiny desks, the alphabet and glitter.

2. We look at the kinds of details the poets used—names of family members, teachers, games they played. I want students to understand that details, very specific details—like Mrs. Hasselbacker's name or Soto's "altar/Of worn baseball cards"—help create a movie or image for their readers.

3. After we read the models, I say, "Think about the age you want to write about. You may not remember every detail from that age and the ages might blur. That's OK. Just try to remember as many details and feelings as you can. We're going to make lists that will help you write the poem." These lists match the ones in the poems we read:

   - Names of games they played, including outdoor games like cartoon tag, hide and seek, school games, imaginary games.
   - Names of clothes—especially the weird or wacky clothes like days of the week underwear or superhero T-shirts, special occasion clothes.
   - School memories from early years—teachers' names, books, special projects.
   - Memories of things they were too small to reach, or things they could not do because they were small—reaching the light switch, playing with the big kids, going on rides at the carnival.
   - Family memories—parents, grandparents, special stories, food, ceremonies. (Hongo's poem pays special tribute to his Hawaiian

grandparents.)

- Strong memories—a memory frozen from that time that replays for them.
- Music they loved, television shows they watched.

4. Students share their lists out loud after they brainstorm. This is a huge piece of the community-building aspect of poetry writing. It is time consuming, but it performs several functions. One student's memory sparks memories for other students, so they can add details to their lists. But students also share common memories and laughter as they tell stories about playing freeze tag at dusk or wearing their Superman T-shirt every day of the week. Sometimes they attended the same elementary school or church, so their collective memory becomes part of the classroom story. This is also the time when students talk about their cultural heritage, including food, religious holidays, names of family members, and words from the language of their ancestors.

5. After students have compiled their brainstorming, I ask them to review their lists and either highlight or circle some of the best items—those details that help the reader understand how the child they were at 5 or 6 became the person they are today. I also encourage them to include words in their home languages when appropriate.

6. Once students have selected their best details, I write Hongo's and Clark's opening lines on the board: "At ____ I lived for. . ." and "I am in the winter of my ____ year." We play with variations—changing the age, changing the season. For example, "At eight, I loved. . ." or "I am in the summer of my eighth year." Poetry becomes boring quickly when a pattern is rigidly followed. I encourage students to incorporate one of these lines into their poem as a repeating line or to create their own repeating line to help move the poem forward. I also tell them to surprise the reader with a memory like Tim McGarry includes in his poem "Six": "I lived for a year when/ Mom's temper got hidden/behind school and a new lover."

7. After students have written a draft, we "read around." Seated in our circle, students read their poems. After each student reads, classmates raise their hands to comment on what they like about the piece. The writer calls on his/her classmates and receives feedback about what is good in the poem. I stop from time to time to point out that the use of a list is a technique they might "borrow" from their peer's poem and include in their next poem or in a revision. I might note that the use of Spanish or their home language adds authenticity to their piece and ask them to see if they could add some to their poem. After a few read-around sessions, I can spot writing techniques that students have "borrowed" from each other and included in their revisions or in their next piece. (See p. 240 for details on using the read-around as a teaching strategy.)

Creating community in our classrooms should not be at odds with developing students' literacy skills. Although I'm not convinced that writing poetry will bring about a revolution, I do believe that learning to share pieces of our personal history and listening closely while others share theirs is absolutely necessary if I want students to write deeply and passionately about their lives. ✻

. . . .

Linda Christensen (lmc@lclark.edu) is director of the Oregon Writing Project at Lewis & Clark College in Portland, Ore. She is a Rethinking Schools editor and author of Reading, Writing, and Rising Up *and* Teaching for Joy and Justice.

Resources

Hongo, Garrett Karou. *Yellow Light.* Middletown, CT: Wesleyan University Press, 1982.

Soto, Gary, *Black Hair.* Pittsburgh: University of Pittsburgh Press, 1985.

Other good models for age poems:

Cisneros, Sandra, "Eleven" in *Woman Hollering Creek.* New York: Vintage Press, 1992.

"The Summer I Was Sixteen" by Geraldine Connolly can be downloaded from Billy Collins' Poetry 180: a poem a day for American high schools (www.loc.gov/poetry/180/003. html).

Five
by Bea Clark

I am in the winter of my fifth year.
My days are filled with kindergarten
And brown readers.
We sit at tiny desks,
In tiny rows
Surrounded by a scaled-down world
With giant alphabet men and woodblocks.
We make paper angels, wrapping circles into cones,
Using Styrofoam balls for heads,
Silver and gold glitter on heavenly
Tissue paper wings.
Too much glue makes no difference.
Add more glitter, stiffer wings—sharp wings.
We have paper angel fights.
Glitter flies into our hair, on our red faces.
Mrs. Hasselbacker calms us down.
It's time for the next activity.

The juice is gone.
And Denise ate glue on her chocolate.

We climb onto the Magic Carpet
And Mrs. Hasselbacker reads stories
From beat-up hardback books.
We clap and laugh and fall asleep
On each other's shoulders.
It's time to go home,
To play,
To build snowmen that glow at night
And wink up at my window
When the moon is out.
 Time to sleep,
And dream,
Of reindeer biting my toes,
Pirates' booty found in the yard,
And smiling alligators.

Six
by Tim McGarry

At six I lived for Evel Knievel
and Pop Rocks
Japanese monster movies
on channel 12
flavored our fantasies
of guts and glory.

I lived for Donny & Marie
and waited for their plate-glass smiles
to lock in a deep kiss.

I lived for the snake
at school
that ate white mice whole.

I lived for a year when
Mom's temper got hidden
behind school and
a new lover.

I lived for Banquet fried chicken
and rocky road ice cream.

I lived to be seven
and one day eight.

I lived for a security
I never knew again.

Six
by Sonia Kellerman

I was too small for bumper cars
or light switches.
I couldn't see myself
in the medicine cabinet like you.
I had to hold myself up
to not fall in the toilet.

My feet never reached the tile.

But I
could stretch way out in the tub
and when
all the water swirled out
down the drain,
I could
slip slide up and down
naked with my feet in the air,

leaving puddles you had to clean up.

Dried and tucked
I still had room for animal friends
in bed with me.
I could drift
songs in my ears
Wink'n Blink'n and Nod.

Her Wedding Day
by Mira Shimabukuro

I am twelve.

I am trembling a pearl strand
Around my mother's neck
She who raises money
For Nicaragua
On her wedding day.

Younger, I squeezed between
My parents' bodies
Sunday mornings in the loft
Afternoons we'd head
To the country, friends
Old playhouses in the rain
Brought my eyes closed by nightfall.

I now stand next to her
Our matching bouquets still.
Faraway relatives and college friends
Breathe in with the minister's words.

My father is in the shadows.
His eyes calm my quaked stomach
Protect each tear from falling.

With an aching smile
I throw my sadness
To his arms as my mother
Places a ring
On the new man's finger.

Celebrating Skin Tone

The poetry of skin color in a 1st/2nd-grade classroom

BY KATHARINE JOHNSON

Dark as leopard spots, light as sand,

SHEILA HAMANAKA

When I look out at my room full of 1st- and 2nd-grade students, I see a symphony of colors. I see this as beautiful and invaluable. Yet, I realize the world does not always embrace my students' multiracial reality. I know that the world will not receive Jamal with his skin the color of summer midnight and his easy laugh the same way it will receive Anita, with her skin the color of late summer wheat and her quiet smile. Young people, like adults, receive countless confusing and negative messages about the implications of skin color. Consistently they get the message that some are better than others—that white trumps black and brown.

Worse than an unwelcoming world is the possibility of an unwelcoming classroom and school. I see racism taking root in the relationships my young learners are establishing. I have had to step in and help my students negotiate their multiracial environment—whether it is stopping a white student from assuming a Black classmate is the one who needs to go with the parent volunteer to work on reading skills, or helping a student of color find a group to join when, once again, she has not been invited into the dramatic play of a group of white girls. Children need help understanding that "race" is socially constructed, but that racism has a serious impact on all of us. Knowing this, I am always on the lookout for learning opportunities that will be accessible and affirming.

When I attended a workshop led by Katie Kissinger demonstrating her approach to celebrating skin tone with her preschool students, I knew I had found a new possibility for beginning to disrupt the skin color prejudice that harms my students on a daily basis. Kissinger's students had celebrated their skin tones and learned about the biological basis of skin color. Young children, like adults, see different skin colors—and assign meaning to these differences. I wanted my students to understand something of the science of skin color in order to challenge the notion that skin color is an indication of anything more than genetic adaptations to one's environment. My aim with this lesson was twofold: First, I wanted students to see their similarities across a skin tone spectrum. This would be the science of skin tone. Second, I wanted them to practice the art of praising their own skin tones as a way to access the connection between skin tone and identity in a positive way. This would be the poetry.

The Science of Skin Tone

I began the lesson by grounding my students in the science of skin tone. Kissinger's own book, *All the Colors We Are*, offers clear explanations for why people have different skin tones. My students were fascinated by the idea presented in Kissinger's book that all people come in shades of brown. Exclamations like "Yes, why do they call me white? I'm not white. I'm pinkish brownish tannish goldish" peppered the cluster of students gathered on the rug for read-aloud. Kissinger's book presents different skin tones as adaptations to different environments. Imagining the evolution of skin tone over millennia is beyond the scope of most 6- and 7-year-old imaginations, but the idea that our skin has tone to make us a good match for our environment, that our skin tone could be understood as a way to make us stronger, offered my multiracial class a path into this conversation. I also used the book *Your Skin and Mine* by Paul Showers to introduce key ideas and scientific concepts. Reading each book aloud, I asked students to turn and talk after most pages so

they could monitor their own growing understanding. We created a word wall dedicated to words related to skin tone. "Melanin," "tone," "genetic," and "heritage" all took places of prominence on the wall.

Using the books and students' understanding, we wrote a kid-friendly definition of each term. We defined melanin as the stuff in your body that gives your skin and hair its color. Students came to understand genetics as the recipe for how one's body will be built. After reading these books, my students stood on solid ground with some basic ideas: Skin tone has evolved over time; it is an adaptation to different environments, especially proximity to the equator; and

I wanted to empower my students to understand the science of skin color and practice the art of praising their own skin tones.

everyone, regardless of how one's "race" is named or misnamed, is a shade of brown.

Once students had some understanding of the science of skin tones, I moved into the language of praise. Following Kissinger's lead again, I stopped by the local hardware store to collect paint chips in dozens of shades of brown and peach and tan. I wanted my 6-, 7-, and 8-year-olds to match paint chips to skin tones, just as Kissinger had done with her preschoolers. I gathered the class on the rug so everyone could see me and the paint chips. Holding out the top of my forearm, I laid a paint chip against my skin. "What do you think? Does this look like my skin?" I asked. Thinking aloud, I modeled deciding which chips seemed too dark or too light, which ones had too much blue or too little red. Soon I asked my students to help me in my matching process, finally landing on a good match. I read the name of the color Caramel Whip to the group and wrote my name on the back of the paint chip.

Then I released students to explore the chips I had spread around the room. They mingled and chatted, helping each other find a good match for their own skin. To close the day's lesson, all the students shared their chips with the class, to applause after each share. Jessica, who had been frustrated by not finding a perfect match, landed on Saddle Brown with help from a few friends. Fergus went with Beach House, Justin and Tyler both identified with Coconut Grove, and Samantha's color match was called Liberty—a great match for her. I collected their paint chips to use when we transitioned to writing poems.

The Poetry of Skin Tone

I began the writing process by reading Sheila Hamanaka's picture book poem *All the Colors of the Earth*. First, I simply read the poem aloud slowly, taking time so we could look closely at each illustration. I had students pair-share their favorite pages, and a few shared favorites with the whole class. Jamal was especially fond of the line "the roaring browns of bears and soaring eagles." As soon as he shared that as his favorite line, six or seven hands went down. Apparently this had been a favorite. Raina offered up the line "like caramel and chocolate and the honey of bees."

"Why do you like that one so much?" I asked.

"Those are all sweet," Raina answered. "I think the poem is supposed to make us feel happy and those things make me happy."

Students continued to share new favorites or restate ones that had already been shared for a few more minutes. It was important to me that students have a chance to simply connect with the language and imagery Hamanaka uses. Often the message students receive, especially white students, is that to talk explicitly about difference is to be racist. We needed our exploration of skin color to begin with a gentle, welcoming discussion.

After students connected with the poem, I moved into the craft of writing. I wanted students to begin to think like poets. I tailored my questions toward the moves Hamanaka used, hoping students might be able to replicate those moves. "Sheila Hamanaka uses a lot of comparisons in her poem," I began. "Who remembers one thing she compared skin tone to?" Students called out bears and eagles and seashells and chocolate. I tried to keep up with the flurry of ideas as I recorded their connections on chart paper.

"Sheila Hamanaka chose her comparisons very carefully," I told my class. "How do you think she feels about skin tone based on the comparisons she chose?" I pushed students to recognize that the poem is a praise poem in celebration of skin tone. I reminded students of Raina's idea that the poem makes her hap-py because Hamanaka compares skin tone to sweet things. Ted thought Hamanaka believes that skin tone makes you strong since she used eagles and bears in her poem. Larry said that the poem made him feel peaceful because it compares skin tone to whispering grass and the ocean.

"How do you feel about your skin tone?" I asked, a little apprehensively. Even though I had laid the path for praise of skin tone, there was still the possibility that some students would have negative concepts of their skin tone and others would claim to have no feelings at all. To maintain a praise focus and offer some additional language support, I suggested that students choose one of the feeling words we had just listed if they did not want to think of their own feeling word. Happy and strong were the most popular feelings, and that was good enough for us to move forward with the poets' work of comparing.

"What is one thing in the world you can compare your skin to?" We closed that day's lesson with students mingling around the room and sharing their comparisons with as many partners as they could. I listened closely to the partner shares, especially eavesdropping on my students of color. I do not want any of my students to feel under a spotlight or that they need to be representatives of their group. What I realized in my eavesdropping was that my students of color were better able to generate lists of comparisons with their partners than some of my white students. I suspect that white students are less practiced at paying attention to their own skin tone. I used suggestive questions and references to nudge some students toward richer language and also toward celebration.

Jeremy, a first-generation child from Eritrea, suggested his skin was the color of dirt. Jeremy's comparison stirred concern in me. Of all my students of color, he was the most socially isolated in the class. I only knew of one other student who had ever played with Jeremy outside of the structured school day. Other students often complained about having to partner with him or tattled about his behavior in P.E. or in the lunch line. Sitting next to him and seeing his paper with dirt as the lone idea listed, I wondered what his motivation was for that comparison, and I wondered why he seemed at a loss for other ideas.

Rather than admonish him for a potentially negative comparison, I probed his connection: "What type of dirt do you imagine? Is it like fresh soil ready to be planted in a garden or like the rich muddy edges of a pond or like the dry patch in front of the soccer goal?" As an expert soccer player, Jeremy ended up with several references to the types of dirt on the field. I cannot be certain Jeremy's original idea of dirt carried negative connotations for him, but I can attest that his face brightened as he added more ideas to his brainstorming chart and his hand went up to share as we closed the lesson. Fergus, a white student, said he couldn't think of anything other than the color of his paint chip. I sent him over to the area of our classroom library with large full-color science books. "Flip through some nature books and see what you find that reminds you of your skin tone and how you feel about it," I suggested. He came back to his seat 10 minutes later with river stones and prairies for his list. Since Fergus spends every summer fishing with his grandfather in Montana, these seemed like excellent choices.

The next day, I introduced another set of poems in praise of skin tone from the book *The Blacker the Berry*, by Joyce Carol Thomas. Each of these poems describes one of the many hues of African American skin color, from deep rich browns to red to seemingly white. Thomas uses images from nature and dialogue between children and elders to celebrate skin tone. For example: "I am midnight and berries/I call the silver stars at dusk/. . . Because I am dark the moon and stars/shine brighter/because berries are dark the juice is sweeter." Thomas links feelings about skin tone to family, referring to grandparents' advice, motherly love, and heritage: "My mother says I am/Red raspberries stirred into blackberries/Like the raspberries I will always be here/Like the blackberries I was here with the first seed." For each of these poems, I asked students, "How does Joyce Carol Thomas describe skin tone?" Students added to the chart that we had started with Hamanaka's poem. Thomas' work gave us additional categories: family memories, berries, sky colors, and feelings. Now we had enough poetic moves and categories borrowed from other poets to move into generating student ideas.

I designed a brainstorming template for students to use based on what they had noticed in Hamanaka's and Thomas' poems. Our categories included: nature, animals, smells, food, and emotions. We gathered on the rug and I showed students a chart paper-sized ver-

sion of the brainstorming template. "These are some of the ways we noticed other poets described skin tone. Today, we are going to think of our own ideas about how to describe our skin tones."

Then I modeled the process of thinking about how to celebrate and describe skin aloud. I pulled my paint chip from the basket of chips and re-read the name of the color: Caramel Whip. "Where would I put this on my chart?" I asked the class. We agreed it belonged under foods. "Let's see if we can think of any other comparisons for my skin." I looked closely at the back of my forearm and showed it to the students sitting closest to me. "What in nature is like this color?" I wondered aloud. "It looks a little like beach sand," I began and added this idea to the chart in the category Things in Nature. When I asked students for more nature comparisons for my skin color, they called out "bunny fur," "dry grass," and "peaches." All of these went onto the chart.

Joyce Carol Thomas' work gave us the categories of family memories and berries, sky colors and feelings.

I wanted students to start thinking about their own skin. "What did you tell your partner yesterday that you compared your skin to?" I told them to share again with a nearby partner. "Who can share their idea?" I asked after a few minutes of partner talk. Many hands went up.

"Cocoa," said Sayla.

"Lovely," I responded. "Where would that idea go on the brainstorming chart?" Working with the students, I modeled placing their ideas onto the chart under the appropriate category. The categories themselves were not that important. My goal was to generate a variety of ideas.

When I felt confident that students had a sense of how to sort their ideas, I released them to work on their own brainstorming charts. "Try to get at least one idea in each section," I recommended as students settled into desks and corners of the carpet to fill out charts.

While students chatted and listed ideas on their brainstorm charts, I again roved and made sure each student came up with ideas celebrating their color. Not every student immediately settled down and brainstormed 10 or 12 poetic images in praise of their skin tone. Many needed one-on-one help to get rolling or to keep going. Neil struggled to come up with ideas, so I paired him with a trusted friend to think together. Katie listed white paper and milk as her skin tone and said she was done. We studied her skin, laying her

"My skin is the color of warm beach sand."

arm next to mine to see that the pinked-up creaminess of her skin tone had little to do with the name of her race as white. She added strawberries to her milk to get closer to the real tone of her skin and came up with one of my favorite ideas—grilled cheese bread. Jason stared into space from his seat, so I pulled up a chair next to him and reminded him to start with the name of his paint chip. We studied his forearm together and imagined lions with their golden hair shining in the sun and cookie dough. Josie's pencil couldn't move fast enough to list all the browns in the world that her skin reminded her of, so I asked her to share her thinking process with the class. Some students ended up with only two or three ideas, but that was enough to get rolling with the poetry.

Poets As Advisors

Now students were ready to sculpt their ideas into poems. I once again relied on think aloud as a modeling technique. I gathered the students on the rug and reviewed the oversized brainstorm chart we had made as a class the day before. "I am going to take these ideas and turn them into a poem today. You are going to take your ideas and turn them into a poem as well. I need some advice on how to do this. First, I am going to take advice from Sheila Hamanaka and Joyce Carol Thomas." I had a couple of student volunteers read aloud once more the skin tone poems we already knew.

"I think I am going to start my poem with an idea from Sheila Hamanaka," I said as I began writing my poem on chart paper. "I am not going to copy her whole poem, but I want to use one of her ideas as a way to jump into my own poem." I wrote: "I am the colors of the earth" at the top of the chart paper. Next, I looked back at the chart of brainstormed ideas and dramatically modeled choosing an idea to add to my

poem. "I think I will use this one next," I said pointing to dry beach sand. I wrote: "My skin is the color of warm beach sand." "What idea should I write next?" I asked the class. Working together, we drafted four or five lines for my poem.

It was time for students to write their own poems. As a way to remind them of the options we noticed in the model poems, I released them from the rug by asking who wanted to start with which type of idea. "Who thinks they will start with a food comparison?" I asked. "Who wants to include a detail about how your skin is like the skin of someone else in your family? Who wants to start with hair instead of skin? Who wants to start by comparing it to an animal? Tell a neighbor how you will start your poem."

We wrote for the rest of the week. Some days we cranked out longer sessions of 45 minutes of writing and sharing. Once or twice, we simply squeezed in 20 minutes before lunch. But each day that week, students touched this work—writing, re-reading, sharing with friends, sharing in small groups, and sharing all together. For students who were ready to stretch as writers, I led a revision lesson on adding more detail to their metaphors. I modeled adding action to the image of an eagle so it became an eagle soaring through the mountains. If students compared their skin to caramel, that caramel could become warm caramel or caramel inside a candy. First- and 2nd-grade metaphors tend toward the cliché, but I wanted them to try to stretch their ideas.

When students seemed satisfied with their poems, we created self-portraits. I let students choose the medium—paints or crayons—that matched how they wanted their portraits to look. Poems and portraits hung in the hallway for several months, the students protesting whenever I wondered if it might be time to take them down.

I know that children see and wonder about skin color. I know that children, even as young as 6, experience racism directed at themselves, their moms, their neighbors, their cousins, the man in front of them in line at the grocery store. I also know that opening my classroom to a discussion about the skin tone differences that we see and the ones that we ignore is one component to disrupting prejudice based on skin color. And I know that this is just the beginning—sharing an experience around loving our skin tones does not suddenly take away the real pain of how the world sees "white" and "black" and "brown" skinned peoples.

The two weeks we spent writing and learning about skin tone opened my classroom in some important ways. Samantha, an African American girl who barely spoke even in morning circle time at the start of the year, read her entire poem aloud to her classmates. Tyler and Justin, one white and one African American, who had never spent free time together before, became friends when they realized they both had skin that matched Coconut Grove. Jeremy, also African American, finished a piece of writing on the same schedule as the rest of the class for the first time.

Maybe Samantha was simply ready to emerge as a more vocal and public presence in the classroom. Maybe Justin and Tyler would have found some other connection and become friends. Maybe the academic support I offered Jeremy finally kicked in. Maybe not. Maybe the discussion of the science of skin tone and the praise of our beautiful differences facilitated these important transformations. I prefer to attribute my students' growth to the poems in celebration of skin tone. Regardless, I plan to continue teaching in ways that might interrupt racist hierarchies and might do so joyfully. ✳

. . . .

Katharine Johnson teaches at Irvington School in Portland, Ore., and is co-director of the Oregon Writing Project. She offers special thanks to Doug Miles and Lisa Hass for their ideas about skin tone poems.

Resources

Hamanaka, Sheila. *All the Colors of the Earth*. New York: Morrow Junior, 1994.

Kissinger, Katie, and Wernher Krutein. *All the Colors We Are: The Story of How We Get Our Skin Color*. St. Paul, MN: Redleaf, 1994.

Showers, Paul, and Kathleen Kuchera. *Your Skin and Mine*. Rev. ed. New York: HarperCollins, 1991.

Thomas, Joyce Carol, and Floyd Cooper. *The Blacker the Berry: Poems*. New York: HarperCollins, 2008.

My Skin
by Teddy

My skin is sweet cinnamon mixed with cream.
It's the color of sand dollars on the ocean floor.
It's like spicy sugar.
It's like light caramel
It's also like a heron's neck.
My skin is the lion's eye.

And it's like a slithering viper on freshly mowed grass,
pebbles under the desert sun.

My skin is beautiful
like my father's and mother's.

. . . .

What Color Am I?
by Sadie

I am delicious mocha with a hint of cinnamon
I am warm caramel in the bottom of the bowl
I smell like spice cake baking in the oven
I am a spicy cinnamon latte.

. . . .

My Skin
by Malcom

My skin is not white
It is caramel whip,
sandy beaches
and the sound of pebbles under the desert sun
My skin is the warmth of the summer sun
And the promise of a day filled with joy.

Skin Tone Brainstorm

Name:

Use this table to brainstorm descriptions of your skin tone.

Things in nature that remind you of your skin tone	Foods that reminds you of your skin tone
Emotions that remind you of your skin tone	Smells that remind you of your skin tone
Animals that remind you of your skin tone	Anything else. . .

Celebrating Student Voice
Lawson Fusao Inada's 'Rayford's Song'

BY LINDA CHRISTENSEN

Lawson Fusao Inada, a poet and professor of literature at Southern Oregon State College, came to my Literature and U.S. History class one year. His visit was one of those lucky circumstances: The class was in the middle of a unit on the history of education and one of the poems he pulled from his book *Legends from Camp* was about a classroom experience. When Lawson read "Rayford's Song" (see p. 88), Bill Bigelow and I realized it was an opportunity for students to remember and explore their own history as students.

In "Rayford's Song," Inada remembered one of his classrooms in the 1930s in Fresno, a town in California's San Joaquin Valley where many people of African, Chinese, Filipino, Japanese, and Mexican descent worked in the fields and canneries. "Our classroom was filled with shades of brown," he recalled. "Our names were Rayford Butler, Consuela and Pedro Gonzales, Susie Chin, and Sam Shimabukuro. We were a mixture. The only white person in the room was our teacher. Our textbooks had pictures and stories about white kids named Dick and Jane and their dog, Spot. And the songs in our songbooks were about Susanna, coming 'round the mountain, and English gardens—songs we

Many of us have experienced the loss of our voices, our songs, our stories as we travel through schools.

never heard in our neighborhood."

Some of the songs mentioned in the poem may not be familiar to today's students. "Old Black Joe," for example, is a Stephen Foster song written in 1860 that attempts to create nostalgic memories of the days of slavery.

"Rayford's Song" arouses strong emotions in students because it speaks to how schools sometimes dampen our hopes and expectations. Many of us have experienced the loss of our voices, our songs, our stories as we travel through schools. We've been told that we are not important, our people are not worth studying, or our language is "wrong." Inada's poem dares to speak about that silencing:

> Our songs, our songs were there—
> on tips of tongues, but stuck
> in throats—songs of love,
> fun, animals, and valor, songs
> of other lands, in other languages,
> but they just wouldn't come out.
> Where did our voices go?

Teaching Strategy

1. I begin this lesson with a technique I call "text rendering." After we've read Inada's poem out loud, I ask students to re-read the poem and underline the words, lines, or phrases that strike them for some reason—perhaps because they seem important to the poem, students like the sound, or a line relates to something in their lives: e.g., "Where did our voices go? . . . I must correct you. . . . One song . . . One voice."

2. Once students have located lines and phrases, I tell them that we are going to create an oral group poem with the words, phrases, or lines they've selected. "Here's how this works: You are going to say your line or phrase when there is a pause. Think about how songs and poems work with repeating lines, repeating words, even an echo. For example, I might keep saying, 'Where did our voices go' throughout our oral poem.' There might be some awkward moments when two voices collide in the middle of the room. That's OK. The big idea is to bring key words from the poem alive in the room."

3. Sometimes I have students begin singing "Swing Low, Sweet Chariot" as background to the poem—or I play a recording of the song softly while we echo the lines of the poem.

4. I encourage students to call out lines or words to form the new poem, in what might be described as the literary equivalent of an improvisational musical composition. To model this, I sometimes invite eight or 10 students to come in front of the room and experiment as an example. Sometimes it takes a few times to get this going. As students re-read lines from the poem, they come to new understandings about the piece.

5. After our oral poem, I ask students to write for five minutes about the poem. "Just take a few minutes to describe how the poem made you feel, your reactions to the poem, or perhaps some memories that the poem evoked for you. There are no wrong answers."

6. When students are finished writing reflections, I begin a discussion. "You can read your response to the poem or you can just talk from your notes. I'd like to hear your thoughts, reactions, and memories."

7. We move on to writing by referring back to "Rayford's Song." "In this poem, Inada speaks of schools silencing students, but he also speaks more broadly about whose lives are included in the curriculum and whose are excluded. This is an event from his life that he witnessed. I want you to

think about times when you witnessed or experienced the silencing of someone's voice. You might also write about times when you felt your history was silenced or left out of the classroom."

8. At this point, I tell a few stories of my own. For example, my 9th-grade teacher made me stand and asked me to conjugate verbs or pronounce words as an example of how not to talk. I tell students that when I was growing up, we never saw or heard women in the curriculum—no history or literature from a women's perspective. I also tell them the story of my junior English teacher, Ms. Carr, who broke that tradition. "You can write about the silencing or the breaking of the silence. Just begin by making a list."

9. After students list times when their voices were silenced or included, or when they felt their history or stories were silenced or left out of the classroom, we share a few ideas to help others who haven't located their memories. "You can write this as a story or as a poem." (See "His Story" by Masta Davis, p. 89.)

10. We finish with a technique that Bill Bigelow, my co-teacher, and I call reading the "collective text." As students read their pieces out loud to the class, I ask them to take notes as they listen to their classmates' papers. I point to the blackboard where I've written: "Collect evidence as you listen. How did your classmates feel about being silenced? Who was silenced? Who silenced them? How did they respond?" (See p. 240 for details on using the read-around as a teaching strategy.)

11. After students listen to their classmates' pieces, I say, "Review your notes. Think about the stories and poems you've heard and write a paragraph or two on the ideas that emerged from the stories. See if you can find a common thread. You might want to mention specific people's poems or stories."

As students listen to the personal stories of their classmates, they can learn to read our society. The silencing and marginalization of the history and literature of people of color and women presents an ongoing problem in many schools. This continued silencing can be evidenced in contemporary school reading lists and syllabi and in the individual and shared experiences of students like Rayford in Inada's poem and Masta Davis and others who peopled my classroom over the years. My hope is by teaching students to read their "collective text," they discover that they are not alone in feeling invisible in the curriculum, and they see their absence as a call for action. ✳

. . . .

Linda Christensen (lmc@lclark.edu) is director of the Oregon Writing Project at Lewis & Clark College in Portland, Ore. She is a Rethinking Schools editor and author of Reading, Writing, and Rising Up *and* Teaching for Joy and Justice.

Resource

Inada, Lawson Fusao. "Rayford's Song," in *Legends from Camp*. Minneapolis: Coffee House Press, 1993.

Rayford's Song

by Lawson Fusao Inada

Rayford's song was Rayford's song,
but it was not his alone, to own.

He had it, though, and kept it to himself
as we rowed-rowed-rowed the boat
through English country gardens
with all the whispering hope
we could muster, along with occasional
choruses of funiculì-funiculà!

Weren't we a cheery lot—
comin' 'round the mountain
with Susanna, banjos on our knees,
rompin' through the leaves
of the third-grade music textbook.

Then Rayford Butler raised his hand.
For the first time, actually,
in all the weeks he had been in class,
and for the only time before he'd leave.
Yes, quiet Rayford, silent Rayford,
little Rayford, dark Rayford—
always in the same overalls—
that Rayford, Rayford Butler, raised his hand:

    "Miss Gordon, ma'am—
    we always singing your songs.

Could I sing one of my own?"
Pause. We looked at one another;
we looked at Rayford Butler;
we looked up at Miss Gordon, who said:

    "Well, I suppose so, Rayford—
    if you insist. Go ahead.
    Just one song. Make it short."

And Rayford Butler stood up very straight,
and in his high voice, sang:

    "Suh-whing a-looow
    suh-wheeeet ah charr-ee-oohh,
    ah-comin' for to carr-ee
    meee ah-hooooome. . . ."

Pause. Classroom, school, schoolyard,
neighborhood, the whole world
focusing on that one song, one voice
which had a light to it, making even
Miss Gordon's white hair shine
in the glory of it, glowing
in the radiance of the song.

Pause. Rayford Butler sat down.
And while the rest of us
may have been spellbound,
on Miss Gordon's face
was something like a smile,
or perhaps a frown:

    "Very good, Rayford.
    However, I must correct you:
    the word is 'chariot.'
    'Chariot.' And there is no
    such thing as a 'chario.'
    Do you understand me?"

    "But Miss Gordon. . . ."

    "I said 'chariot, chariot.'
    Can you pronounce that for me?"

    "Yes, Miss Gordon. Chariot."

    "Very good, Rayford,
    Now, class, before we return
    to our book, would anyone else
    care to sing a song of their own?"

Our songs, our songs were there—
on tips of tongues, but stuck
in throats—songs of love,
fun, animals, and valor, songs
of other lands, in other languages,
but they just wouldn't come out.
Where did our voices go?
Rayford's song was Rayford's song,
but it was not his alone to own.

    "Well, then, class—
    let's turn our books to
    'Old Black Joe.'"

His Story

by Masta Davis

Sittin' in the class,
the only spot of color in the place.
We're talkin' about history,
but mine's gone without a trace.
I turn the pages looking for color
at a vigorous pace.
Ahh.
Stop and it slaps me in the face.

Pictures of Africans,
sardines packed in ships.
Damn!
It looks like I'm gettin' ripped.
Ooops!
Here's King.

They always got the brotha'
who had the Dream.

I turn the page and reached
the end?
Slavery ain't how my history began.

Lies, fibs, and mistruths must be corrected.
It's time for my people to be honored and
Respected.

Remember Me
A farewell poem

BY LINDA CHRISTENSEN

MARY TREMONTE

On the last day of school, there is no final, no "free day," no signing of yearbooks in my classroom. Instead, as a going away present to my students, I make a book of their favorite writings from the year. In addition to the poem, story, or essay that students submit to the book, each student writes one "Remember Me" poem about a fellow classmate. As we gather for the last time in our circle, students honor each other in a final read-around with a poem in their classmate's memory, and a sparkling apple juice toast.

Many years ago I ran across a short paragraph by the Irish writer Dylan Thomas that delighted me. I loved his playful language, rift of r-words—round, red, robustly raddled—his comical metaphors and oddball list of details about himself:

Remember me? Round, red, robustly raddled, a bulging apple among poets, hard as nails made of cream cheese, gap-toothed, balding, noisome, a great collector of dust and a magnet for moths, mad for beer, frightened of priests, women, Chicago, writers, distance, time, children, geese, death, in love, frightened of love, liable to drip.

Thomas' paragraph inspired my farewell poem.

One year, when the new schedule crunched the ending of the year into a mad scramble to finish up portfolios, I decided to forgo the poem with my juniors. A few seniors stopped by my room, and I discussed my decision with them, weighing the merits of a portfolio review and the "Remember Me" poems. They convinced me that I had to continue the tradition.

Jalean Webb was the ringleader advocating me to keep the "Remember Me" poem. "These poems create bonds between students that carry into their senior year. The person I got I didn't know at all. I never noticed her before I drew her name. We never talked once during our first three years of high school. We talk all of the time this year," Jalean said when I asked the group why these poems were worth writing.

The three other visiting seniors agreed that the poems had to stay. Desiree Duboise said, "I drew the name of someone who I knew since middle school. I had a lot of memories. [The poem] was a great way to showcase that, to go back in time and write those memories. Also, at the end of the year, it was a great way to end on a personal note. Everyone is stressed; people don't even like each other any more. This poem made the class end on a positive note."

When I asked students to describe their process for creating the poem, Jalean responded, "I interviewed Desi and Gabby about Loan because they had classes with her. Desi told me, 'When Loan asks me for help, I feel smart.' I incorporated their quotes into the poem. Loan is Vietnamese, so I put that in the poem to make her feel special. I think that's the point of these poems—to make our classmates feel special."

Desiree Barksdale, said, "I drew Antonio, who I didn't know, but everyone else did. Antonio is a dancer, and I've seen him dance, so I knew I wanted to put that in the poem. From talking to other people, I found out

that he's a fantastic brother, and he has a younger sister who he takes to school. I put all of that in my poem."

"I also interviewed other classmates to get quotes in my poem about Sinnamon," Gabby said. "But I know Sinnamon well, so I included things I could praise about her."

Teaching Strategy

1. I ask students to write their names on slips of paper and place them in a basket. After everyone's name is included—those who are absent as well as the teacher—each student draws one name out of the bowl. If students draw their own names, they put them back. In some classes, I remind students not to groan, roll their eyes, or say they don't want to write about someone. I create a master list of who is writing about whom, so I make sure everyone has a poem on the final day—and I know who to nag.

2. I talk about the necessity of grounding their poems in details about their classmates. I select one student in the class and talk about some positive things the class will remember about this person to get students beyond the "he was nice" generalities in their poem. For example, in our class we might remember that Matt was always the first one in the door in the morning. We might remember that he wrote wonderful historical fiction and was passionate about chess. We might talk about how he remained friends with his buddies from Ockley Green Middle School or tell about the day he played Raheem's grandfather in the improvisation.

3. I read Jessica Rawlins' poem "Remember Sihaya?" (see p. 93). It is playful—evoking Sihaya Buntin's love of dance with the "tap, shuffle, tap" and the "electric angel with the dancer's feet" references. Jessica shares details about Sihaya that we remember: her tardiness, the fact that she was a

Students honor each other with a poem in their classmate's memory.

Jefferson dancer, her constant movement in class. We also read Jalean's tribute to Loan. The diverse models help students see a way into the poem if they are stuck.

4. After looking at the models, the class creates a list of items that may be included in the poem. We keep the list on the board, so students can look up and remind themselves if they run out of ideas: Quotes about the person, things the person said in class, memorable poems, stories, or essays that she or he shared in class, a list of details about the person—from where she sat to what he wore, to sports, hobbies, sayings, and a metaphor or simile about the person.

5. I start this process a couple of weeks before the end of the year, so students have time to watch their assigned classmate and collect ideas from

These poems create bonds between students.

others before they write. This needn't be a "private" piece of writing. I urge students to ask their classmates or me for details they might include. Also, I make sure that everyone has a poem written about them and that all poems are positive. In my class, students keep the name of their person secret until the last day when the class books are distributed and the poems read.

6. I check over the poems before they are read. I make sure that everyone has a poem and that the poems are tributes, not jibes. I also write a poem about the class as a whole because every class has a personality and shared memories that I want to capture. And, up until the last day, I model myself as a writer and member of the class, not a bystander or evaluator.

7. On the final day of school, our class is arranged in our typical circle. A volunteer starts off our read-around. After students read their poems, they walk across the room and hand the poem to a classmate. Then the classmate reads a poem about the person she drew. I end the class by reading the class poem.

Students need to learn how to build new traditions—ones that don't involve corporations telling them how to think and feel about death, birth, illness, goodbyes, celebrations, or each other. By creating practices in our classrooms that honor our time together, our work, and our community, we can teach students how to develop meaningful new traditions and remind them of the power of poetry up until the last minutes of the school year. ✳

. . . .

Linda Christensen (lmc@lclark.edu) is director of the Oregon Writing Project at Lewis & Clark College in Portland, Ore. She is a Rethinking Schools editor and author of Reading, Writing, and Rising Up *and* Teaching for Joy and Justice.

Remember Sihaya?
by Jessica Rawlins

I am the electric angel
with dancer's feet,
the slick sister who grins,
strolls into class only ten minutes late,
toting too many bags for a lady.
I am the laughter that echoes.
With a tap, shuffle, tap,
I practice my moves
to the silent beat in my head.
I am the Jefferson Dancer
who loathes geometry
and classes that I *know* I won't need later in life.
So I roll
and let it all slide by.
When grades come in,
I'm swimming upstream.
I am the party girl,
who lived for my friends
and thinks hell is getting stuck at home.
I am the fire,
who doesn't wait for details.
I'll catch up sooner or later,
just watch me.
I am Sihaya.

Mary
by Erika Howard

Mary, Mary, child of grace.
Long slim fingers, baby face.
When the boys catch at your skirt,
do you kiss or court or flirt?
When you marry charming Jim,
how many kisses will you give him?
Two four six eight ten.
Two four six eight twenty.
Two four six eight thirty.
Two four six eight forty.
Two four six eight. . .
Did you jump rope when you were a very little girl?
Or did you climb
wild in the branches of the play structure?
Perhaps you sat serenely
on the grass with a friend and a doll,
but I doubt it.
You, with the book of bright colors,
bright pictures,
and your own smooth pen.
You, with the smile that never stops.
Do you have sorrow or is your life,
a huge joyous rave?
Sometimes I wonder,
but your smile gives a hand to my limping heart,
and your laugh in the silence
nudges my elbow to include me.
You, with the clogs and wild tights.
You, with the red hair to almost match Lulu's.
You, who sat in the window,
silhouetted by the rich blue sky.
Mary, I'll always remember you.

Jalean
by Uriah Boyd

I recall football
in the front yard,
camping in the back.
Those Bambi eyes
and teddy bear demeanor
remind me of the boy I once knew,
but he is a boy no longer.
He's the big brother I always had:
varying,
protective, cheerful,
the one to make you smile
in the middle of a cry.
He's a poet—once slowly peering
out of his shell.
Now he enters unapologetically:
Fists clenched, uttering spine-chilling words.
I remember him as the class clown,
the kid with a smile that tickled my soul, and
my pigeon-toed neighbor,
but you can just call him
Jalean.

Remember Loan Vu
by Jalean Webb

The petite girl
whose Vietnamese culture brings diversity
to our class.
Her shy intelligence
is the X that marks the spot
on the treasure map that is our class.

She's the woman
Desi, Gabby, and I adorn with praise:
"Her shyness is only matched
by her brains."
"When she asks me questions,
it makes me feel smart."
"A person to look for when
you need a calm moment."

She's the learner
who won't quit,
who hits the books harder
when they hit back,
who strikes to put education
on a pedestal,
who is a quiet thinker
who will achieve greatness.

Remember Loan?
Once she touched our lives
we refused to forget.

Remember Junior English?

by Linda Christensen

Who could forget you?
You came in with your chins up
and fists cocked,
ready to take on two white women
who appeared new to the school,
full of rules like:
put your phones away
respect air time
listen when others speak.

Remember the day I
asked you to sign up to be Scholars
and you said, "Hell, no?"
well maybe,
but I'm not saying, "I will be a scholar."

I fell in love with you that day.
Even when you talked back,
because you didn't bow down to anyone.
You rebelled.
And could never resist cracking silence with your
    voices.
And I love you for it.

I love the cross between your Ninja Turtle Trayvon
    Martin hoodies'
vulnerability
and the amazing courage
you forged to write your lives.

I love the way you crackled and resisted
at the beginning of each assignment,
then wrote and rewrote.
I loved it when you complained, "I can't stop."
"This is my novel."
You squeezed my brain.
You pounding the keyboard
made poetry,
made literature,
made this old teacher's year.

Father Was a Musician
by Dyan Watson

In the basement they played.
"Jam session" he called it,
halting only to mend a chord or two.

The house swayed from side to side
dancing freely, carelessly
while neighbors shut doors and windows.

Sometimes I would sneak into his bedroom
just to see it, touch it,
pluck a string or two.

At night, I dreamed
of concerts and demos.

I want to be just like him.

CHAPTER THREE

Poetry for the People
Breathing life into literary and historical characters

THEA GAHR

Becoming American
by Khalilah Joseph

I looked into the eyes of my Japanese doll
and knew I could not surrender her
to the fury of the fire.
My mother threw out the poetry
she loved;
my brother gave the fire his sword.

We worked hours
to vanish any traces of the Asian world
from our home.
Who could ask us
to destroy
gifts from a world that molded
and shaped us?

If I ate hamburgers
and apple pies,
if I wore jeans,
then would I be American?

Poetry for the People
Breathing life into literary and historical characters

We believe that our classrooms need to tell the untold stories that are often submerged beneath the weight of official curriculum. In many schools, names and dates celebrate the historical winners; novels feature stories of white people in an airbrushed world, and too many of our students and their families are absent, silent, or marginalized. In this chapter, we encourage teachers to bring those untold stories of historical and literary characters to life through poetry.

When writing poems from history or literature, students find different ways of expressing knowledge about a fictional character or a historical decision. Our skin, our blood, our bones sometimes understand events before our minds catch up and process the information. Writing poetry helps unleash sorrow or joy, the human understanding of loss and creation across cultures, centuries, and continents. In this chapter teachers share poetry lessons that helped students connect across lines that typically divide—race, class, gender, language, sexual orientation. Students' poems demonstrate how they imagined forgotten histories—Khalilah Joseph from the point of view of a Japanese American girl on the brink of entering an internment camp, Meg Niemi imagining a father killed in Vietnam, Kyle Christy stepping into the world of a Chinese woman sold into prostitution.

If we think of a curricular unit as a journey, then poetry is an invitation for classes to stop at cafés and linger over conversations about books, read historical plaques in rest areas, and picnic by the ocean, sucking on morsels of texts as if they are Dungeness crab legs. Writing poetry about literary and historical texts isn't a make-work assignment designed to keep students busy; it fulfills vital functions. It provides entry points for students to see the texts with fresh eyes. Through persona, dialogue, and "Write that I" poems, students imagine both the literary and historical past, but these poetry lessons also teach students to "read" the untold stories in the daily news and their own lives as well. Whose stories are told? Whose are left out? By immersing students in literature and history, they learn to unearth the details that the powerful seek to bury: A granddaughter remembering her family home as gentrification sweeps through her neighborhood or a girl searching for her sister after the U.S. bombing of Hiroshima.

Poetry encourages students to respond on an emotional level, providing a vehicle to excavate not only these untold stories, but also anger and despair—and sometimes joy.

"Poetry for the People" also implies poetry as activism. Poetry awakens consciousness through truth telling. In "Dropping the Bomb Was a Clean Job," student poet Keely Thrasher evokes the human lives that war destroys—of the living and the dead, reminding us that there is no clean war. By stepping into other people's lives, children develop the ability to empathize. Part of our job as teachers includes nurturing students' capacity to imagine the effects of historical and literary events on other human beings. ✳

Other People's Lives

Persona poems teach insight and empathy

BY LINDA CHRISTENSEN

BEC YOUNG

On the best days in my class-room, students learn to read novels and primary sources, to critique news and popular culture, to write passionate essays, narratives, and poems, but I would consider my-self a failure if my students didn't also develop an empathetic heart. Empathy, or "social imagination," as Peter Johnston calls it in *The Reading Teacher*, encourages students to get inside the head and heart of another human being. Poetry (as well as interior monologues and historical fiction) allows students to inhabit the lives of others, to use their imaginations to humanize the abstractions of poverty, war, racism by making literary and historical situations vivid enough for the reader—and the writer—to be moved by people and their circumstances: The unaccompanied minors riding trains and crossing deserts from Central America, the children ducking and dodging drones and bomb blasts shattering the concrete walls of their homes in Gaza, the women and children in Honduras and China and Vietnam sewing shirts for U.S. teenagers, the Yakama fighting coal exports on the Columbia River. I want my students to use poetry to cross the boundaries of race, nationality, class, and gender to find their common humanity with people whose history and literature we have studied.

I return to the persona poem again and again as an anchor poetic strategy in my classroom. Unlike most poems I use, there isn't an easy trick that helps students write the poem—a repeating line and a list, an extended metaphor, a model poem providing a road map. This poem leads with heart and imagination, asking students to find that place inside themselves that connects with a moment in history, literature, life—and to imagine another's world, to value it, to hold it sacred for a moment as a way of bearing witness for another human being. This poem demands emotional honesty, intellectual curiosity, poetic craft, and the ability to imagine stepping into someone else's life at the moment when their life changes.

The poet Patricia Smith described the persona poem in her *Torch* interview:

> There's got to be some wrinkle in the life of the person you're writing about. Something they're angry about. There's a texture to it. . . . A lot of times, it's not just the job or whatever. It's something that's happened in their life that's making them talk, that has them angered or sad or about to jump off of a building. You put them in a situation that is interesting.

These "wrinkles" can be the result of decisions imposed on people by governments—like the Japanese American internment—but they might also be personal, like Celie, from *The Color Purple*, rising up and fighting back against the men who abused her. By giving voice to historical and literary characters, I hope students see the possibility of the past being different, but also learn to see the future as unwritten, a field of possibilities, the outcome dependent, in part, on their actions.

Using History, Film, Literature, News

Students enter the persona poem through a literary or historical character. Typically, I saturate them in a unit—reading historical texts, novels, plays, short stories, poetry, and film clips. Throughout the entire unit, they take notes, both to understand the unit—from language colonization to Pygmalion to the gentrification of our neighborhood—and to collect evidence toward discussions and essays, but also to figure out what piques their interests. Along the way, I ask them to "capture language or images that sear into you, watch for words or phrases that evoke memories or feelings."

To prepare students to write the poem, I ask them to brainstorm potential key moments and turning points that a historical or literary character faced in the unit we are studying. Students have written persona poems from the point of view of a young girl after the Student Nonviolent Coordinating Committee (SNCC) and Bob Moses entered her small town in Mississippi, of a sister whose brother was killed during the Soweto uprising, of Ma Joad in *The Grapes of Wrath* when the sheriff tries to evict her family, and of Henry David Thoreau about the Mexican-American War.

After studying the Japanese American internment and reading Monica Sone's *Nisei Daughter* and selections from Jeanne Wakatsuki Houston and James D. Houston's *Farewell to Manzanar*, students wrote persona poems. I asked students to "choose the scene, the circumstance, the 'wrinkle' from our readings." We brainstormed key scenes from the books, places that made tears well up or anger burn in our chests. I listed these on the board.

This poem demands the ability to imagine stepping into someone else's life at the moment when their life changes.

Once we itemized potential scenes, I enlisted students to call out details. "What do you remember about the scene? Remember, a poem must create a picture in the reader's head. You need specific details to make that happen: People's names. Street names. Names of parks or boats or buildings. Clothing. Language from the characters. Slogans. What details do you recall?" I put these on the board, too.

I encourage students to return to the specific pages of the scene or book to re-read the language the author used. When we watch a film, I stop after the first couple of minutes and ask students for details to model how to take notes. We never watch or read all of the way through without stopping to gather words and images from the "text"—whether it is a novel, a film, or a field trip. "Lift off from the writer's words and details to fuel your poem."

I use my former student Khalilah Joseph's poem "Becoming American" as an example for my current students to examine because I like the way she takes the situation and details from the original text to create her poem. We also read Patricia Smith's and Martín Espada's poetry, but my previous students' poetry offers more accessible models. Reading the writing of graduates from their school makes possible the idea that they can also produce this level of work. Sometimes students know the poet. Nowadays, the "older" student poets who still "speak" from the pages of our literary magazine are the aunts and uncles or parents of some of the students I currently work with. Legacies.

Khalilah wrote from a segment in *Nisei Daughter* where the family burned their Japanese possessions because neighbors warned them about "having too many Japanese objects around the house." I pass out the segment from Sone's book that Khalilah wrote from, and we read it out loud:

We worked all night, feverishly combing through bookshelves, closets, drawers, and furtively creeping down to the basement furnace for the burning. I gathered together my well-worn Japanese language schoolbooks. . . . I threw them into the fire and watched them flame and shrivel into black ashes. But when I came face to face with my Japanese doll which Grandmother Nagashima had sent me from Japan, I rebelled.

Then we read the poem Khalilah created from the scene. As we read, I ask students to think about what details Khalilah used from Sone's book. How did she take that scene and make a poem?

Becoming American
I looked into the eyes of my Japanese doll
and knew I could not surrender her
to the fury of the fire.
My mother threw out the poetry
she loved;
my brother gave the fire his sword.

We worked hours
to vanish any traces of the Asian world
from our home.
Who could ask us
to destroy
gifts from a world that molded
and shaped us?

If I ate hamburgers
and apple pies,
if I wore jeans,
then would I be American?

Students typically note that Khalilah put in the particulars of what Sone burned and refused to burn—her beloved Japanese doll, her mother's poetry, her brother's sword. This is the point where I need to push students: "Why did she use these details? What do they tell us about what was happening to Japanese Americans?" These particular and concrete specifics help the reader "see" the loss; they are also the characteristics of great poetry that I want students to notice and use. By bringing us to the fire with the Sone family, Khalilah distills one moment from the memoir and the internment to depict the inhumanity, the attempt to erase a people and culture.

I ask students to think about who the "I" is in the poem and what other perspective Khalilah could have chosen. Persona poems are typically, but not always, written in first person. We also discuss how Khalilah wrote from Monica's point of view. Students point out that she could have written from the mother's or brother's perspective or from the perspective of inanimate objects, like the fire, poem, sword, or doll. Over the years, students have written spectacular poems from the point of view of objects—the last building standing after the fire destroyed Tulsa's Black neighborhood, the branding iron used to "brand" enslaved Africans, Hector Pieterson's shoe after he was killed in the Soweto uprising.

Writers' Choices

In order to get students to pay attention to how word choice helps create the sense of resistance, submission, anger, and defiance, we read the poem a second time. "For a moment, let's return to the poem and think about why Khalilah might have chosen the words she did." Students usually point out the words like "surrender" in the lines "I could not surrender her/to the fury of the fire." We talk about how the word "surrender" depicts the stance of giving up, like her brother does with his sword, but it's also a term used in warfare. Because Monica does not "surrender" her doll to the "fury of the fire," Khalilah also demonstrates her resistance to the "fury" of the events unfurling around her.

Let me pause to say that students often bring up these points on their own. If they don't, I might. What I don't want to do is dissect the poem for them. There's no better way to kill poetry than to tell someone else what it means.

The other poetic craft Khalilah employs is the use of questions at the end of the poem, turning to face the reader. Because questions are another writing craft I want students to incorporate, I ask students to think about why she uses questions in her poetry. "Who could ask us/to destroy/gifts from a world that molded/and shaped us?" And again in the last stanza: "If I ate hamburgers/and apple pies,/if I wore jeans,/then would I be American?" Of course, many students aren't sure why she uses questions. I'm not sure why, either, but I want them to talk about how questions push the reader to think about what it means to be American.

My intention in carefully reading and re-reading Khalilah's poem is to show students the specific tools at work in her piece—concrete details from the reading, word choice that matches the content, and evocative questions. Before students write their pieces, I write this list of poetic tools on the board that they might use in their poems.

Using the persona poem, students write the heartache, tragedy, joy, the stumbling footsteps, the missed opportunities, the unspoken and wish-it-had-never-been-spoken words of the many characters who crowd our classrooms: The warriors for justice in our Civil Rights unit, the church lady who turned activist in our gentrification study, Troy and his son who fight across the pages of *Fences*, Eliza Doolittle attempting to learn "proper" English to escape poverty in *Pygmalion*, or Dante and Aristotle, the two gay Mexican American boys in *Dante and Aristotle Discover the Secrets of the Universe*. Through writing, students imagine different lives, give voice to the voiceless, carve poetry out of the "rock experiences" of their daily lives, and, as the poet Martín Espada wrote, "document the presence of such social forces as racism, sexism, and poverty, and in so doing make those abstract terms painfully concrete." ✳

I hope students learn to see the future as unwritten, a field of possibilities, the outcome dependent, in part, on their actions.

. . . .

Linda Christensen (lmc@lclark.edu) is director of the Oregon Writing Project at Lewis & Clark College in Portland, Ore. She is a Rethinking Schools editor and author of Reading, Writing, and Rising Up *and* Teaching for Joy and Justice.

Hiroshima
by Kamaria Kyle

(Written in the "persona" of a young girl whose sister
was killed during the bombing of Hiroshima.)

"Sister, where are you?"
I see the shadow where you were,
but only surrounded by ashes.
Your beautiful smile,
your enchanting face
are the ashes at my feet.
The quiet of death surrounds me,
and I hope for a noise,
something to break the silence.
Your voice would prove
the shadow wrong,
but I only hear the cries of children
whose sisters disappeared
as quickly as you did.
I know you're not just ashes.
"Sister, where are you?"

'Dropping the Bombs Was a Clean Job'
by Keely Thrasher

(Written in response to the film *Hearts and Minds*
about Vietnam. The title of the poem quotes a soldier
who dropped bombs during the war.)

What you didn't see were the women
Too weak to cry
Wrinkled hands holding broken bodies
Chapped lips kissing open wounds.

What you didn't hear were the children
Lost in the smoke
Running naked through the burning fields
Curling up next to their dead mother
Waiting for her to wake.

What you didn't smell was the flesh
Caught in barbed wire
Torn like an old rag
Soft brown skin heated to black.

What you didn't taste was the blood
Mixed with dirt and rice
Staining the walls of the huts
Splashed on the faces of young girls.

What you didn't feel were the men
Their faces frozen
Thrown hard against the earth
Like the end of a statement.

You must have missed those things
If you hadn't, you would have turned back
Picking up every shell you dropped
Bandaging every scrape you caused.

You must have missed those things.

Vietnam: No Scissors to the Truth
by Meg Niemi

(Written after a unit on Vietnam that included reading
In Country by Bobbie Ann Mason.)

They sent Dad back
in an army green
ziplock freezer bag,
the kind Mama
shells sweet peas in
and stocks in the icebox
as a reminder of
sunnier days.

They sent him as
a reminder, a token of the war
that his three-month-old child
would spend
the rest
of her life
trying to thaw.

There were no scissors
to cut through to
the truth.
They even made sure
he was double-sealed
for our protection—
leaving a number
as his only identity.

If Mama had shaken that bag
to spill the truth,
would he have rattled
like those summer sweet peas
shaken from a pod?
Would I have heard
Sunday talk
of Kentucky catfish,
Jesus bugs,
and days 'in country'?

Opened Eyes
by Adiana Wilmot

(Interior monologue written as a poem from the point
of view of Janie, the main character in *Their Eyes Were
Watching Go*d, talking back to her husband, Joe.)

I knew you weren't the rising sun
who caused pollen to work its magic.
I knew you wouldn't make the trees bloom,
but something inside of me blossomed
when you spoke of the horizon.
How was I to know
that my hands were needed
to hold up your imaginary sky?
You based our lives on a fairy tale,
a story easy for you to read,
but for me,
the pages turned slowly,
and with each turn
the paper sliced my skin.
It became too much for me to clean up.
If only you would've picked up a cloth
and scrubbed the redness off the floor with me,
maybe then your horizon could've been saved.
But I guess you had your own cuts to heal.
Your blood was more important than mine.
And instead of mixing our wounds into a marriage,
our fenced-up horizon began to crumble
until only a few boards remained.

Poetic Storytelling

Selecting details from coat pockets and dresser drawers

BY LINDA CHRISTENSEN

BEC YOUNG

Many years ago, I found a wonderful poem about a woman on a balcony. The poem started, "Write that I. . . ." In the jumble of my file cabinets and moves, I lost the original poem, but I didn't lose my love for this opening. I wrote a poem from the point of view of Molly Craig, the main character in the movie *Rabbit-Proof Fence*, to use as a model with students.

This poetic model is a variation on the persona poem, meaning that it is written from the perspective of a historical or literary character, but students can also write about their own lives. The format encourages students to get inside the head and heart of another human being, to become the "second throat" that poet Patricia Smith writes about in her essay "Keepers of the Second Throat" (see p. 205).

The "Write that I. . ." poem drives students to select significant details to use in their poems—to search among the chest of drawers, closets, pockets of old coats; to eavesdrop on family arguments, corporate discussions; to find the just-right crumbs, lint, and detritus of a life. Over the years, I have taught the poem in both literature and history units, with most of the novels and plays I teach, during our study of Tulsa Race "Riots" and gentrification, and in the opening of the year to build community.

Writing the Poem

I begin by reading my poem "Molly Craig" out loud (see p. 109). I ask students to highlight the poem with two colors of highlighters. "Highlight the repeating lines in one color. For example, 'Write that I' is a repeating line. What other lines repeat and carry the poem forward? Highlight the details about Molly's life in the other color." Students usually identify the lines "write that I," and "tell them," etc. I point out that the poem uses a series of phrases that help weave the content together: Write that I; tell them that I; when you write my story, say that I.

Students point out details from Molly's life, where she grew up, that she was a tracker, and so on. We work to categorize these details, the specific information I included in the model: Names of people and places, dialogue from the movie, characters' actions. I also direct students to notice my use of negatives and questions as a pushback to the whites' assessment of Molly's conditions:

No there weren't walls,
And no there weren't beds,
And yes, we were poor,
But when did love come in units
Counted up in dollar bills?

The trick to teaching students how to write poetry is to instruct them at the point of writing, to show them the tools in process—repetition, negation, questions, lists.

Now that I also have student models, we look at what pieces of the mentor poem Kyle Christy used in his poem about Lalu Nathoy from the novel *Thousand Pieces of Gold* (see p. 110). We also examine how he uses the details from Lalu's life in lists to celebrate her life and her defiance of tradition:

Tell the world how I was so stubborn
Stood up for what I wanted
Did what I felt was right
Despite what society asked

I broke the stereotype
Of a normal Chinese women
Led my own life. . .
Lived it how I wanted

No more bound feet to hold me back
No slavery
No husband
No falling into stereotypes
But also. . .
No disrespect

In Kyle's poem, I point out his great use of repetition of "no" with the "No more bound feet" stanza. He uses the format of the poem—lists, repeating and changing lines like "tell that," but he breaks it to create his own rhythm.

The poem encourages students to get inside the head and heart of another human being.

Alyss Dixson's poem, "Write that I . . . (A Frederick Douglass Narrative)," started in our Literature and U.S. History classroom at Jefferson (see p. 111). When she was a freshman at Yale, Alyss revised it and won the Meeker Poetry Prize with this piece. As we read Alyss' poem, I again encourage students to notice what pieces she lifts from the original poem. I also push students to observe how she not only uses evidence from Douglass' life, but also line breaks and spacing to tell his story.

Once students understand the frame of repeating lines—write that I, say that I, when you tell my story—I encourage them to add phrases that would hook their poems forward. "What other phrases could you use to anchor your stanza?" I list their alternatives on the board. "Your poems will all sound the same unless you find your own verbs here." Students will invariably come up with ones I hadn't considered.

Then we generate a list of characters for their poems. As we make the list, I encourage them to think about minor characters, bystanders, as well as objects in the landscape. For example, when we studied the Soweto uprising, students not only listed Hector Pieterson, who was killed by the police during the uprising, Hector's sister, the photographer, and a teacher whose students walked out, but also the school building, the flag, the bullet that killed Hector.

After students decide on a character—human or inanimate—I ask them to list details from the event or person's life that will make them come alive. We do this first with a common, well-known character, as a way to put an island of words under students who struggle. Depending on the strength of the writers in the room, I sometimes have students construct a poem together.

My final instructions are: "Write the poem. Use

The "Write that I" poem allows students to more deeply understand events and characters, to develop empathy, to step outside of their own lives. I love the freestanding persona poem, but sometimes students need a few more hooks to get into the writing, especially at the beginning of the year. The structure of the "Write that I" poem provides that poetic footstool. ✻

....

Linda Christensen (lmc@lclark.edu) is director of the Oregon Writing Project at Lewis & Clark College in Portland, Ore. She is a Rethinking Schools editor and author of Reading, Writing, and Rising Up *and* Teaching for Joy and Justice.

The trick to teaching students how to write poetry is to instruct them at the point of writing.

the lines as hooks to move the poem forward. When you run out of details, begin a new stanza. Write a new linking line and add new details."

When students complete the poem, I send them back for immediate revision. "When you finish, stand back and see if you have the right order. Notice if you have repeated yourself. Is there any new way you could pull the poem forward? Can you rearrange words? Add something? Substitute a different word to create more rhythm? Is there any place where you can eliminate words that don't add anything to the poem?"

When students are satisfied with their drafts, we read the poems around the circle. In this read-around, I say, "As usual, I want you to notice the great moves of the poet, but I also want you to think about what you learn from the poem. What does the poet teach us about the incident or the people?" Because this is typically a content-driven poem, I use the poems to launch discussions about the book or historical event we are investigating.

Molly Craig
by Linda Christensen

Write that I grew up in Jigalong
With my mother and grandmother.
Say that it was my home,
No there weren't walls,
And no there weren't beds,
And yes, we were poor,
But when did love come in units
Counted up in dollar bills?
When did family become something you could count
Instead of something you could count on?

Tell them that I learned to read animal tracks,
Filter water from roots in a desert, cook over an open fire,
And find my spirit bird
Before most kids learn to read words.
And yet, Mr. Devil calls me uneducated.

He wants to teach me to sweep, empty buckets,
Wring water from white people's sheets.

Tell them instead of beating me and shaming me
For my color, my dirty hair, my language,
My mother taught me through praise,
Good tracker, she said,
"You brought us a fat one."

When you write my story, tell Mr. Devil that my mother's grief
Could not be counted, not tallied up in his books,
My mother's grief strummed along 1,200 miles of rabbit-proof fence
And hummed me home.

Say that I wasn't half anything,
Not half caste, not half black, not half white,
Yes, when you tell my story,
Say that when I'm home,
I'm whole.

Thousand Pieces of Gold
by Kyle Christy

When you tell my story. . .
Tell it all
Tell the truth

Tell the world how I was so stubborn
Stood up for what I wanted
Did what I felt was right
Despite what society asked

I broke the stereotype
Of a normal Chinese women
Led my own life. . .
Lived it how I wanted

No more bound feet to hold me back
No slavery
No husband
No falling into stereotypes
But also. . .
No disrespect

But that's how I like it. . .
Free

Even when things were the worst
Tell the world how I still fought
I always fought
Never gave up
No matter how bad it got
I stayed strong

When you tell my story. . .
Tell about. . .
Me

When You Speak of Me
by Dylan Mitchell

When you speak of me
tell them about how lonely
I really am,

tell them a story of
a kid who can't find himself,
a wonderful story
stitched together with
yo-yo string.

Speak of a kid who wants
to find freedom, of a life
that wants to drag him
to the deepest parts of hell.

Tell the story of a kid
who is tightrope walking
across a cauldron bubbling
a stew of a world full
of tweakers, debt,
and minimum wage jobs.

But what I want you to
tell them is that this kid
will make it across that
rope. No matter how bumpy
the rope may be, he will
make it.

Write that I. . .
(A Frederick Douglass Narrative)
by Alyss Dixson

Write that I started in Freedom
praising my God
        feet inscribing the circle of my tribe
Tell how I described paradise
in pounding rhythms
      the sting of skin
          against drum
and the reassuring heat
        rising from the earth

Write that I grew up   in chains
praising my Master
with the sweat rolling from my back
   humbled by cotton in the field
Tell how I described paradise
in a bowl of rawhide soup
flea-infested hay
and the regular cracks!
        Rising and falling from the whip of
         the overseer

Write that I reached   "Manhood"
less than a man
barely stirring in my sleep
at the sound of my master
taking what was "his" to claim
from my Sisters

Tell how I described Freedom
in a chain
wrapped around a pale wrinkled
    neck
the satisfying crunch!
      of bone and
         the bulging of blue eyes in
         a moon-shaped face

Tell how
with fevered brain
I ran north
  ran
    from bloodhounds
    and bounty hunters

blood still
wet   upon my fists

I
   ran   streams   forests
      through   and
the words of slave spirituals
     and
the faint   sounding of   the train whistle
      my only guides

Say I was bitter
and disappointed
knowing my children
and their children
would cry out
    against these silent chains
    another kind of bondage
    restricting their lives
    binding them
        to poverty

Tell how I described   Freedom
In pounding syllables of   Revolution
                Education
                Equality

Write that I died
praising my Lord
    singing
        of Amazing
          Grace
and Write
     that I was proud.

Learning About Inequality
A poem for two voices

BY LINDA CHRISTENSEN

THEA GAHR

The two-voice poem, or dialogue poem, became a full-time resident in the Literature and U.S. History class Bill Bigelow and I co-taught for years. Our love affair with this poem started when Gail Black, our colleague in the Language Arts Department at Jefferson High School in Portland, Ore., gave us "Two Women," a poem written by a working-class Chilean woman in 1973, shortly after the overthrow of Salvador Allende, Chile's socialist president (see p. 116). The poem was originally published in *Sojourners* magazine. The paired voices of the two Chilean women— one poor and one rich—show how the historical events in their country changed their lives, from Allende's election to his overthrow.

The poetic format of the dialogue poem helps students get at something fundamental about social reality: Different social groups are affected differently by the same historical events. Writing the poem alerts students to inequality—from the coup in Chile to slavery in the United States to immigration policies. This disparity can be seen in the Chilean women's dialogue:

I am a woman.
I am a woman.

I am a woman born of a woman whose man
    owned a factory.
*I am a woman born of a woman whose man
    labored in a factory.*

I am a woman whose man wore silk suits, who
    constantly watched his weight.
*I am a woman whose man wore tattered clothing,
    whose heart was constantly strangled by
    hunger.*

I am a woman who watched two babies grow into
    beautiful children.
*I am a woman who watched two babies die
    because there was no milk.*

I use the dialogue poem to evoke discussion about literature as well as history so that students can understand how race, class, and gender differences impact their own lives as well as the lives of historical and literary characters. Students explore the contradictions between social groups as they focus on inequality by contemplating and writing from diverse perspectives. When writing these pieces, students can also discover surprising commonalities between groups.

Students need the solid foundation of content knowledge prior to writing this variation on the persona poem. Because Bill and I asked students to partner up to write the poem, the assignment also facilitated collaboration between kids. The poem forced them to return to the materials we studied as they struggled together to make sense of the history or literature, discussing both overview and detail to create their poem. To make this piece work, students must pinpoint the conflict, or inequality, so they have something to write about.

Because of the history of inequality in our country, there is no shortage of topics. In a unit on slavery and resistance, for example, our students focused on dialogues between enslaved women and women in the "big house," slave and master, and abolitionists with differing positions about how to end slavery. In *The Grapes of Wrath*, students constructed conversations between tenant farmers and bank owners, Ma Joad and the sheriff. In the young adult novel *Esperanza Rising*, students identified the inequality between the field workers and the owners/bosses, but also between workers who went on strike and those who didn't, between the authorities who rounded up and deported Mexicans and the deportees. The sharp edges of class in Mexican society created friction between Esperanza, whose father owned land, and Miguel, whose father worked the land.

Writing the Poem

Before class on the day I launched the poem, I found two students, strong readers, and asked them to rehearse reading the poem out loud a few times to get into the voice and rhythm of the speakers. I started class by giving students a brief overview of a piece of Chilean history, so they could understand the poem: Salvador Allende was elected president of Chile in 1970. His Popular Unity government initiated changes, like nationalizing the copper mines and other

Students explore the contradictions between social groups by contemplating and writing from diverse perspectives.

pro-working class reforms. These reforms angered both the wealthy of Chile as well as the U.S. government. The coup took place on Sept. 11, 1973. Allende and many others were killed or imprisoned, and the dictator Augusto Pinochet came to power and instituted a radical free market, pro-rich reform. That flip from a government that supported the poor to a government that supported the rich is the wrinkle in history from which the poem was written. After I distributed the poem, I asked the two readers to stand on opposite sides of the room as they read "Two Women" out loud. I get goose bumps every time I hear the poem.

Once students heard the poem, I asked them to talk about the poem. "What did you notice about the poem?" Often students' first responses were about the format. When I taught the poem to a class reading *Fools Crow* by James Welch, Elisa noticed that one line was written in italics and the other in bold to help the reader follow the two voices. Llondyn pointed out that sometimes the women had the same starting point on the line, but depending on their class, the line ended differently. Llondyn's observation led to

The poem provides a way to move deeper into the content of the class.

others' comments about how the writer showed the difference by using details like clothes, children, husbands, or food. Hannah drew us to the line about the husbands. "One owns a factory, the other works in a factory." Using the students' remarks, I constructed a T-chart on the board so they could visually see how the poet used the same items in each line. (See chart on p. 120.)

After students located the major points in the format of the poem, I asked, "Where can you see the history we discussed earlier reflected in the poem? Where can you find the 'beats' or changes in history that we talked about before we read the poem?" Maya directed our attention to how the lines that the women say together point out the change: In the beginning they are both women, but their lives are very different. Later when the women say, "But then there was a man," the line signaled a change—Allende coming to power. And the third time the women speak together again, "And I saw a man" indicated another change: Pinochet coming to power. Although students didn't remember the names and dates from my brief overview, they could see how the writer took those historical events and created a flow to the poem.

Once students understood the model, we turned our attention to *Fools Crow*, a novel about the invasion of whites into Blackfeet land, which threatened to change their traditional ways of life. The Blackfeet had

to choose to fight or assimilate, and the author, James Welch, deftly portrays the multiple perspectives of the tribe about the invasion, the consequences, and their choices. "Where do you see that historic 'wrinkle' or tension in the book? Can you isolate two people or two groups of people who might see the world differently, like the two Chilean women?" Students began shouting out pairs: Napikwans (whites) and Blackfeet, elders and young warriors, Fast Horse and Fools Crow, Owls Child and Fast Horse, men and women in the Blackfeet society. They also named particular characters who had different ideas about how to address the coming of the settlers.

Next, I drew another T-chart on the blackboard (and yes, it is still a blackboard in 2014), and said, "When we looked at the "Two Women" poem, we made a list of the different historical moments that surfaced the women's responses. Now let's make a list of those moments in *Fools Crow*, as well as the items that you might compare to show the different reactions of the Napikwans and the Blackfeet or whatever pair you choose to write from." Kevin started out the listing, "The raid on the Crow Camp, when the Napikwans arrived, when they started taking over the land, setting up forts, bringing small pox." As a class, students listed the "beats" of the novel together. We wrote the poem about two-thirds of the way through the book, so we didn't have the entire novel listed.

After going through the historical beats, I asked students to think about what items might demonstrate the difference between the people they chose. "Let's go back to the 'Two Women' poem, and remind ourselves how that poem is constructed. We have the two voices, we have the historical 'beats.' Now let's go back to the items the writer chose to show the difference. Remember how you all pointed out that the writer *showed* the difference by using details like clothes, children, husbands, or food? What items would you use to show the difference between your two people?"

Taylor pointed out that for the elders and the young warriors, they could use the points of disagreement—whether they should trade with the whites, make war on the whites, try to assimilate. We looked at a couple of other pairings to make sure students understood how to proceed with the poem, then I said,

"Partner up. Find someone to work with, decide who you will write about, and get started."

Now, to be honest, some students hadn't read the book or weren't deep enough into it to write this poem. And although this is frustrating, it is also a fact of life in most classrooms. The upside of this is that students had to *read* at least some of the book to fulfill the assignment. Listing the beats of the novel helped them and partnering them with someone who had read helped them. We also reminded students to look at the walls of the classroom, which was filled with previous work on the book: quotes, debate notes, and character silhouettes that include character traits, quotes, and page numbers.

We didn't write this straight through. I roamed the room checking on the students' character charts, seeing who was stuck, who had filled out their charts, who had interesting insights. Once most of the students were rolling, I stopped the class and said, "Let's take a look at how a few partners have tackled the poem." I had a few students show their charts on the document camera and explain their rationale of who and what they were comparing to help the students who were still flailing around. During the last five minutes of the class when students started actually writing the dialogue lines, I invited a few partners up to share their poems.

Savannah and Brianna chose to write from the points of view of two leaders, one who wanted to fight the whites and the other who believed that in order to survive, the Blackfeet had to assimilate:

I am a leader.
I am a leader.

Let us fight.
Let us make peace.

They want our land.
We are willing to share.

If we surrender, we die.
If we fight, we die.

They call for us to stand down and give up.
They called for us to negotiate and reassured us.

I will not go and hear more lies.
I made sure they knew we were allies.

As students bent their attention to the poem, they returned again and again to the book, discussing points of view, agreements and disagreements, choice points.

Once students completed the poems, they shared their pieces in class. In addition to literary show-and-tell, these dialogues also provided a platform for students to discuss the historical beats of the novel, the points of difference between generations, races, and genders on the coming of whites into Blackfeet land. In other words, the poem provides a way to move deeper into the content of the class.

The poem can become a framework or a position for an essay. In an essay on *Fools Crow*, students have explored the divisions between members of the Blackfeet nation on how to deal with the coming of the whites, and examined how the different perspectives or worldviews of whites and Blackfeet led to conflict. In Andy Kulak and Wendy Shelton's classroom at Jefferson High School, the students wrote their *Fools Crow* dialogue poems on long pieces of "butcher" paper, creating what Andy calls "an interactive wallpaper" that he leaves up as students work on their final essays. "Thus, if one line of thinking in building their essay proves to be a dead end, or students have difficulty providing evidence for their ideas, they can 'look up' and hear another previously unconsidered voice that might lead them to a more successful essay."

For me, the dialogue poem is more about content than poetry. This poetic vehicle forces students to examine fundamental disparities in our society through literature, history, and their own lives as it develops their analytic capacity in preparation for future encounters with inequality. It is this awakening of consciousness that schools should be about. ✳

. . . .

Linda Christensen (lmc@lclark.edu) is director of the Oregon Writing Project at Lewis & Clark College in Portland, Ore. She is a Rethinking Schools editor and author of Reading, Writing, and Rising Up *and* Teaching for Joy and Justice.

Two Women

I am a woman.
   I am a woman.

I am a woman born of a woman whose man owned a factory.
   I am a woman born of a woman whose man labored in a factory.

I am a woman whose man wore silk suits, who constantly watched his weight.
   I am a woman whose man wore tattered clothing, whose heart was constantly strangled by hunger.

I am a woman who watched two babies grow into beautiful children.
   I am a woman who watched two babies die because there was no milk.

I am a woman who watched twins grow into popular college students with summers abroad.
   I am a woman who watched three children grow, but with bellies stretched from no food.

But then there was a man;
   But then there was a man;

And he talked about the peasants getting richer by my family getting poorer.
   And he told me of days that would be better, and he made the days better.

We had to eat rice.
   We had rice.

We had to eat beans!
   We had beans.

My children were no longer given summer visas to Europe.
   My children no longer cried themselves to sleep.

And I felt like a peasant.
   And I felt like a woman.

A peasant with a dull, hard, unexciting life.
   Like a woman with a life that sometimes allowed a song.

And I saw a man.
   And I saw a man.

And together we began to plot with the hope of the return to freedom.
   I saw his heart begin to beat with hope of freedom, at last.

Someday, the return to freedom.
   Someday freedom.

And then,
  But then,

One day,
  One day,

There were planes overhead and guns firing close by.
  There were planes overhead and guns firing in the distance.

I gathered my children and went home.
  I gathered my children and ran.

And the guns moved farther and farther away.
  But the guns moved closer and closer.

And then, they announced that freedom had been restored!
  And then they came, young boys really.

They came into my home along with my man.
  They came and found my man.

Those men whose money was almost gone—
  They found all of the men whose lives were almost their own.

And we all had drinks to celebrate.
  And they shot them all.

The most wonderful martinis.
  They shot my man.

And then they asked us to dance.
  And then they came for me.

Me.
  For me, the woman.

And my sisters.
  For my sisters.

And then they took us,
  Men they took us,

They took us to dinner at a small, private club.
  They stripped from us the dignity we had gained.

And they treated us to beef.
   And then they raped us.

It was one course after another.
   One after another they came after us.

We nearly burst we were so full.
   Lunging, plunging—sisters bleeding, sisters dying.

It was magnificent to be free again!
   It was hardly a relief to have survived.

The beans have almost disappeared now.
   The beans have disappeared.

The rice—I've replaced it with chicken or steak.
   The rice, I cannot find it.

And the parties continue night after night to make up for all the time wasted.
   And my silent tears are joined once more by the midnight cries of my children.

And I feel like a woman again.
   They say, I am a woman.

. . . .

This reflection was written by a working-class Chilean woman in 1973, shortly after Chile's socialist president Salvador Allende was overthrown. A U.S. missionary translated the work and brought it with her when she was forced to leave Chile.

Two Young Women

by Deidre Barry

I'm 18, and years older than that.
I'm 18, and I can't believe I'm that old.

I get up before sunrise, because I have to be at work.
I get up at 6, because I need time to do my hair and makeup before school.

I walk two miles to work, the blisters on my feet open from wear.
I drive to school, and walk carefully, because I need to keep my shoes clean.

I spend my day inside a factory, with hundreds of other girls, unable to take breaks, and unable to leave.
I spend my day in classes, wanting only to get out.

I would give anything to go to school, to learn, to be able to get somewhere in life.
I would give anything to be done with school. Who cares anyway?

I would quit, but I can't. I have parents, brothers, and sisters to support, and jobs are hard to find.
I'd drop out, but then my parents would be pissed.

At 4:00, we get a five-minute break for water, and then it's back for more work.
At 3:30, we get out, and I head for basketball practice.

I sew the Swoosh on, time after time, hour after hour, until my fingers bleed, and my knuckles ache.
I lace up my Nikes, my new ones.

I earn barely enough to live, and not even near enough to help my family. I get paid per pair, and I can only make so many.
These cost me $130, and everyone has a pair.

My lungs burn with every breath, and I cough up dust every night when I get home.
My lungs sear as I run up and down the court, but I know it only makes me stronger.

I sew pair after pair, trying to earn enough to buy food and clothes.
These shoes hurt my feet. I think I'll buy a new pair.

I go home, and cry. I want out, but it's such a vicious cycle. I work to get out, but I always need to work a little more before I have enough.
I go home, and lie on my water bed. I can't wait till college. I can get out.

. . . .

Rethinking Globalization, 2002.

Dialogue Poem: Charting Difference and Commonality

After reading the poem "Two Women," fill out the chart below. Where do the women's lives intersect? What common points of contact—husband, children, education, food—demonstrate their inequality? What historical points create differences?

	Poor Woman	Rich Woman
Gender	Woman	Woman
Husband	Works in factory	Owns factory
Husband	Hungry	Watches weight

Based on the unit you are studying, whose points of view could you write from? List below.

Once you have determined your two voices, fill in the following chart. Again, think of commonalities as well as differences between the two.

As you begin to write, think about where the two voices might speak in unison (commonalities) and where they might speak on different lines based on their life experiences.

Brown Doll, White Doll

Partner poems help students talk back to stereotypes

BY SHWAYLA JAMES AND HEIDI TOLENTINO

MEREDITH STERN

As women of color who both grew up in predominately white communities, we continuously worked to assimilate rather than celebrate who we were. It was difficult for a young African American woman and a young half-Japanese, half-Caucasian woman to truly fit in to the places where we grew up. We longed to be what society portrayed as beautiful. Institutionalized images in magazines, on television, on school posters did not reflect who we were. We tucked it all inside, hoping it might disappear. But there are some aspects of our identities that cannot be hidden.

One summer at the Portland Writing Project, we read *Warriors Don't Cry*, the remarkable autobiography of Melba Pattillo Beals, one of the Little Rock Nine, that brings students inside the lives of a family in the center of the Civil Rights Movement. We developed a writing lesson plan that used the themes in the book.

We knew we wanted to create a lesson that would help our students celebrate who they were. We both taught in diverse classrooms: Heidi at the Monroe Teen Parent Program, a program in Portland Public Schools for middle school and high school teen mothers; and Shwayla at Harriet Tubman Middle School. As we reflected on our own feelings, thoughts, and experiences growing up as people of color, we realized we had seen our students dealing with these same scarred self-images that hold them back. These scars manifest themselves through our continuous negative self-talk: "What guy is going to want to be with me with stretch marks all over my body?" "I got bad, nappy hair. I wish I had your good hair." "Ooh, she's too dark. I like light-skinned girls."

When our students were brave enough to share their writing, we recognized their feelings of inferiority. They shared stories of isolation, eating disorders, drugs, poverty, abuse, being picked on, struggling

We want students to fight back against the images and stereotypes that devalue who they are.

with language, and wanting to be more like someone else. We want students to fight back against the images and stereotypes that devalue who they are.

Whether they are students of color struggling to find a sense of themselves, teen mothers wanting to fit back into their size 3 jeans, or students feeling disconnected from their culture and language, we want to validate who and what they are.

During the Writing Project, we wrote a partner poem (see "A Woman of Color," p. 125), both to celebrate our own identities and to use as a model for our students.

One of our goals in this lesson was to help our students learn to speak about what makes them unique and resist changing who they are just to "fit in." In our partner poem lesson, students created two-voice po-

ems that celebrate what is often devalued in our society. We believe these poems are one way for students to fight back against the negative images that keep them disconnected from themselves. Writing partner poems also gives students opportunities to work collaboratively and to combine voices that are often unheard to create powerful pieces of writing.

Talking Back

Before we began the partner poem lesson in each of our classrooms, we reflected on the year with students, especially discussions of stereotypes and racism. In Shwayla's class these discussions were prompted by studying *Roll of Thunder, Hear My Cry*, the moving historical fiction set in Mississippi at the height of the Depression. It is the story of one family's struggle to maintain their integrity, pride, and independence in the face of racism and social injustice. Heidi's class reflected on the unit in which they read *Warriors Don't Cry*. We both reviewed the media stereotypes that we had examined with our classes. One student in Heidi's class said, "Women are always shown as needing to be rescued." Another said, "People are always supposed to be skinny." Another added, "And women are suppose to have nice figures, be pretty, have tiny feet, and be searching for the perfect man." In Shwayla's class, a Latinx student said, "Latinx are seen as gang-affiliated criminals with scruffy facial hair and strong accents." Another student added, "They also think all Black people are uneducated."

In both classes we reviewed the year and then introduced the partner poem, explaining that our critical analysis of these stereotypes led us to a place where we needed to talk back to them. Shwayla, for example, shared a time in middle school when she was stereotyped and hurt, and she lashed out at classmates for calling her "ebony and ivory." Heidi talked to her students about a time in high school when she verbally attacked another student who made "Chinese eyes" at her and called her a "gook." After sharing these personal examples, we handed out "A Woman of Color," the poem that we had written. We each explained that this was our attempt to fight back at the stereotypes. In each of our classes we chose a student to read the poem ahead of time to get the feel and the flow. That student was then able to read the poem with each of us for the rest of the class.

Because we wanted to teach students how to write a partner poem and not just appreciate ours, in each of the classes we asked the students to read the poem on their own and to highlight some of the categories they recognized in our poem—like hair, eyes, or culture. Some students struggled with this. In Heidi's class many felt they should just highlight the entire poem because they found categories they identified with in each line. In retrospect, we should have encouraged them to look for one or two words that clarified the category and only highlight those.

Once students finished highlighting, we created a T-chart, with categories on the left side and colorful descriptions on the right, of all of the categories they found running through "A Woman of Color." Categories included skin color, hair, language, culture, food, family, etc. We both asked students to add other categories that we had not listed. Then we also asked them to add their own descriptions to get a feel for the flow. For example, our students' descriptions in the "skin color" category included the following:

Rich color of rice paper
Swirling taupe
Yellow and cream
Caramel colored latte
Hershey's special dark chocolate
Vanilla mixed with strawberries
Peaches mixed with cherries
Smooth creamy vanilla ice cream

And here are some of their descriptions from the "language" category:

The native tongue whispered quietly, poetically
The rhythms of Ebonics call and answer
My gospel tongue thick with scripture
The teenage language that has to be quick to flip the scrip
The laid back and civilized language of natives

Once students finished their lists, Shwayla's class had further discussion on "juicy language," while Hei-

di's students were ready to write. Students in both classes created T-charts like the one we made, with categories such as skin color, language, and generations or with physical attributes on one side and descriptive words and phrases for each category on the other side. We reminded students that they were talking back to stereotypes that boxed them in, so they should use powerful words.

Naturally, in both of our groups, there were students who couldn't write fast enough and others who just stared at us defiantly. "This is stupid and I have nothing to write about!" "What is the point of

We reminded students that they were talking back to stereotypes that boxed them in, so they should use powerful words.

this poem?" "I don't want to work with a partner!" We both found it helpful to sit down with individual students and remind them of some of their comments in our discussions throughout the year. In Heidi's class, one student talked about her anger at being kept out of sports her whole life because she was a girl. Heidi encouraged her to use "being a woman" as a category. In both classes we noticed students who were reluctant to work with partners, so we sat with individuals and asked them to compare a few categories with the person next to them to see what they had in common. In retrospect, asking students to list for a few minutes and then share with the class might have taken some of the anxiety out of it for those who were struggling.

Once we sensed that students were slowing down in making their charts, we paired them up with another student—someone we believed they could work with and might feel comfortable sharing personal information with. Once they were in pairs, we both asked them to find a category they had in common and use the idea to write a line of the poem. This wasn't always easy. An African American student and a European American student in Shwayla's class who were working together had trouble identifying common categories.

One student explained, "We don't even hang out with the same guys, what do we have in common?" Shwayla asked them to start by looking at each other. "We don't have anything that looks alike," one of them said. Shwayla explained that when we wrote "A Woman of Color" together, we were virtual strangers, of different races and nervous about sharing personal information. We found it helpful to start by sharing our lists, then asking each other questions about lines before we created sentences for our poem. The two boys used their eyes as their starting point. They began their poem with:

> My eyes are not a common color, but they are
> a beautiful color.
> *I may wear glasses, but four eyes are better
> then two.*

Heidi explained to students that they did not have to share all of the same categories. Two students volunteered their lines as an example that did not match:

> I don't have to wear daisy dukes to be a woman.
> *I love my life and the way that I live it because I
> choose to live that way.*

The students seemed encouraged when they heard their classmates read aloud. We also reminded students that sometimes new lines arise from hearing a partner's lines, so discussing each other's words might spark ideas.

There are a number of ways that our students worked as partners. Some pairs compared categories, found what they had in common, and used those to create their lines together. Others read through their lists, called out lines, and had the other person answer back. And some students wrote out their own lines and then combined them with their partner's lines.

To make the poems easier to read aloud, we asked the students to create scripts by writing down their lines in the correct order.

Once students finished their first drafts, we asked them to read to each other to check the flow, word choice, and rhythm. They seemed to find this the most enjoyable part. For many of our students, this is where it clicked. This is where their poems came to life. In each of our classes we heard shouts, laughter, and support as students encouraged one another with "That's a good one" or "That sounds good together."

Finally, pairs of students volunteered to share their poems with the class. These poems were powerful enough that in Heidi's class some students suggested they find other ways to share them. Students brought these poems to student art performances and displayed them on school bulletin boards. In hearing the exciting summaries from Heidi's class, Shwayla decided to do a poetry slam, with microphone, spotlights, and a student DJ, incorporating other poetry lessons completed in her class.

Reflections

These activities allowed us to celebrate each other and ourselves. We laughed, joked, and learned about each other. Instead of focusing on what was different about one another, we celebrated our commonalities and have since become good friends. This is what we want to happen in our classrooms—a sense of community.

This partner poem lesson allows students an opportunity to find their own voices. It allows students to talk—and sometimes yell—back at stereotypes and unachievable images. Together, we as teachers found strength in our poem, and we hope that others will do the same. ✳

. . . .

Shwayla "Shay" James is an administrator in Portland Public Schools and Heidi Tolentino is a counselor at Cleveland High School in Portland, Ore.

A Woman of Color
by Shwayla James and Heidi Tolentino

I am a woman of color.
I am a woman of color.

I am the rich color of rice paper, swirling taupe, yellow and cream.
I am caramel-colored latte with a drop of Hershey's special dark chocolate.

The slant of my almond eyes denotes honor.
The deep brown specks in mine line the Nile River.

My highlighted curls defy the tradition of straight, long, and black.
Remnants of pin curls, hot pressing combs, and ragtag scarves proudly lie on each strand of my head.

I am proud to be half Barbie's height, twice her weight, and capable of kickin' her butt.
I got your back, girl!

Don't call me Chinese, call me Asian, or call me nothing at all.
African American—a name I grew to love, and I now embrace.

I am from generations of proud Samurai and religious European peasants.
I am from slaves who were whipped and beaten, but who left a strong-willed people.

I am a bamboo cane that bends, but will not break.
I am sugarcane, whose ancestors knew bamboo canes on their backs, who have defied the odds.

The native tongue of my family is not one to be mocked or imitated, but whispered quietly, poetically.
The rhythms of Ebonics call and answer when chosen in the right company.

Sushi glistens, the work of my tireless fanning, my job, and my heritage.
The scraps given to my people by their master which have become a specialty, made with seasoned soul.

Raised by two parents, four grandparents, and eight great-grandparents, generations of people pleasers.
Daughter, granddaughter, and great-granddaughter, who's been passed the torch of our Matriarch.

I am not yet a mother.
I am a single mother who is not a statistic; I am focused, determined, and a homeowner, too!

No, I'm not a genius, I can't do math, and I drive faster than you do. Don't box me in!
Are you surprised I can read, write, and spell, too? I'm educated and have never been in a jail with jumpsuit blues.
Don't box me in.

I am a loud-talkin', gum-snappin', name-callin', in your face kind of Asian woman.
I am a soft-spoken, leg-crossin', passive don't mess with me Black woman.

We are women of color.
We are powerful, strong, and whole.

Why I Use Poetry in Social Studies

BY DYAN WATSON

THEA GAHR

"Economics. Geography. History. Government. Writing. These are the disciplines within social studies." When I announce this to my preservice teacher education students, a few folks cock their heads to one side, some crinkle their eyebrows, a couple nod slowly. "If you are a social studies teacher," I go on, "you are a writing teacher." This declaration is the easy part. Now what?

Because social studies is so often regarded as a date-rich discipline about wars and treaties and conquests and inventions and presidents, we can sometimes forget the root of social studies: *social*; i.e., people. Fundamentally, social studies is a discipline about people, and discovering why they do what they do. It's about empathy. And that is good reason why poetry is such a key piece of my social studies curriculum: because it helps students imagine the lives of others so powerfully.

Poetry also encourages the struggling or hesitant writer in ways that other forms of writing may not. It is playful writing, forgiving writing. I want my graduate students to recognize how poetry builds community, historical empathy, and helps us recognize how perspectives are influenced by social location.

For My People: Building Community

In my classes, we regularly explore issues of social location—race, gender, class, nationality, sexual orientation—and the cultural lenses that teachers bring to teaching. I tell my students: "We'll spend a lot of time examining our lenses, trying to understand our personal filters and how they work for and sometimes against us as teachers to educate all children, no matter their religious, sexual, racial, or ability background. All children can learn and it is our job to teach them."

The "For My People" poem by Margaret Walker is an easy way to surface the cultural pieces that shape our identity. In this poem, Walker walks through U.S. history, exploring major and minor events and their effects on Black Americans. Through this analysis, she details aspects of Black culture and describes some of her family practices.

"List seven groups to which you belong." I give my students this instruction each year as we prepare to write "For My People" poems. Most of my white students do not include affiliations that are explicitly racial. Most of my students who are parents include "mom" or "dad" or some other indication that they belong to a group of "parents." Most students mention athletic and political associations. "How you see yourself and the memberships you value affect how you see others. What might it mean if you don't see yourself as a racial being? What might it mean if this is one of the first things you think about when you see yourself? How will this affect your teaching?" Some of my white students echo Kevin's reaction: "This is the first time I've ever thought about being white."

From this discussion, we generally follow Linda

Christensen's "For My People" lesson (see p. 40).

Christensen's "For My People" lesson (see p. 40).
"What do you notice about either the content or the form of the poem?" I ask. Among noticing the lists, the repeating lines, the punctuation, and other moves that make this poem so incredible, my future history teachers say:

"She lists historical events that have happened to Black people."

"She talks about cultural things that probably only Black people would know about."

"She critiques the cultural narrative of certain historical events such as desegregation."

I probe each of these, asking students to provide support for their ideas—"Which line did you get that from?"—because I want them to constantly think about evidence and perspective as they interpret any piece of writing.

As Linda suggests, I create and share my own list of groups that I may want to write about on the board:

Students need to know they can be real with raw emotions and question conventional understandings.

Black, Jamaican, teacher, aunt, bused, musician, vertically challenged, Jackson Five fan, Portland transplant, Jefferson High School Democrat, and middle-class newbie. I want to demonstrate broad categories that students can mimic. Even though my teaching strategy follows Linda's, my goal is for these future teachers to understand these steps so that they can replicate them with their students. I want them to grasp both the pedagogy and the social justice moves that make this lesson work.

"What do you notice about my categories?" I ask. "What broad categories do my groups represent?" Students call out race, location, class, family, body size. "Notice there are social locators that for some students will be difficult to name, but also other places that will feel safe such as musical preference. It's important that you model that all of these are acceptable and welcome. You need to send the message that race, sexual orientation, disability, and other social locators all are OK to talk about in your class."

I always write an example of what I ask my students

to write. My "For My People" poem is titled "For My Sisters Whose Wombs Are Silent." I purposely share this poem (even though I now have children) and not one that centers on history or race so that everyone in the class feels that she or he has a "people." I want these preservice teachers to see that everyone has culture and sometimes you choose how you are seen. Equally important is that sometimes people choose for you. I also continue to use this poem because as history teachers, I want them to think about and then teach

Poetry is how we teach empathy. It's how we explore social contradiction and connection.

about whose story is valued and what ordinary people write and talk about.

For My Sisters Whose Wombs Are Silent

For my childless women: not a part of the club,
not in the inner circle, not included on That Day
crying alone, vacuuming alone, watching alone.
Thinking, wondering, dreaming full of envy, relief,
and hope.

For my sisters everywhere whose wombs are
silent. We long to be a mother, to hear a child
call out to us, to have random people open doors
for us with our baby on our right hip and diaper
bag in our left hand. Can I help you, ma'am? How
many children you got? Oh, he looks just like you.

For my mothers with no kids who always thought
they'd be a mom, who look like a mom, who
think like a mom. Which ones are yours? Oh, I
don't have any kids; I'm here for my nephew.
There he is.

Reactions to my poem vary from laughter to teary eyes from students who desire to be parents or who simply are touched that I would share something so personal. And that's the point. Writing poetry together builds community. I want teachers to demonstrate their vulnerability, share their cultural identity, and have an early opportunity to see their students as whole beings. In my class, as in hundreds of classes

like it across teacher education, we deal with social issues that make students shift in their seat. Students need to know they can be real with raw emotions and question conventional understandings. This is part of what it means to be a good social studies teacher. Ultimately, we want K–12 students to gain these same sensibilities.

Over the years, my students have used this poem in their classrooms. I encourage them to use it to think about the history of our nation and the world. In addition to my poem, I purposely use model poems that give homage to women, to Latinx, to the working class. I tell my class: "I chose these particular models to demonstrate my belief about whose story is told. By choosing poems about Blacks, Latinx, Asian Americans, and other people too often neglected in the curriculum, they are visible whether or not they are present in my class." These poems bring a real-life testimony to the textbook accounts of marginalized people. I believe that the more individuals can connect to their roots and understand the triumphs, struggles, and shortcomings of their "own" people, the more likely they are able to connect with the students in their classroom and the more likely they are willing to bring students' lives—past and present—into the classroom.

Persona Poem: Building Historical Empathy

A crucial aspect of being a social justice social studies teacher is helping students understand and apply historical empathy. Historical empathy involves cognitive and emotional effort. It requires one to reconstruct the past using historical sources while paying attention to the attitudes and feelings one has toward historical characters. One way to develop students' ability to employ historical empathy is to construct persona poems. Persona poems get inside characters' thoughts and feelings and are written from their point of view.

Using persona poems can help young people make connections to the history they learn, and take them more deeply into that history. Through poetry, students hear points of view that are often left out of mainstream textbooks. We begin this persona poem activity by focusing on an upcoming unit. "Write down at least five essential people or groups that you will explore with students in this upcoming unit. You decide who is essential. For example, you could do Patrick Henry or one of the 77 people he enslaved. Franklin D. Roosevelt or an interned Japanese American."

Again, borrowing from Linda Christensen's persona poem lesson plan (see p. 100), we read aloud the following handout:

Persona Poems

The excerpt below comes from a segment in Monica Sone's *Nisei Daughter* where the family burned their Japanese possessions because neighbors warned them about "having too many Japanese objects around the house."

We worked all night, feverishly combing through bookshelves, closets, drawers, and furtively creeping down to the basement furnace for the burning. I gathered together my well-worn Japanese language school-books. . . . I threw them into the fire and watched them flame and shrivel into black ashes. But when I came face to face with my Japanese doll which Grandmother Nagashima had sent me from Japan, I rebelled.

Becoming American
by Khalilah Joseph (student at Jefferson High)

I looked into the eyes of my Japanese doll
and knew I could not surrender her
to the fury of the fire.
My mother threw out the poetry
she loved;
my brother gave the fire his sword.

We worked hours
to vanish any traces of the Asian world
from our home.
Who could ask us
to destroy
gifts from a world that molded
and shaped us?

If I ate hamburgers
and apple pies,
if I wore jeans,
then would I be American?

I then ask: "What do you notice? What historical event is Khalilah Joseph referring to? What is the moment the poem is about? What is historical fact and what is historical fiction?" Students point out that this is about the Japanese internment and what many families did shortly before they were interned. Both Henry and Joey mention how they can't get past the line about the sword—how fire wouldn't burn a Japanese sword. I turn the comment back to my students: "What would you say if this were your student?" Gillian responds: "I would say, 'You know you're right. The sword wouldn't burn. Then I'd ask the class, 'So what might be some reasons you think the author put that in there? How might the sword serve as a metaphor for their identity?'"

Eventually it becomes my students' turn to write. "Choose one of the people or groups that you wrote down. Everyone have a person or group? Now, close your eyes." I take them through visualizing the context of their character by having them answer the following, with their eyes closed, pausing between each question: "Where is this person? What sounds do you hear? What does it smell like? Are you outside? If so, what's there? Trees, buildings, sand?" I continue this for a few minutes. Then I say, "Open your eyes and write your persona poem."

The poems allow students to recreate a historical scene with real or imagined historical figures. These figures are acting and are acted upon, have emotions and feelings; and further, evoke strong reactions from the reader.

The Dialogue Poem:
Where We Are Shapes What We Think

In my "What Counts as Evidence" unit, one of my main goals is for teachers to create assessments that break out of the traditional paper/pencil tests: multiple choice, short answer, true-false, etc. The dialogue poem can help students demonstrate their understanding of multiple and contrasting views, pivotal events, and the influence of these events and views on everyday people. These skills are the foundation for social studies.

"In the persona poem, we focus on and learn about whose voice is left out. In the dialogue poem we are contrasting voices—often those with privilege with those who are marginalized." We begin learning the versatility of the dialogue poem in our "What Is Justice?" unit. Although there are many good lessons that use the dialogue poem, I like to start this unit by doing Bob Peterson's "The World Is Just" cartoon activity. (For more on this lesson, see *Rethinking Globalization*.) I display "The World Is Just" cartoon and ask

'The world is just'

students: "What is the message of this cartoon? What does it say about the ideas of 'power' and 'justice'?"

"Justice depends on where you are situated," Marco replies.

"Say more."

"Well, if you're the middle fish, there are certain things that seem right to you and you have some power, but at the end of the day, there is someone with more power than you."

Cynthia adds, "There is always the little guy who gets squashed by more powerful people, corporations, and systems of injustice."

"Did you get all that from this cartoon?" I ask.

"Well, no. The cartoon just reinforces what I already know."

"I think the cartoon is inaccurate because of what you're always saying to us about situated privilege. How people get messed over isn't always that linear. Like Marco said, it's going to depend on what event or circumstance that's going on at the time whether or not you feel the world is just and whether or not you see yourself as the biggest fish or the smallest fish," says Cheryl.

"Good, Cheryl. In other words, different social locators influence your perspective. This is one of the reasons why I like this cartoon and think you should use it: It gets students thinking about multiple perspectives. You are going to write a dialogue poem. The

dialogue poem helps students understand the very idea we're discussing about multiple perspectives and social location even more directly."

We then take a look at a short dialogue poem that I wrote while in high school in Bill Bigelow and Linda Christensen's language arts/U.S. history class. The poem is inspired by a scene in the 1974 documentary *Hearts and Minds*, which chronicles the Vietnam War.

VIETNAM: Two Perspectives

> I wanted them! I wanted them!
> *All we wanted was freedom, independence,*
> *   and unification.*
>
> And I remember there were two guys that were
>   going through some grass—
> *And I remember there was my daughter*
> *   standing in the fields, feeding the pigs—*
>
> And bam!
> *And bam!*
>
> I dinged in on one of them and I nailed him.
> *The sky lit up and my daughter's body*
> *   exploded.*
>
> And I felt good, and I wanted more.
> *And I wept and cursed the god of America.*

I ask my usual questions: "What do you notice? What historical event or moment in history is this about?" In this scene, Lieutenant Bobby Muller talks about how he fired on a couple of Vietnamese while he was on patrol. ("I wanted them. I wanted them."). This time I add, "Imagine I'm your student. What does this poem demonstrate about what I know about Vietnam?"

"You know that the same moment in time had very different meaning for two people. And that in this scene of violence, the people who perpetrated the violence were proud of themselves and excited, and the people that received the violence—their lives were destroyed."

I show them two common social studies standards: Describe various perspectives on an event or issue and the reasoning behind them; and analyze characteristics, causes, and consequences of an event, issue, problem, or phenomenon. Although this poem is short and would need more fleshing out, teachers can see how a student could demonstrate her ability to describe multiple perspectives about various issues in the Vietnam War. This is how powerful the dialogue poem can be.

In a world as unequal as ours, and with a history to match, the dialogue poem allows students to explore how the same event can be experienced in profoundly different ways: a U.S. soldier in Vietnam and a Vietnamese peasant; a young Nike-wearing teenager in the United States and a young worker in a Nike factory in Indonesia; one of Columbus' men and a Taíno cacique; a West Virginia coal baron and someone living in a hollow beset by mountaintop removal coal mining; a police officer in Ferguson, Mo., and a Black youth fearful of any police encounter. But power and inequality do not always appear so neatly. People within oppressed groups can dominate others in their group. Race matters, but so do class, gender, sexual orientation, nationality, language, and a host of other ways that our society assigns wealth, power, and privilege. Still, dialogue poems can capture the fundamental truth that our perspective is shaped in large part by where we exist in the social landscape.

When the world was chopped up and put in different curricular boxes, poetry ended up in the box labeled language arts. But poetry "belongs" every bit as much to social studies. It's a key way to touch students' hearts with people's lives. It's how we teach empathy. It's how we build community. It's how we explore social contradiction and connection. It's one important way we help students recognize that social studies is more than dates to memorize; it's about lives to learn and to care about. ✳

. . . .

Dyan Watson teaches in the Graduate School of Education and Counseling at Lewis & Clark College in Portland, Ore. She is an editor of Rethinking Schools.

Resources

Walker, Margaret. "For My People" in *This Is My Century: New and Collected Poems*. Athens, GA: University of Georgia Press, 1989.

"For My People" by Margaret Walker is available in the Poetry Foundation's *Poetry* magazine (www. poetryfoundation.org/poetrymagazine/poem/11053).

Singing Up Our Ancestors

Teaching Myrlin Hepworth's 'Ritchie Valens'

BY LINDA CHRISTENSEN

Myrlin Hepworth's poem "Ritchie Valens" is a Swiss army knife kind of poem, providing multiple functions—mentor text for poetic devices; biographic poem to help students praise family members, literary characters, or historical figures; tutor text that examines both racial and language discrimination in the United States; accessible model to launch students' own poetry.

In the poem, Hepworth tells the story of Valens' rise to fame, but also his brushes with racism because of his Mexican American heritage. Valens was born Richard Steven Valenzuela, but his producer at Del-Fi Records shortened his name to give him "broader appeal":

Richard Valenzuela,
they called you Ritchie.
Said Valenzuela
was too much for a *gringo*'s tongue.
Said it would taste bad in their mouths
if they said it,

so they cut your name in half to Valens,
and you swallowed that taste down,
stood tall like a Pachuco
and signed that contract
para su familia para su música.

In eight months, Valens, who was 17, went from playing in local theaters in his hometown of Pacoima, Calif., to playing on Dick Clark's *American Bandstand.* He wrote his own music and

Took an old folk song
from Veracruz,
La Bamba,
Swung that Afro Mexican rhythm into rock and
    roll, "*para bailar la bamba!*"

Valens is considered the founder of Chicano Rock.

Hepworth, who is Mexican American and Anglo, works as a teaching artist in Arizona. His poem includes a line underscoring the linguistic racism that still exists 55 years after Valens' plane tumbled from the sky into Clear Lake, Iowa:

Sang all Spanish lyrics at a time when speaking
    Spanish
came with a wooden paddle punishment.

In a line close to the end of the poem, Hepworth returns to the same theme:

And America is still trying
to shape you into Hollywood,
still trying to bleach the memory of your skin.
Wrote a movie and said you never spoke Spanish,
even though you understood each *cariño* your
    mother
placed into your ears as a child.
The movie chalked your death
up to superstition and Mexican hoopla.

Yes, Hepworth's poem has it all. I've used the poem with freshmen through seniors (and adults) as a model, but it could be used with younger students as well. After my junior class studies the politics of language discrimination, they write biographic poems about literary and historical characters whose native tongues had been lost or severed. After reading Au-gust Wilson's play *Jitney*, sophomores write poems about people they know whose lives have been disrupted by gentrification. During a break between units, seniors write about people in their own lives they want to praise.

Setting the Mood, Learning the History

When I teach the poem, I play Valens' signature song, "La Bamba," and project his image across a large screen as students walk in. Most students are familiar with the song, and some even sing along and dance as they move into their seats. "Hey, I watched that movie with my mom," Trina remembers. "He's the singer who died in a plane crash with Buddy Holly, right?" Vince asks. The "La Bamba" upbeat rhythm is a great start to any day.

Once students settle into their desks, I tell them that we are going to watch a video clip of Hepworth performing a poem that we will use as a model for our own writing. "Hepworth is writing a poetic biography of a famous singer. You will also write a poetic biography. In this poem, Hepworth tells the story of Ritchie Valens, who sang 'La Bamba.' Notice how he tells the story. Think about what pieces of his story stand out for you." (Of course, my introduction varies depending on the content—politics of language, *Jitney*, Civil Rights Movement, or personal writing. This introduction is for my juniors.)

Then we watch Hepworth's amazing performance of "Ritchie Valens" (see Resources). Students fill the post-poetry silence with a variety of comments: "It's a history." "He talks about the night Valens died." "He uses Spanish."

Over the years, I've discovered that struggling readers often screech to a stop when they see words or phrases in another language. Usually, there is enough context in the reading to provide an understanding of the text. I use Hepworth's poem to teach students how to push through their hesitancy to engage with the unfamiliar. "As you read the poem, you will come across words in Spanish. We will let the Spanish speakers in our midst help us, but first, I want you to try to figure out what Hepworth means in the line on your own. Guess. Write notes in the margin of your poem as you listen and read. Then we'll come back and talk about it."

I distribute copies of the poem and ask students to listen again as they read the text, but this time to look

Raising the Bones of the Poem

At this point, I'm getting on students' nerves, but we return to the poem again. "What are Hepworth's poetic landmarks? What do you notice about how he moves the poem forward? What are his hooks?" Let me pause to say that these are questions I ask about almost every poem we examine—and about essays and narratives as well. These are the "raise the bones" questions necessary to get students to read like writers. Instead of reading for information and content, at this point I want them to read to understand the poetic "moves" Hepworth makes to shape his poem. This, in turn, helps students learn to make those moves themselves—to learn from his style, but also to improvise or "lift off" from his poem as a model.

We travel through the poem, looking at information in each stanza. In the first stanza, for example, Hepworth has a hook:

> You were the child
> of R&B and Jump Blues
> Flamenco Guitar and Mariachi.

This lead, "You were the child," is a great way to open a poem, to introduce the reader to the person.

The second stanza tells more about the subject of the poem and what others said about them: "They called you. . ." Again, students can lift that line to fill out more details about their person. In the following stanzas, we notice incidents and obstacles that reveal more about Valens—little details like "playing a guitar with only two strings" and a neighbor helping "a left-handed boy playing a right-handed guitar."

I point out the line "At 16 you were signed to Del-Fi Records" and suggest that it is a wonderful hook to tell another story and use their person's age as a landmark. And, later in that stanza, we take note of Hepworth's use of repetition:

> But you did not have old blue eyes.
> No, yours were young and brown,
> brown like the dirt in the San Fernando Valley,

for the kinds of details Hepworth chooses. "What stands out about the story? What pieces of Valens' history does he choose to tell?" After the second reading, students pull out more details. My juniors, fresh from their study of the politics of language, notice the part about shortening Valens' name and about being paddled for speaking Spanish in school—two common practices used by colonialists throughout the world to discourage Indigenous people from using their native languages. Most students also pick up on the "bleach the memory of your skin," which leads to a discussion about how many artists—and people in general—have been forced to try to "become white"—assimilate into the dominant culture—in order to be "successful." When students fail to notice these aspects, I point them out, because when they write their poems, I want them to remember how Hepworth handled historical information.

"What are Hepworth's poetic landmarks? What do you notice about how he moves the poem forward? What are his hooks?"

When we circle back to the words in Spanish, students realize that they can guess the words *familia* and *música* because they look like family and music in English. The words they can't figure out, like *para bailar la bamba*, they can understand well enough to continue reading for the gist of the poem. This is also a time for the Spanish speakers in our class to shine as they translate for us.

brown like the hands of your *tíos* and *tías*
who worked in the fields for pennies,
died inside cantinas with broken hearts

Later we point out the historical references to the Zoot Suit Riots, to names of musicians—Chuck Berry and Bo Diddley—and places that Valens played. "Poetry resides in the specific," I remind the students. "Give us details."

Writing Our Poems

I tell students, "Ultimately, this is a love poem, a praise poem, a biographic poem, so think about who you want to write about." In my junior class, students start with a list of people they studied in our language unit. In other classes, students have written about their family members, their personal heroes, or people from their cultural/racial background who deserve praise. My friend and colleague Gretchen Kraig-Turner, who teaches biology at Jefferson High School, asked students to write about scientists they'd studied.

We return to the "bones" of the poem, and I write some of the landmarks students noticed or I've pointed out on the board. "When you get stuck, return to Hepworth's poem and notice how he moved his poem forward. I've listed some questions and leads to get you started":

"You were the child of. . ."
"They called you. . ."
"At 16 you. . ."
What did people say about this person?
How did the person react?
What's an incident you can tell about this person?
Did something happen at a significant age?
When you think of this person, do historical events arise?
What can we see? Hear? Watch on TV?

Student Poems

In our language pieces, Bridgette Lang wrote about Joe Suina, who is currently a professor at the University of Arizona. When he was 6, Suina was taken from his Cochiti Pueblo, an Indian reservation in New Mexico, to a Native American boarding school. Now Bridgette uses Hepworth's opening line to start her poem:

You were the child of a thousand years of heritage,
Cochiti blood flowed through your veins,
Joseph Suina,
You were the child of pride and honor,
And you grew out of it.

Later, she uses Hepworth's age hook to share more of Suina's story:

So you turned 6 and went to school:
a classroom of white walls and white values.
You were so far from home that you forgot
    yourself, too.
You had to leave your Indian at home,
You had to forget your language,
Forget Cochiti, forget your Pueblo,
A beating ensued when you remembered.

Shabria Montgomery writes about Molly Craig, made famous in the movie *Rabbit-Proof Fence*, who was a mixed-race Aboriginal child stolen from her family in Australia and placed in a boarding school. Shabria lifts off from Hepworth's line "You were the child of. . ." and creates a repeating line for her poem:

You are the daughter of love.
Ripped away from your mother
Forced to leave home.
You are the daughter of the desert.
The rabbits running wild
The fence to keep them away.
You are the daughter of color.
Light skinned but not light enough
Still forced to forget your home.

Hepworth's poem encourages students to intersect with their own cultural, linguistic, and familial interests. Baqi Coles, a sophomore, writes about his great-great-uncle Nat King Cole, who intrigued him, but he knew little about him. My time with Baqi's class turned into a day of learning for me, too, as I watched students use their smartphones to find historical details for their poems. Baqi writes:

Nat, you were the child of rhythm,
    destined to alter the course of jazz
    with your classic vocal and piano style.

They called you the King of Jazz,
the kind who held in his heart
the beat of drums inherited
from his African forefathers.

The King who at 15,
dropped school to become
a jazz pianist full time.
You knew your destiny.

Sydney Broncheau Shimaoka, a student in Amy Wright's junior class at Jefferson, explores her musical heritage by writing about Bruddah Israel Kamakawiwo'ole, a Hawaiian singer and ukulele player:

Started as just a "kid with a ukulele"
to a young Hawai'ian man with native dreams
From the most sacred "Ni'ihau"
Slowly you became a legend,
Slowly you became an idol

Poems like Myrlin Hepworth's "Ritchie Valens" help students see that poetry isn't just about flowers and rainbows and unrequited love. It's also about history, language, race, and resistance. Poets can use their voices and their space to sing up the past and to remember those who have gone before. ✳

. . . .

Linda Christensen (lmc@lclark.edu) is director of the Oregon Writing Project at Lewis & Clark College in Portland, Ore. She is a Rethinking Schools editor and author of Reading, Writing, and Rising Up *and* Teaching for Joy and Justice.

Resource

Hepworth, Myrlin. "Ritchie Valens." www.youtube.com/watch?v=AvVulbbm85s

Ritchie Valens
by Myrlin Hepworth

You were the child
Of R&B and Jump Blues
Flamenco Guitar, and Mariachi.

Richard Valenzuela,
they called you Ritchie.
Said Valenzuela
was too much for a *gringo*'s tongue.
Said it would taste bad in their mouths
if they said it,
so they cut your name in half to Valens,
And you swallowed that taste down
Stood tall like a Pachuco
And signed that contract
para su familia para su música
Ritchie Valens
It was always about your music.

You felt it tumble inside your chest as a boy
playing a guitar with only two strings.
When the neighbor caught you,
you thought he would be angry over your racket,
instead he helped you repair the instrument,
and taught you how to grip it correctly.

And you
left-handed boy playing a right-handed guitar
repaid him by making the notes fly.
You could play and sing.

At sixteen you were signed to Del-Fi Records
and America wanted to pass you off as Italian,
But you did not have old blue eyes.
No, yours were young and brown,
brown like the dirt in the San Fernando Valley,
brown like the hands of your *tíos* and *tías*
who worked in the fields for pennies,
died inside cantinas with broken hearts.
California's hands were filled with hate then—
    bleeding
brown and white—master and slave.
And there you were in the midst of it all—young
    Chicano
kid from the barrio on American Bandstand shredding
guitar strings while Dick Clark applauded.

I swear Ritchie when I listen. . .
I can hear it all. I can hear the screams from the Zoot
    Suit Riots,
I can hear the young gringo hipsters swarming you
    after a concert,
how you made them dance and sing in their
    ballrooms—the children
on the bleachers at your old middle school swaying to
    your rhythm and blues—
the old men in your neighborhoods listening to you
    play *rancheras*
as they shouted out, "*Cántalo muchacho! Órale!*"

How you made them all smile,
in a nation at war with itself
ashamed of the blood on its hands
You were never ashamed
of who you were.
Took an old folk song
from Veracruz
La Bamba
Swung that Afro Mexican rhythm
into rock and roll, "*para bailar la bamba!*"
Sang all Spanish lyrics at a time when speaking
    Spanish
came with a wooden paddle punishment.
You played live at The Apollo
while Chuck Berry and Bo Diddley rocked!

You were a legend then Ritchie,
before that night, before you boarded that plane,
A legend before you fell from the sky like a comet
mere months before your 18th birthday.
Your body frozen near that lake in Iowa the phrase
    "what if"
still sits on our tongues.

And America is still trying to shape you into
Hollywood, still trying to bleach the memory of your
    skin.
We made a movie and said you never spoke Spanish
even though you understood each *cariño* your mother
placed into your ears as a child. The movie chalked
    your death
up to superstition and Mexican hoopla.

There are myths scattered in your legacy
but I know Ritchie,
we know

It was always about your music and that music
can never be disfigured. It plays forever in our hearts.
It is stuck inside Carlos Santana's fingertips.
It drifts through neighborhoods and walkways
inside television sets and elevators.
It continues to fall into backyards
where there is some boy, some place,
desperately trying to make music
from a guitar with only two strings.

Bruddah Israel Kamakawiwoʻole
by Sydney Broncheau Shimaoka

Started as just a "kid with a ukulele"
to a young Hawaiʻian man with native dreams
From the most sacred "Niʻihau"
Slowly you became a legend,
Slowly you became an idol

You could taste the music that slipped from your
    tongue
Playing my soul with your fingers
With only four strings and a couple of words
I could feel your music as it whispered harmoniously
    into my ears

"*Imua Kamakawiwoʻole!*" burned in your blood
The past would play right before your eyes
You held words so poetic they came alive, they grew
    sublime
Flowing through my veins was the blood of our history,
the blood you sung upon
I became mesmerized
Your music would soon become lullabies, gently sung
    before a child's eye
Gently sung through the crowd, followed by a fierce
    "*Hana hou!*" of Hawaiʻi

To many, the remembrance of you,
like the rainbow you have once sung about,
is a beautiful sadness
Waiting to be awakened by the voice of a father
    singing to a daughter
Waiting for a young Hawaiʻian musician far from home
to use their fingertips to play their soul
Playing your music with just one strum
remembering that you, too, were once "just a kid
    with a ukulele"

Nat King Cole
by Baqi Coles

Nat, you were the child of rhythm,
destined to alter the course of jazz
with your classic vocal and piano style.

They called you the King of Jazz,
the kind who held in his heart
the beat of drums inherited
from his African forefathers.

The King who at 15,
dropped school to become
a jazz pianist full time.
You knew your destiny.

You understood that love and positivity
is the key to a path of abundance.
Nat, your music brought harmony
to souls in despair.
For that is the greatest contribution
one could possibly make to
better the world.

So as I stand here today,
in the shadow of your legacy
determined to keep love
and positivity
and wisdom
and inner peace
alive in myself
as well as my loved ones.

No matter the setbacks,
you prevailed. And shared knowledge
through your classic unforgettable music.
To this day it brings joy to people
of all shapes forms, and sizes,
as it will for years to come.

Bill Bigelow
by Linda Christensen

You were the poster child
for the '6os.
Dead concerts at the Fillmore,
protests in Union Square
busted for blocking the draft board
in Tiburon.

William Gaston Bigelow
your name and roots
a legacy
of freedom fighters
lining the cemeteries of old Boston:
Bigelows and Lowells
abolitionists and writers.
It has always been about justice
for you.

I felt the tumble in your chest
when we stood with the Women in Black in Jerusalem.
I saw you swallow back tears
when we waded the polluted stream in Chilpancingo.
Your footsteps never once stuttered
when we walked with Basque farmers
in Northern Spain,
fighting for land rights and language,
And, Billy, your smile lit the sky
the day we watched our students
pull together like a fist,
protesting yet another negative article
about Jefferson.

I swear Bill when I listen to you speak
I hear the Taínos rise up to turn back Columbus' ships,
and the sisters from Seneca Falls to Title IX
straighten their shoulders
and step up instead of stepping back.

How you've made me smile, Billy Bigelow,
for these many years,
because you've never once drifted or strayed
from the path of justice,
you, a boy born in the city of angels,
you, blue eyed, anglo man
who could have taken a different, easier path,
chose the path of justice.

Mrs. Luella Bates Washington Jones
by Carrie Strecker, teacher, Neahkahnie, Ore.

*"I have done things, too, which I would not tell you,
son—neither tell God, if he didn't already know."
—Mrs. Luella Bates Washington Jones in Langston
Hughes' "Thank You, Ma'am"*

You were the child of Harlem,
Hughes, and hope
amidst the illusions
and disillusions of a country.

Mrs. Luella Bates Washington Jones,
they called you big.
They called you loud.
They called you why does she have such a long name?
But it fits you—big, loud, long name.
Big as your heart that allowed you to forgive,
loud as the love you gave a lost boy,
long as the time you would open your home.

I swear, Mrs. Luella Bates Washington Jones,
I can hear it all. I can hear your food cooking,
your sink running, your blue-jean sitter kicking,
your reaching into your pocketbook and heart.

How you made a little boy shocked and scared
and confused. And how you told him,
"Yeah, I've made mistakes, too."
When out in the streets was hate,
out in the world was blood,
out in the hearts of many was fear,
yours only held forgiveness.

You may be written off as big and loud,
but I know, Mrs. Luella Bates Washington Jones,
we know:

It was always about your love and that love
cannot be afraid. It lives forever in our hearts.
It is stuck inside the pages and minds of readers.
It drifts through classrooms and libraries,
sits on nightstands, rides through internet waves,
drifts into the words of a student
who has made a mistake once or twice,
desperately trying to be good,
and needing someone's unconditional love.

Integrating Poetry into the Elementary Curriculum

BY BOB PETERSON

CROWBERT/FLICKR.COM

oetry doesn't have to end in a writing assignment. Sometimes in my classroom we read and discuss a poem because it is relevant to the topic. This has the dual advantage of reinforcing or providing another viewpoint on the topic, as well as showing students the power of words set to poetry.

By the start of the second week of the school year my 5th graders are well into a whole class read of the *Sidewalk Story* by Sharon Bell Mathis, which is about a young girl fighting the eviction of her best friend's family.

To deepen students' understanding of the social issue of homelessness and to give it some historical context, I insert two poems into the study of this book: Langston Hughes' "The Ballad of the Landlord" and Lucille Clifton's "Eviction" (also called "The 1st"). I start with "The Ballad of the Landlord." I explain that I'm going to read a poem by my favorite American poet, and tell a little about Langston Hughes. I first explain that in the poem Hughes uses the word "Negro" instead

of African American or Black, because that was the respectful term used at the time. Since I've worked in a
two-way bilingual school and students know that "negro" means "black" in Spanish, this is rarely a point
of confusion. I ask my students to listen carefully and
then I recite the poem.

Before asking students what they think about the
poem, I pass out a three-hole punched copy to each
student, ask them to get out their three-ring binder.
I tell them to write title and name of the poet on the
"Poems We've Read" log sheet. I then ask if anyone
knows the meaning of three phrases—"copper's whistle," "precinct station," and "bail"– and we collective-
ly define them. After the second read I ask students
what they think Langston Hughes' message is. "What
images does each stanza create in your mind? Why is
the renter angry? Why does he want to withhold his
rent money?"

> Landlord, landlord,
> My roof has sprung a leak.
> Don't you 'member I told you about it
> Way last week?
>
> Landlord, landlord,
> These steps is broken down.
> When you come up yourself
> It's a wonder you don't fall down.

To end the lesson I ask students to join me in a
choral reading of the poem. I assign one stanza to each
cluster of six desks and we read it out loud, one stanza
at a time. Reading out loud and examining the poem
helps students understand not only how to read poetry, but also how to read inequality and injustice in life.

The following day I take 10 minutes during literature time, and we re-read the poem again and watch
a two-minute video a previous class made acting out
the poem.

Before the end of the *Sidewalk Story* unit, I teach
another mini lesson on the shorter, more subdued
poem by Lucille Clifton, "Eviction," which tells the story of a child witnessing the eviction of her family. Clifton's specific details evoke the sense of a family being
exposed and "emptied":

> what I remember about that day
> is boxes stacked across the walk

> and couch springs curling through the air
> and drawers and tables balanced on the curb
> and us, hollering,
> leaping up and around
> happy to have a playground;
>
> nothing about the emptied rooms
> nothing about the emptied family

I don't use these two poems as models for class
writing assignments. I want my students to appreciate and learn to love poetry. I point out that while the
Sidewalk Story clearly details the fear and problems
surrounding homelessness, these short poems do so
as well. I ask my students how each poem shows these
problems to the reader. The responses vary widely—"it
paints a picture in your head of all the furniture on the
street," "it shows how angry the guy is"—but they inevitably underscore the power of poetry.

If the poems I share are always models for a written
assignment, I won't be able to share as many poems,
and it would decrease some students' interest. For my
class I classify these two poems as "story poems" as
we construct a list of poem "types" that we keep post-
ed throughout the year. This reminds students of the
variety of poems we study throughout the year. When
a student has some extra time I say, "Check out the
list, look in your binder for a model, and write your own
poem." ✳

. . . .

*Bob Peterson (bob.e.peterson@gmail.com) is a founding
editor of Rethinking Schools. He taught 5th grade in
Milwaukee Public Schools for many years and is currently the
president of the Milwaukee Teachers' Education Association.*

Resources

Clifton, Lucille. "Eviction," in *Good Times*. New York:
Random House, 1969.

Hughes, Langston. "The Ballad of the Landlord," in
Rampersad, Arnold (Ed.), *The Collected Poems of Langston
Hughes*. New York: Alfred A. Knopf, 1994. Available at
allpoetry.com/The-Ballad-Of-The-Landlord.

The Metaphor Poem
Making knowledge visible

BY LINDA CHRISTENSEN

MEREDITH STERN

Over the years, I've come to value the metaphorical poem and drawing as a way to find out what my students understand about the novel/unit we're studying. I'm not talking about the old-school quiz on the difference between metaphors and similes; I'm talking about extracting exactly how students are making sense of the curriculum. What do they know? What don't they get? What pieces are missing in their understanding? Sometimes students know things intuitively that they have difficulty explaining. The metaphor poem allows that different way of knowing to emerge.

For example, when we studied a unit on the colonization of languages, students drew lips sewn shut, voice boxes removed, names of languages on coffins. Their metaphors—and subsequent explanations—demonstrated deeper understanding than the mere recitation of the facts: colonial boarding schools "stole" Indigenous languages in many places in the world, colonial powers extracted both material and cultural resources, like language. Metaphors help students pull together peculiar and significant stories as well as ungainly elements into a unified vision, a thesis, about a character or unit of study—like language colonization or gentrification or corporate control of the media, or Celie, from *The Color Purple*.

Metaphorical poems and drawings level the playing field in the classroom. Often the students who craft the most interesting and provocative metaphors don't do school in the read, test, read, test way. The metaphor poem allows for their Technicolor view of world to shine.

Ultimately, metaphors give students an opportunity to step back from our study, meditate on the details stacked throughout the unit, and reflect on what they mean.

Creating Metaphors

I begin this poem about two-thirds of the way through a unit. I ask students to give me a definition of a metaphor and an example. Typically, they recite the mantra "A metaphor is a comparison between two things without using like or as." We look out the window of my classroom on C-floor at Jefferson High School and create metaphors from what we observe. "The track is a ribbon of blue, surrounding the green sea of the football field. Mount St. Helens is a snow cone (or for the daring) a breast pressed against the sky." Students have been drilled in this since their legs dangled in the short chairs of their 1st-grade classroom, and as poet William Stafford noted, children create metaphors naturally, so I don't spend a lot of time on it—about two

These poems provide student-driven platforms that evoke discussion.

to five minutes. I find the action of creating is far more effective than the naming and defining.

When we created metaphorical poems for *Their Eyes Were Watching God* by Zora Neale Hurston, I asked, "How would you describe Janie's relationship with her husbands?" Kirk said she was like a possession for Joe. He wanted to show her off. "How would you draw that? What metaphor could you use to show that relationship?" Stephanie said Janie was like a ring on Joe's finger. Emma said Joe put her on a pedestal,

which kept her away from the other people in town. "So if she's a ring or she's on a pedestal, what other words would you use to extend the poem? What words go with ring and pedestal?"

After we have established that a metaphor is a comparison, and we've started thinking about the book—or unit—we're studying, we list potential topics to write about: names of characters from the novel we're reading or history we're studying. Sometimes students call out abstract ideas that can be made visible through poetry like apartheid, Jim Crow laws, gentrification.

After reading *Their Eyes Were Watching God*, for example, I hand out sample poems from my former students, like Lila Johnson's "Celie." We read the poem out loud, then I ask, "What comparison does Lila use?" Students note that Lila compares Celie to a record.

"Here's what I want you to notice—writers don't metaphor hop. Lila didn't start with a record and then move to a teapot. What words stay with her metaphor? Look back at how Lila used terms related to records. Highlight words or phrases that show something about how Celie is a record."

Natalie points out, "She shows the record on a shelf, she describes it 'dressed/in dust and age/full/ of cracked songs/you play/when you are blue.'"

"Let's ponder that 'cracked songs' phrase. What do you think Lila's poem is saying about Celie? I know many of you haven't read *The Color Purple*, but you can still read the poem and make sense of it." We continue to explore Lila's poem, examining how she used the record metaphor to describe Celie's relationship with someone who abused her. "How do you know someone abused her?" I ask. "Where's the evidence in the poem?" LaDonna raises her hand, "Because she says his 'liquor-heavy fingers' and 'red watery eyes' play her when he is 'blue.'" "Yeah," James says, "it's like when he's drunk he finds her and uses her."

Once we've discussed Lila's poem and students have a sense of how to proceed with their own poems, I pass out paper and crayons, which is always a big hit in the high school classroom. "Create a metaphorical drawing for one of the characters (literary or historical depending on the unit). I'm not concerned about your artistic ability. I want to see your thinking about the characters. Think metaphorically. Remember the initial comparisons you made—Janie as a ring on Joe's finger, Janie as a mule."

I've discovered that the time students spend drawing allows them to think more deeply about their work. Most days, students sink into silence as they color and draw. That said, it's not unusual for students to get stuck, so when it looks like a few students have a strong grasp on their drawing and the shape of their metaphor, I ask them to share their drawings and discuss the comparison in order to get other students started.

After students create their metaphorical drawings, I encourage them to expand the language of the metaphor in the same way that Lila did in her poetry. I say, "On the back of your paper, write an explanation of your metaphor. Then list the vocabulary or language to expand the metaphor. If it's a garden, go for flowers, hose, water, vegetables, etc. Kirk, you said Janie was a ring on Joe's finger. What other words do you have to extend that metaphor?" Before we start writing, students share quickly, holding up their drawings and outlining their metaphors.

As students move into writing their poems, I remind them to look back at the models. "When you are not sure how to move forward, look back at how Lila, Don, Jessica, and others wrote their poems (see p. 146). Think about whether you want to use first person like Lila and Don did in their poems about Celie. If you do, then begin your poem with either the name or the metaphor: 'I am Celie.' Or you can begin in third person, "Celie was a record." I also want them to notice the line breaks. "Line breaks tell the reader to take a breath. This isn't a paragraph. So once you've written, read your poem out loud and see where you want the reader to pause for effect."

Metaphor Poems Evoke Discussion

Of course, any writing of poetry is about the poem, the metaphor, the collection of words that delight us, but these poems also provide student-driven platforms that evoke discussion. As students read their poems the next day, we talk about the metaphors that students use. In a Literature and U.S. History class that Bill Bigelow and I co-taught, for example, students pointed out that Don Pendleton compared Celie to the floor, then to the ceiling. We asked, "What is he saying

about her? What does that metaphor imply about how Celie changes?" In other words, this is a great way to explore the ways that characters change or what happened to them.

Students become co-teachers as we move through the poems. The discussions that follow student poetry are simply more engaging than those in which I provide all the questions and topics. What struck students, what moved them in the novel or unit is focused and concentrated into a poem—the heart of their interaction with the ideas. Class discussion peers into this heart and reads it. Students are more involved because they had a hand in shaping the content of the class talk.

Not every aspect of the novel will be revealed in the students' poetry, perhaps not every character will be written about. But I can weave in important points that escape the students' lines and discuss missing characters in the context of those who were present. In students' poems from *The Color Purple*, for example, Mr. _____ was rarely, if ever, written about. This omission alone gave us an opportunity to raise questions.

The poem can serve as a rough draft, or an outline, for an essay. Once they've found their "passion," students can translate it into another form. Getting students to write poetry is not enough. They must learn to extend their metaphors, to articulate the flashes of insight they found in their poems. Don can use his floor/ceiling metaphor as a framework to describe Celie's change. Ednie and Stephanie can write about the objectification of women. "The essay just grows out of the poem," my student Sonia Kellerman said one year.

Getting students to write poetry is obviously not enough, nor is it the only strategy we use to discuss the novels, stories, and autobiographies read in class. But metaphor poems provide an opportunity for students to demonstrate their understanding of our curriculum in a way that more typical methods don't offer. ✳

. . . .

Linda Christensen (lmc@lclark.edu) is director of the Oregon Writing Project at Lewis & Clark College in Portland, Ore. She is a Rethinking Schools editor and author of Reading, Writing, and Rising Up *and* Teaching for Joy and Justice.

Celie
by Don Pendleton

I am Celie.
I am the cold hard black floor
everyone walked on.
People have stained me and laughed
but I stayed solid under them
and did not squeak.
I am the floor now
but once you go downstairs
I become the ceiling.

. . . .

Celie
by Lila Johnson

I am a record
on your shelf
the one
dressed
in dust and age
full
of cracked songs
you play
when you are blue
the one
pushed
behind the others
cool black jackets
smooth golden sounds
the one
your liquor-heavy fingers
find
on days
your red watery eyes
don't know the difference
just an old record
you play me
when you are blue

Shug Avery
by Jessica Rawlins

I am Shug.
I am the sweet breath
every man holds onto at night.
I am the lingering scent
that stays
to bring memories of violets
and lily kisses.
I am the sugar perfume
that comes on strong,
burns the senses,
then vanishes
leaving nothing
but the life of a stolen thought.

. . . .

Janie's Garden
by Hasina Deary

I am tired of being ready to bloom,
ready to grow
only to have you pull my roots
out beneath me.

I'm tired of looking for sun and rain
to nourish me
only to have you shade me
with your hopeless darkness.

I stand tall
with my stem firmly planted.
You sigh winds to blow me down.
I'm tired,
but I will not sleep.

I will wait here
in this garden
for a strong hand,
a loving hand
to pick me from my sorrow.

CHAPTER FOUR

Standing Up in Troubled Times
Creating a culture of conscience

TOM HANNIGAN FLICKR/CREATIVE COMMONS

Imagine the Angels of Bread

by Martín Espada

This is the year that squatters evict landlords,
gazing like admirals from the rail
of the roof deck
or levitating hands in praise
of steam in the shower;
this is the year
that shawled refugees deport judges
who stare at the floor
and their swollen feet
as files are stamped
with their destination;
this is the year that police revolvers,
stove-hot, blister the fingers
of raging cops,
and nightsticks splinter
in their palms;
this is the year
that dark-skinned men
lynched a century ago
return to sip coffee quietly
with the apologizing descendants
of their executioners.

This is the year that those
who swim the border's undertow
and shiver in boxcars
are greeted with trumpets and drums
at the first railroad crossing
on the other side;
this is the year that the hands
pulling tomatoes from the vine
uproot the deed to the earth that sprouts the vine,
the hands canning tomatoes
are named in the will
that owns the bedlam of the cannery;
this is the year that the eyes
stinging from the poison that purifies toilets
awaken at last to the sight
of a rooster-loud hillside,
pilgrimage of immigrant birth;
this is the year that cockroaches
become extinct, that no doctor
finds a roach embedded
in the ear of an infant;

this is the year that the food stamps
of adolescent mothers
are auctioned like gold doubloons,
and no coin is given to buy machetes
for the next bouquet of severed heads
in coffee plantation country.

If the abolition of slave-manacles
began as a vision of hands without manacles,
then this is the year;
if the shutdown of extermination camps
began as the imagination of a land
without barbed wire or the crematorium,
then this is the year;
if every rebellion begins with the idea
that conquerors on horseback
are not many-legged gods, that they too drown
if plunged in the river,
then this is the year.

So may every humiliated mouth,
teeth like desecrated headstones,
fill with the angels of bread.

. . . .

Espada, Martín. "Imagine the Angels of Bread" in Imagine the
Angels of Bread. *New York: W. W. Norton, 1996.*

Standing Up in Troubled Times
Creating a culture of conscience

Many years ago, a colleague who taught down the hall told our students, "Art and politics don't mix. If you want to send a message, send a telegram." But the colleague was wrong. In our experience, students write most passionately when they try to understand the world, when they use their empathy and their creativity to shout back to injustices—past and present.

In this chapter, students come to see themselves as truth-tellers and change-makers, to draw inspiration from historical and contemporary poets who use their words to stand up and talk back to the injustices they have experienced or witnessed. Lucille Clifton, Martín Espada, Aracelis Girmay, Langston Hughes, Lawson Fusao Inada, Katharine Johnson, Willie Perdomo, Patricia Smith, and many others who generously gave us permission to use their poems illustrate how poetry serves as a tool to touch gravestones, to name the war camps, to cradle the victims of violence. They teach us that poetry can be used to remember tragedies and call attention to policies and actions that harm society's most vulnerable, to make the invisible visible.

Although this might sound grim, in fact the act of standing up and talking back empowers students, gives hope. It's inaction that leads to despair. In this chapter, Renée Watson teaches students to bear witness in times of tragedy, to refuse to avert their eyes at the suffering of others, to ask questions instead of swallowing official platitudes and phony explanations. Kelly Gomes retools a traditional poem to push students to see social issues from a variety of perspectives. Bob Peterson creates space for a poetic talk-back to top-down decisions that affect his students' lives. Jefferson High School students in Portland, Ore., publicly speak back to administrators, refusing to quietly accept school district mandates.

In *What Is Found There*, Adrienne Rich writes: "Any truly revolutionary art is an alchemy through which waste, greed, brutality, frozen indifference, 'blind sorrow,' and anger are transmuted into some drenching recognition of the *What if?*—the possible. *What if—*?—the first revolutionary question. . . ."

Once students learn about historical and contemporary wrongs, we must offer the possibility of change, the possibility that when we speak out, when we stand together, when we no longer allow injustice to fester and continue in silence, we can begin to imagine a world where justice is possible. With students, we can begin to imagine: What if—? ✳

. . . .

Rich, Adrienne. What Is Found There: Notebooks on Poetry and Politics. *New York: W. W. Norton & Company, 2003.*

The Poetry of Protest
Martín Espada

BY LINDA CHRISTENSEN

RAM DEVINENI

Tony tossed the Tootsie Roll paper over his shoulder as he entered my room. "I'm not your mama, Tony. Pick up that mess."

"Ms. Christensen, the custodians are paid to clean up. If I didn't leave anything on the floor, they'd lose their jobs."

Ruthie Griffin, the custodian, would disagree. But Ruthie, like Marlene Grieves, the cafeteria worker who serves them lunch, is largely invisible to students. Their brooms or spatulas might as well be held by robots. That's one reason why I teach the poetry of Martín Espada in my classroom.

Espada's poetry is a weapon for justice in a society that oppresses people who aren't white, who don't speak English, whose work as janitors and migrant laborers is exploited. His poetry teaches students about the power of language—both Spanish and English—as he makes "invisible" workers visible. What Espada writes about Pablo Neruda's poetry is also true for his own: "[T]he poet demanded dignity for the commonplace subject, commanding respect for things and people normally denied such respect."

I want to introduce students to writers, like Espada, whose art speaks out against injustice, as well as give them the tools to write their own poems of empathy and outrage.

A while back, Espada refused Nike's offer to produce a poem for them for TV commercials they planned to air during the 1998 Winter Olympics. *The Progressive* magazine published Espada's letter to an ad agency listing the reasons he refused Nike's poet for-hire offer:

> "I could reject your offer based on the fact that your deadline is ludicrous. . . . A poem is not a pop tart.
>
> I could reject your offer based on the fact that, to make this offer to me in the first place, you must be totally and insultingly ignorant of my work as a poet, which strives to stand against all that you and your client represent. Whoever referred me to you did you a grave disservice.
>
> I could reject your offer based on the fact that your client Nike has—through commercials such as these—outrageously manipulated the youth market, so that even low-income adolescents are compelled to buy products they do not need at prices they cannot afford.
>
> Ultimately, however, I am rejecting your offer as a protest against the brutal labor practices of Nike. I will not associate myself with a company that engages in the well-documented exploitation of workers in sweatshops. . . ."

Espada's public refusal to serve as yet-another-artist-for-sale is reason enough to present his work to students. In my curriculum I want to highlight writers who put their talents at the service of humanity, not profits. Espada is right: Nike must be ignorant of his work. But my students shouldn't be.

I use Espada's poetry, in English and Spanish, to teach students how to use metaphors and how to write a "persona poem," but I also use Espada's poetry and letter because he shows how to make visible the work of those who toil in physical labor. For example, in his poem "Jorge the Church Janitor Finally Quits," Espada writes from a janitor's perspective:

> No one can speak
> my name,
> I host the fiesta
> of the bathroom,
> stirring the toilet
> like a punchbowl.
> The Spanish music of my name
> is lost
> when the guests complain
> about toilet paper.

Espada's poem reminds us that part of the political work of poetry is shaking people awake, making them look at the world and people with a new awareness.

In *Rethinking Our Classrooms* (1994, 2007), the editors write about the need to ground our teaching in our students' lives, equip students to "talk back" to the world, pose essential questions, be multicultural, anti-racist, and pro-justice, participatory, joyful, activist, academically rigorous, and culturally sensitive:

> A social justice curriculum must strive to include the lives of all those in our society, especially the marginalized and dominated.

Many of my students' parents work in the service industry—as custodians, waitresses, bus drivers. I want this poetry lesson to bring respect to their lives as well. Too often, I have witnessed counselors or teachers point to this kind of work as the reason to stay in school, teaching students to look down or feel shame for their parents' work. "If you don't want to pump gas or flip burgers for the rest of your life. . . ."

Teaching students to respect the custodian who mops their halls, the short-order cook who makes their

I want to introduce students to writers, like Espada, whose art speaks out against injustice.

tacos, or the field worker who picks their strawberries should be a part of our critical classrooms. Martín Espada's poetry includes the lives of the marginalized, giving them dignity, but also demanding justice.

Teaching Strategy

1. Prior to reading Espada's letter to Nike, I ask students if they would ever turn down money if it compromised their beliefs. What are some exam-

ples? Then I read Espada's letter and discuss why someone would give up a chance to earn $2,500. Would it really be such a big deal if he let them use his poem? What does he stand to lose by not agreeing to write a poem for them? What does he gain? Why did he make his letter public? "We are going to return to this letter after we read a couple of Espada's poems. I want you to think about why Espada refused Nike's offer."

2. We read "Jorge the Church Janitor Finally Quits" in both languages. (This validates students who speak Spanish and also locates writing in the broader linguistic world. I encourage students who speak more than one language to write in either or both languages.)

3. Once we have read the poem, I ask some opening discussion questions: Who is the narrator of the poem? How do people treat Jorge? What evidence in the poem tells us that? What does he compare the mop to? What does Espada want us to know about Jorge? How do we learn that? What do we learn about Espada?

Part of the political work of poetry is shaking people awake, making them look at the world and people with a new awareness.

4. After reading and discussing "Jorge the Church Janitor Finally Quits," we read "Imagine the Angels of Bread." I ask students, "What do you notice about this poem? Talk about content or style of writing." Dylan pointed out the repeating line. Desi brought the class attention to the way he turns the world upside down. "How does he do that?" Other students jumped in, finding the places where Espada shows what justice might look like: "He talks about people who have been lynched getting justice."

5. Once we have examined Espada's poems, we reread his letter to Nike. I ask students to identify evidence in the poems that indicates why Espa-

da would turn down Nike's money. Espada wrote, "you must be totally and insultingly ignorant of my work as a poet." I ask the students, "What ideas in Espada's work talk back to Nike's view of the world? Write for five minutes, using evidence from his poems in your answer." This is a quick write meant to saturate students in the poems and review how to use evidence to support a claim.

Writing Poems About Workers

6. To begin this poetry assignment, we read two students' poems about invisible workers—"Mr. Ruffle" by Rachel Fox (see p. 155) and "Two Young Women" by Deidre Barry (see p. 119)—to see how they brought workers to life. "For this assignment, we are looking at how to make visible work that is often invisible. Espada does this with Jorge. How does Rachel Fox do that in her poem? What details about working in a potato chip factory does she show us?" We do the same close reading of "Two Young Women," examining how details of the worker's life are imagined—bleeding fingers, sewing on the swoosh, etc.

7. After we've read and discussed the student model poems, I ask students to make a list of "invisible workers" they know whom they could make visible: for example, hotel maids, strawberry harvesters, the seamstress who sewed their shirt or blouse. A few students share their lists to help stumped classmates find a topic.

8. Because many students in Portland have experienced picking berries, sometimes for money in the summer, sometimes with their families on a mission to make strawberry ice cream or jam, I choose berry picking as a model for our work. "When we write these poems, we need to imagine what goes into the work. What are some details about berry picking?" Bunky led the list: "Buckets tied to your waist. You have to find a row that has berries on it." Adele added, "Long rows, you have to bend over." Another student remembered, "They smell sweet. They stain your fingers." "My back started hurting after about five minutes. Then you get down on your knees." "So, if we were going to write a poem

about berry picking, we would want to put in all of those details. We would want to describe the land, the smell of the berries, the stains."

9. "Go back to your list of invisible jobs and choose one. List the details that make a reader see and feel the work. Once students have created lists, I ask them to share with a partner. "Your job," I tell them, "is to help your partner get as many details as possible. What details do they have that bring the work to life? What else could go on their list?"

10. "Find a way into your poem. Let's remind ourselves of the different ways that the poets we're using as models wrote theirs." As a class, we quickly review the poems: Espada wrote his about Jorge on the night he quits. It is written in third person. Rachel wrote hers as a letter to Mr. Ruffle, reminding him of what his workers have suffered. Deidre Barry wrote hers as a dialogue poem, comparing a teenage worker's life with someone who bought the clothes she sewed. "Write it as a letter. Write a poem describing the work. Go back to the models if you get stuck."

The next day, we read around the poems, making invisible work come to life, celebrating the people—many of whom are family members—who pick our fruit, cook and serve our food, and clean our schools, like Ruthie Griffin. ✳

. . . .

Linda Christensen (lmc@lclark.edu) is director of the Oregon Writing Project at Lewis & Clark College in Portland, Ore. She is a Rethinking Schools editor and author of Reading, Writing, and Rising Up *and* Teaching for Joy and Justice.

Jorge the Church Janitor Finally Quits
by Martín Espada

No one asks
where I am from,
I must be
from the country of janitors,
I have always mopped this floor.
Honduras, you are a squatter's camp
outside the city
of their understanding.

No one can speak
my name,
I host the fiesta
of the bathroom,
stirring the toilet
like a punchbowl.
The Spanish music of my name
is lost
when the guests complain
about toilet paper.

What they say
must be true:
I am smart,
but I have a bad attitude.

No one knows
that I quit tonight,
maybe the mop
will push on without me,
sniffing along the floor
like a crazy squid
with stringy gray tentacles.
They will call it Jorge.

Por fin renuncia Jorge el conserje de la iglesia
by Martín Espada
(translated by Camilo Pérez-Bustillo and the author)

Nadie me pregunta
de dónde soy,
tendré que ser
de la patria de los conserjes,
siempre he trapeado este piso.
Honduras, eres un campamento de desamparados
afuera de la ciudad
de su comprensión.

Nadie puede decir
mi nombre,
yo soy el amenizador
de la fiesta en el baño,
meneando el agua en el inodoro
como si fuera una ponchera.
La música española de mi nombre
se pierde
cuando los invitados se quejan
del papel higiénico.

Será verdad
lo que dicen:
soy listo,
pero tengo una mala actitud.

Nadie sabe
que esta noche renuncié al puesto,
quizá el trapero
seguirá adelante sin mí,
husmeando el piso
como un calamar enloquecido
con fibrosos tentáculos grises.
Lo llamarán Jorge.

. . . .

Espada, Martín. "Jorge the Church Janitor Finally Quits" in
Rebellion Is the Circle of a Lover's Hands. *Willimantic, CT:*
Curbstone Press, 1990.

Mr. Ruffle

by Rachel Fox

To Mr. Ruffle, making the money off the potato peelers' blisters:
tomorrow night, in your sleep,
dreams will come of workers sharpening their knives
tearing their aprons off, dropping them in the puddles of their sweat
and then a knock on your door.
Your office door, or your bedroom door
you won't be able to tell.
You'll try to wake up,
to focus on something,
but you'll be too fast asleep;
you are
too fast asleep.
And then you'll reach for your secretary or your wife
to go get you some tea
like she always does when you have these dreams,
but she won't be at her desk or in bed.
She'll be standing at the door
with the men and women who cut
that extra something—you know what it is—
into your pockets;
who go home with numb hands every day
from washing thousands of dirty potatoes in ice water;
who sit up all night picking splinters out of calloused hands
from chopping trees for paper bags that you put your name on;
she'll be standing there with them
and the hugest, sharpest potato peeler you've seen
in her hand.
She'll walk over to your desk, or your bed
and look you right in your foggy-dreamed eyes
say, Good morning, sir
or, Good night, dear
and, starting at the top of your head,
she'll peel your skin off
until you're a puddle of grease to be cooked into chips.

Federico's Ghost

by Martín Espada

The story is
that whole families of fruitpickers
still crept between the furrows
of the field at dusk,
when for reasons of whiskey or whatever
the cropduster plane sprayed anyway,
floating a pesticide drizzle
over the pickers
who thrashed like dark birds
in a glistening white net,
except for Federico,
a skinny boy who stood apart
in his own green row,
and, knowing the pilot
would not understand in Spanish
that he was the son of a whore,
instead jerked his arm
and thrust an obscene finger.

The pilot understood.
He circled the plane and sprayed again,
watching a fine gauze of poison
drift over the brown bodies
that cowered and scurried on the ground,
and aiming for Federico,
leaving the skin beneath his shirt
wet and blistered,
but still pumping his finger at the sky.

After Federico died,
rumors at the labor camp
told of tomatoes picked and smashed at night,
growers muttering of vandal children
or communists in camp,
first threatening to call Immigration,
then promising every Sunday off
if only the smashing of tomatoes would stop.

Still tomatoes were picked and squashed
in the dark,
and the old women in camp
said it was Federico,
laboring after sundown
to cool the burns on his arms,
flinging tomatoes
at the cropduster
that hummed like a mosquito
lost in his ear and kept his soul awake.

. . . .

Espada, Martín. "Federico's Ghost" *in* Rebellion Is the Circle of a Lover's Hands. *Willimantic, CT: Curbstone Press, 1990.*

Concentration Constellation

by Lawson Fusao Inada

In this early configuration,
we have, not points of light,
but prominent barbs of dark.

It's all right there on the map.
It's all right there in the mind.
Find it. If you care to look.

Begin between the Golden State's
highest and lowest elevations
and name that location

Manzanar. Rattlesnake a line
southward to the zone
of Arizona, to the home
of natives on the reservation,
and call those *Gila, Poston*.

Then just take your time
winding your way across
the Southwest expanse, the Lone
Star State of Texas, gathering
up a mess of blues as you
meander around the banks
of the humid Mississippi; yes,
just make yourself at home
in the swamps of Arkansas,
for this is *Rohwer* and *Jerome*.

By now, you weary of the way,
It's a big country, you say.
It's a big history, hardly
Halfway through—with *Amache*
Looming in the Colorado desert,
Heart Mountain high in wide

Wyoming, *Minidoka* on the moon
of Idaho, then down to Utah's
jewel of *Topaz* before finding
yourself at northern California's
frozen shore of *Tule Lake*. . .

Now regard what sort of shape
this constellation takes.
It sits there like a jagged scar,
massive, on the massive landscape.
It lies there like the rested wire
of a twisted and remembered fence.

. . . .

Inada, Lawson Fusao. "Concentration Constellation" in
Legends from Camp. *Minneapolis: Coffee House Press, 1993.*

Death Toll from Tulsa Race Riots Estimated Between 300 and 3,000
by Katharine Johnson

What is the difference made by one zero,
One digit placed to the right of a collection,
One circle, one nothing,
one absence of quantity?
What legacies linger in the void
between 300 and 3,000?

What little girls, hair
plaited for sleep,
cool, white nightgowns
for a hot Tulsa night
slipped through the hole in that zero?

What grandma rests
somewhere around 2,186
clicking her tongue along her teeth
rocking and moaning,
"Not again, Lord, not again."

Which young man, framed
by a tiny house and soot-soaked camellias,
his legs wide, arms cradling a rifle
is silenced by the denial of 892?

Whose brother waits at 1,753
for someone to call his name,
etch it into a slab of solid marble
and set his soul free?

Is there a Bernice lost to history at 2,127
or the restless ghost of a Walter
still searching at 582 for safe harbor, for freedom?

Whose last moment of terror
is secreted away in the yawning chasm
of one wide zero?

Whose final act of courage is rendered
invisible by such a grave miscalculation?

How can a soul, told it never existed, find peace?

How might one zero bring them all home?

Katharine Johnson teaches at Irvington School in Portland, Ore., and is co-director of the Oregon Writing Project.

Happening Yesterday, Happened Tomorrow
Teaching the ongoing murders of Black men

BY RENÉE WATSON

"I CAN'T BREATHE"
ERIC GARNER - RIP

Emmett Till.
Medgar Evers.
Henry Dumas.
Fred Hampton.
Mulugeta Seraw.
Amadou Diallo.
Sean Bell.
Oscar Grant.
Trayvon Martin.
Jordan Davis.
Eric Garner.
Michael Brown.

There is a history in our country of white men killing unarmed Black boys and men with little to no consequence. I taught the murders of Sean Bell and Amadou Diallo, using Willie Perdomo's "Forty-One Bullets Off-Broadway" as the model poem, to a class of 7th graders ("From Pain to Poetry," fall 2008). But then there was Trayvon Martin, then Jordan Davis, then Michael Brown, and the list keeps growing.

After the murder of Trayvon Martin, I taught a version of "From Pain to Poetry." I wanted to use Perdomo's poem again—it is a strong example of how writers use facts and their imaginations to tell a story. I wanted to add a research component because my students needed to develop researching and note-taking skills and, just as important, I needed to

Young people need space to learn and practice positive ways of coping with and processing emotions.

show students that racial profiling and police brutality are not new.

Aracelis Girmay's poem "Night, for Henry Dumas" is a perfect pairing with "Forty-One Bullets Off-Broadway." We get the intense immersion into one man's story in Perdomo's poem, while Girmay plays with time and place, making us acknowledge that the list of Black men who have been unjustly killed is long and painful and ongoing. I wanted students to see both as approaches in their own work.

One of my objectives was to have students explore ways that poets use their work to respond to injustice. I also wanted them to create a collaborative performance by the end of the unit, so scaffolding in opportunities to work together was something I needed to think about. I decided to ask students to work in small groups for the entire unit and focus on a person who was killed as a result of racial profiling or police brutality.

'They Were Murdered'

When they came to class on the first day of the unit, there was a plastic bag with jigsaw puzzle pieces in the center of each table. Each group's puzzle, when put together, was a photo of one of five of the slain men: Henry Dumas, Oscar Grant, Amadou Diallo, Sean Bell, or Trayvon Martin. I made the puzzles by printing the photos on cardstock, turning them over to the blank side, drawing jigsaw pieces, and cutting them out. The pieces were big and easy to assemble, about 10-15 pieces for each photo.

The goal was to get the students to collaborate on creating something. "You have five minutes to work as a group to put the puzzle together," I told them as they began to pour the pieces out. I walked around the classroom, checking to make sure everyone in the

groups was actively participating.

When each group finished, they received an index card with the name of their person written on it.

I called out to the class, "Who has Henry Dumas?" The members of that group raised their hands. I taped his photo on the board and wrote his name underneath so that the whole class could see Dumas. I continued this, making a chart on the board with five columns. The last person we added to the board was Trayvon Martin.

I asked the class: "Do you recognize anyone on the board?"

All of the students knew who Trayvon Martin was.

There were a few students who felt they had seen Oscar Grant before. "There's a movie about him, right?" one student asked. *Fruitvale Station*, a movie that reconstructs the last 24 hours of Grant's life, had been released the same weekend as the Zimmerman verdict. (George Zimmerman, who killed Martin, was found not guilty by a jury in Sanford, Fla.)

I asked someone to give a very brief account of what they knew about Martin.

"He was shot by a neighborhood watch guy," a student answered.

"He was shot because he was wearing a hoodie," another student shouted.

I asked the class to hold off on adding more. "Based on what you know about Trayvon and Oscar, why do you think these other men are on the board?"

"Because they got shot, too?" James suggested.

"Yes. They were all murdered," I told the class. "Looking at these photos, what do you notice? What do they have in common?"

Lakeesha noticed that they were all Black.

"And they're all men," Sami added.

"And they probably didn't deserve to die," James blurted out.

I asked him, "What makes you say that?"

He considered what he knew about Martin and Grant. "They didn't even have weapons on them when they got shot. The others probably didn't, either."

"You all are being great critical thinkers. Let's find out more about these men—what happened to them, how their stories are similar, and where there are differences." I passed out an article to each of the five groups about the person whose photo they had. "Your group should take turns reading the article out loud.

Underline important facts that stand out. If there are strong images in the article, underline those, too." I ask students to mark up their papers, whether it's an article or a poem. I think it's important for them to engage with their handouts, to write questions in the margins, to highlight phrases that grab them. "When you are finished reading the article, let me know."

Students were eager to learn what happened to the men in the photos. When the groups finished reading, I gave them a handout with three columns—Facts, Emotions, Images—and asked them to write at least four words under each heading. I explained that the images could be from their imaginations. "Even if the article doesn't mention bloodstained cement, that might be something that comes to your mind as you read the article. Think about the pictures your mind sees as you read the article and write them down." For the list of emotions, I told them they could write their own emotion or an emotion that they believe people in the article felt. "So, when I read about Henry Dumas, I felt shocked. I'm going to write 'shock' on my chart. I'm also going to write 'frustrated' because I think his family might have felt that way."

Students went back to their articles and searched for compelling facts, strong emotions, and vivid images. Shavon was in the group that read about Martin. Under Facts she wrote "acquitted" and "a voice can be heard screaming for help." Fania, who studied Diallo, listed "betrayal" and "resentment" under Emotions. Lakeesha, who focused on Bell, wrote "a wedding dress hanging on a hanger" and "a child standing at a casket" under Images.

After they filled out the charts, I asked for a representative from each group to share what they learned. "Give us at least three important facts," I said. I wrote on the board under the picture of each person. "Make sure you copy this list in your notebook," I told the class. I wanted to keep them engaged, and I also needed them to have this information for the poems they would be writing.

Seeing the faces of five Black men who had been murdered side by side, with facts about their lives written under their names, was sobering. Once all groups had shared, we had a class discussion. "What did you learn? What more do you want to know?"

Sami wanted to know why this kept happening.

Jason wanted to know why, in the cases of Diallo and Bell, there was such excessive force. "I mean, 41 bullets being shot is just not right!"

I asked students to share how they felt. I took the first risk and shared that I felt angry and sometimes hopeless. That I cried when I heard the verdict because I thought about my 17-year-old nephew and how it could have been him walking home with snacks from a corner store but never making it. Maria said she felt sad. Jeremiah shared that it made him afraid sometimes. Fania told the class: "It just makes me angry. It makes me so angry."

Poetry Holds Rage and Questions

It was important to me not to censor students, but to welcome their emotions into the space. Just as I invited their boisterous laughter, their hurt was allowed here, too. Even if that meant tears. I believe young people need space to learn and practice positive ways of coping with and processing emotions. Art can provide a structured outlet for them to express how they feel.

I wanted them to know that poetry could hold their rage and their questions. The first poem we read was "Forty-One Bullets Off-Broadway." I played the audio poem and students read along. As I had asked them

The point is to make people remember. If people don't write their stories they could be forgotten."

to mark up their articles, I asked them to do the same on the poem. "I'd like you to think about when Willie is using facts from the article and when he is using his own imagination."

Usually, as a ritual, we give snaps after a poem is shared in class, following the tradition of poetry cafés. But after listening to Perdomo's poem, students clapped.

Before discussing the poem, I asked them to number the stanzas. "I'd like us to talk like poets, OK? So name the stanza you're referring to and, if you notice any literary devices that Willie is using here, we can talk about that, too." We noted when he used a fact from the case. "In the second stanza, he mentions the exact number of bullets," Maisha pointed out.

Jeremiah read from stanza four:

Before you could show your
I.D. and say, "Officer—"
Four regulation Glock clips went achoo
and smoked you into spirit

He recognized that Diallo reaching for his wallet was factual and noted Perdomo's use of personification in making a gun sneeze. He also noticed that Perdomo used his imagination to describe the "bubble gum-stained mosaic" floor where Diallo's body fell.

The next poem we read was Girmay's "Night, for Henry Dumas." Just as we did when discussing "Forty-One Bullets Off-Broadway," we talked about where Girmay used facts, where she used her imagination. Students liked how she referenced Dumas' science fiction writing by saying he did not die by a spaceship. Most of them had underlined the moment of the poet's imagination when she writes that Dumas died "in the subway station singing & thinking of a poem/what he's about to eat."

We talked about the different approaches each poet took. "Willie Perdomo focused on one incident and took us into Amadou Diallo's story," Lakeesha said. "Aracelis Girmay wrote about Henry but also talked about other black men who have been murdered."

I asked the class: "What do you think the phrase 'happening yesterday, happened tomorrow' means?"

Maisha touched the puzzle at her table, moved the pieces even closer together. "I think she's saying that it happened in 1968 and in 2008 and in 2012—"

"And it's probably going to keep happening," James blurted out.

I asked him why he thought that.

"Well, there was Emmett Till," he said. James was

"The first brave thing you did was make yourself vulnerable enough to write this poem. Now what are you going to do with it?"

in my class last year when we studied Marilyn Nelson's "A Wreath for Emmett Till" and watched excerpts of *Eyes on the Prize*. I was glad to see him making connections to previous lessons. "And in her poem, I think that's what she's saying. It happened way back

in the day and it happens now and it will continue to happen everywhere."

"Where do you see that in the poem?" I asked.

"This part," Jason said. He read the lines to the class:

under the ground & above the ground
at Lenox & 125th in Harlem, Tennessee,
Memphis, New York, Watts, Queens.
1157 Wheeler Avenue, San Quentin, above which
sky swings down a giant rope, says
Climb me into heaven, or follow me home

Lakeesha noted Girmay's list of Black martyrs. "There could be so many names added to that list," she said.

"How does this make you feel?" I asked the class.

"It makes me want to be careful."

"It makes me worry about my brother."

"I feel really angry because it isn't fair and it's not a coincidence that this keeps happening."

Then I asked: "Why do you think Aracelis Girmay and Willie Perdomo wrote these poems? Does it change anything? What's the point?"

"It makes people aware of what's going on."

"I think the point is to make people remember. If people don't write their stories they could be forgotten."

"And it honors them."

Writing from Facts, Emotions, and Images

With that, it was time to write. "You can choose to write your poem like Willie did, and focus on one person. Or you can include the stories or names of others, like Aracelis." I told them to be sure to use the brainstorming chart to help them with writing their poem. "Your poem should include at least three facts, three emotions, and three images from your chart." I also gave them options for point of view. "You can write in first, second, or third person. You can write a persona poem in the voice of one of the people involved in the story—for example, you can be Oscar Grant or maybe his daughter. You could even speak from the bullet's perspective or the ground."

I wrote line starters on the board, but most students didn't use them. They had a lot to say and already knew how they wanted to craft their poems. Since that day, I have taught this to racially diverse groups of students, as well as to professionals who work with young people, including teachers, counselors, and administrators at the college level; the words have spilled out of almost everyone.

I was deeply moved by the poetry my students wrote. For example:

Never Written
by A. M.
for Henry Dumas

1968, underground,
day or night,
coming or going,
under the eternal florescent
flicker of subway lights

the clamor of wheels,
crackle of electric current
maybe muffled the shooting
sound that silenced.

One cop's "mistake"
two boys now to forever
wait for their father's face.

A mind full of memory and make believe,
stretched from sacred desert sands
to sci-fi space and mythic lands,
spilled out, running thick
on worn concrete spans

as subway doors open and close
empty cars rattle ahead
blank pages blown behind
nothing but another man's
black body laid down
in haste and waste.

For All of Them
by L. V.

Who scrubs the bloodstained train track, tile,
    lobby, car, sidewalk?
Who tears down the yellow tape?

Who sends the flowers and cards?
Who sings at the funeral?
Who watches the casket sink into the ground?
Who can get back to their normal life?
Who is holding their breath waiting for the next
    time?
Who takes a stand?
Who demands justice?
Who knows justice may never come?
Who keeps fighting anyway?
Who fights by protest?
Who fights by teaching?
Who fights by writing a poem?
Who fights by keeping their names alive?

After students revised their poems, I encouraged them to take a small action. "The first brave thing you did was make yourself vulnerable enough to write this poem. Now what are you going to do with it?" I asked. "Remember the reasons you said it was important for poems like these to be written. How can you share your poem to get it out into the world?" We made a quick list that included posting the poem on Facebook, tweeting a line or phrase from the poem, recording the poem and posting the video, reading the poem to a teacher, parent, or friend.

Later in the semester, a few students shared their poems at our open mic, when we invited parents and the community to witness the art their young people had created. Some students shared their poems through social media outlets. I encouraged them to not let this just be an assignment but something they took out of our classroom. I challenged them to pay attention to the news, to continue to use their pens and their voices to respond to what is happening in their world. ✱

. . . .

Renée Watson (reneewatson.net) is an author, performer, and educator. Her children's books have received several honors, including an NAACP Image Award nomination. She teaches poetry at DreamYard in New York City.

Forty-One Bullets Off-Broadway

by Willie Perdomo

It's not like you were looking at a
vase filled with plastic white roses
while pissing in your mother's bathroom
and hoped that today was not the day
you bumped into four cops who
happened to wake up with a bad
case of contagious shooting

From the Bronx to El Barrio
we heard you fall face first into
the lobby of your equal opportunity
forty-one bullets like silver push pins
holding up a connect-the-dots picture of Africa
forty-one bullets not giving you enough time
to hit the floor with dignity and
justice for all forty-one bullet shells
trickling onto a bubble gum-stained mosaic
where your body is mapped out

Before your mother kissed you goodbye
she forgot to tell you that American kids
get massacred in gym class
and shot during Sunday sermon
They are mourned for a whole year while
people like you go away quietly

Before you could show your
I.D. and say, "Officer—"
Four regulation Glock clips went achoo
and smoked you into spirit and by the
time a special street unit decided what was
enough another dream submitted an
application for deferral

It was *la vida te da sorpresas/sorpresas
te da la vida/ay dios* and you probably thought
I was singing from living *la vida loca*
but be you prince/be you pauper
the skin on your drum makes you
the usual suspect around here
By the time you hit the floor
protest poets came to your rescue
legal eagles got on their cell phones
and booked red eyes to New York
File folders were filled with dream team
pitches for your mother who was on TV
looking suspicious at your defense
knowing that Justice has been known
to keep one eye open for the right price

By the time you hit the floor
the special unit forgot everything they
learned at the academy
The mayor told them to take a few
days off and when they came back he
sent them to go beat up a million young
black men while your blood seeped through
the tile in the lobby of your equal
opportunity from the Bronx to El Barrio
there were enough shots to go around

. . . .

From Smoking Lovely *by Willie Perdomo (willieperdomo.com).
Copyright © 2003.*

Night, for Henry Dumas
by Aracelis Girmay

Henry Dumas, 1934-1968,
did not die by a spaceship
or flying saucer or outer space at all
but was shot down, at 33,
by a New York City Transit policeman,
will be shot down, May 23rd,
coming home, in just 6 days,
by a New York City Transit policeman
in the subway station singing & thinking of a poem,
what he's about to eat, will be, was, is right now
shot down,
happening yesterday, happened tomorrow,
will happen now
under the ground & above the ground
at Lenox & 125th in Harlem, Tennessee,
Memphis, New York, Watts, Queens.
1157 Wheeler Avenue, San Quentin, above which
sky swings down a giant rope, says
Climb me into heaven, or follow me home,
& Henry
& Amadou
& Malcolm
& King,
& the night hangs over the men & their faces,
& the night grows thick above the streets,
I swear it is more blue, more black, tonight
with the men going up there.
Bring the children out
to see who their uncles are.

. . . .

This poem originally appeared in Girmay, Aracelis. 2011. Kingdom Animalia. BOA Editions Ltd. (www.boaeditions.org/ bookstore/poetry/kingdom-animalia.html)

What If?
The first revolutionary question

BY LINDA CHRISTENSEN

Weave RADICAL TRANSFORMATION

MEREDITH STERN

The "What If?" poem is embedded in both loss and social action, straddling the line between what is tragically present in our lives and what is possible through a vision of change and action. In her brilliant essay "What If?," Adrienne Rich wrote:

> Any truly revolutionary art is an alchemy through which waste, grief, brutality, frozen indifference, "blind sorrow," and anger are transmuted into some drenching recognition of the *What if*—the possible. *What if—?*—the first revolutionary question. . . . Naming and mourning damage, keeping pain vocal so it cannot become normalized and acceptable.

And this is the challenge in our schools—to create critical classrooms that analyze the grim details of the way money, power, and race have contributed to the incredible inequality of both the past and the present, while also maintaining hope. Poetry gives students a way to "name and mourn" the damage occurring in their lives but also space to voice their protest against intolerable conditions and their vision for possibilities of a different future.

I first taught the "What if" poem at a time when Portland Public Schools faced a huge budget crisis. The district held hearings to discuss potential cuts to the arts, sports, and teachers, as well as a proposal to close schools 10 days early. Josh Branch, an outstanding football player and wrestler, wrote a poem to express his sense of what would be lost if sports were cut (see p. 168).

What If?
What if there were no football fields
or goal posts?
No sidelines covered with chalk
and drops of blood and sweat?

Who will remember
sweat running into the eyes of coaches,
voices of cheerleaders
like a chorus line being sung,
the feel of a football caught and thrown?

What if the hearts of thousands
of would-be athletes
are never recognized
because there is no football?

Josh read his poem at a rally to save Portland Public Schools. His poem was also made into a poster, which was distributed at nearby elementary and middle schools. During his senior year, he developed a poetry video by slicing together cuts from videotapes of himself running for a touchdown or tiptoeing down the sidelines during a particularly tense football game. He set the images to background music and then read his poem as a voiceover.

During the final days of the 1998 school year another crisis rocked our school. Josh visited my class as the Portland school board toyed with plans to reconstitute Jefferson High School. I thought it was a good time to dust off his "What If" poem and video. My students had just organized a news conference and invited the press to hear the "Whole Truth About Jefferson High School" as a challenge to the school board's proposal to "fire" all of the current staff and force all of us to reapply for our jobs. During the press conference, students handed out press packages challenging the vision of Jefferson as a failing school; they performed dances they had choreographed and recited poetry they had written

for the occasion. In addition, students came forward and spoke about how Jefferson had helped them. But the school board's determination to reconstitute did not wane in spite of student effort.

On May 21, 1998, Jefferson High School teachers, cafeteria workers, custodians, secretaries, and administrators lined up to receive our official "pink slips," notifying us to "vacate" our positions. Jefferson was "reconstituted" because of low test scores and falling enrollment. After the school board voted to reconstitute Jefferson, students organized a community performance to showcase Jefferson's talent. Josh's visit came as we reeled with grief over the impending reconstitution. Students needed to mourn and they needed to fight. Josh's poem allowed them to do both.

During the final student "recital," Djamila Moore's, and Jessica Knudson's "What If" poems were read as students danced to pieces they had choreographed for the poems.

After the performance, I received a letter from a parent who wrote about how moved she was by the student showcase, especially the poems. She said the students' work was a demonstration of using a teachable moment to intersect tragedy, how students had moved beyond despair to action.

Our students will intersect tragedy, again and again during their lives. Poetry will not keep it at bay. But as Adrienne Rich wrote, what poetry can do is help them mourn and remind them to remain vocal so that inequality and inhumanity cannot become "normalized and acceptable." ✳

....

Linda Christensen (lmc@lclark.edu) is director of the Oregon Writing Project at Lewis & Clark College in Portland, Ore. She is a Rethinking Schools editor and author of Reading, Writing, and Rising Up *and* Teaching for Joy and Justice.

Resource

Rich, Adrienne. "What If?" in *What Is Found There: Notebooks on Poetry and Politics*. New York: W. W. Norton & Company, 2003.

What If?

by Joshua Bishop Branch

What if there were no football fields
or goal posts?
No sidelines covered with chalk
and drops of blood and sweat?

What if there were no bone-
crunching hits that rock the stands,
that make the crowd ooh and aah?

What if there were no more
tiptoeing down the sideline
for the touchdown?
No more one-handed catches
in the end zone for the TD?

What if the game of football
ends all together?

What will young men
do if they aren't playing football?

Who will remember
sweat running into the eyes of coaches,
voices of cheerleaders
like a chorus line being sung,
the feel of a football caught and thrown?

What if the hearts of thousands
of would-be athletes
are never recognized
because there is no football?

What If?

by Djamila Moore

What if spirits no longer joined in dance?
What if education were confined to an 8 1/2 by
    11 paper
instead of flowing through veins?
What if there were no more young muscles flexing and
    stretching?
What if the makeup and fake eyelashes fluttered to
    the ground,
and the lights snapped to darkness one by one?
What if there was no rhythm to tap your foot to
or your breath no longer caught in your throat,
anxious for the dancers lifted to the sky?

What if stories only sounded through words
and the stage was an empty canvas numb with loss?
What if calloused feet softened to tender skin,
easily ripped on the unfamiliar earth?

What if drops of sweat cooled to stains of salt,
never to warm again,
and dreams of dance smoldered
like fiery embers praying for breath?

Using Poetry as a Tool for Justice

BY BOB PETERSON

ERIK RUIN

One year during the spring budget cycle our school was informed that because we were $51,000 short we'd have to cut our librarian. The 4th- and 5th-grade teachers agreed to tell the news to our students, but we decided to ask for volunteer representatives to come to my room during lunch to talk about what might be done. These students formed the "Rescue the Librarians Club"—making sure it was plural because as Olivia declared, "all schools deserve librarians." Meeting several times the following week, the 12 students agreed to speak out at an upcoming school council community meeting. Half of the club got permission to stay after school for the meeting, and they put up posters. They also composed a group poem:

A Library Without a Librarian
by members of the "Rescue the Librarians Club"

A library without a librarian
is like a beehive without bees
A tree without leaves
A brownie without chocolate
A forest without trees
A head without a brain
A book without words
An ocean without water
A bird without wings
A zebra without stripes
A tailor without clothes
A barber without scissors
Blood without iron
A bank without money
A fish without gills
A turtle without a shell
All these things are bad, but a library without a
    librarian is worse.

Later the students shared the poem at a public hearing held by an official from the U.S. Department of Public Education and again at a school board meeting, where several students and parents testified.

The school board came up with enough money to keep the librarian at Fratney.

A few years later in the midst of great social turmoil in Wisconsin, after the governor had stripped

I used writing to help students deal with the pending cuts—this time the art teacher.

public sector unions of most of their rights, and implemented the largest budget cuts of any state in the union, I used writing to help students deal with the pending cuts—this time the art teacher.

In one of my post-lunch "sit down and write in your journal now!" assignments, I put a seven-word prompt on the document camera: "What the budget cuts mean to me."

As I walked around my classroom encouraging students, I came to Edie Redwine, a student of Irish

and Objibwe origin. She appeared finished, and she said I could read her journal entry.

I read it quickly and said, "great poem." She looked up at me expressionless, but her penetrating glare reminded me of how my two daughters would look at me after I said something that they thought was one of the stupidest things in the world. Edie's reply: "It's not a poem, it's a letter to the governor."

A Letter to Governor Scott Walker
Budget cuts: an unfair mutiny
that destroys the economy
and slowly tears apart all humanity
and makes the flaws of ourselves
that much deeper
that much bigger
and that much more hurtful.
It is hard to believe
that all this circles
around Governor Walker
the King of destroying schools and jobs
So congratulations, Scott,
you ruined kids' lives!
Now isn't that a sport?

Sincerely,
Just A. Student

P.S. Kids are the future.
Frightened?

At the end of year completion celebration Edie read it to the large crowd. She called it a poem and received a standing ovation from several hundred parents.

She also sent it to Gov. Walker as a letter and never got a reply. ✳

. . . .

Bob Peterson (bob.e.peterson@gmail.com) is a founding editor of Rethinking Schools. He taught 5th grade in Milwaukee Public Schools for many years and is currently the president of the Milwaukee Teachers' Education Association.

Bearing Witness Through Poetry

BY RENÉE WATSON

RICARDO LEVINS MORALES

"This is an oral history lesson
just in case the textbooks neglect the truth:
Natural disaster holocausts
are destroying the poor.
Tens of thousands of bodies lie in Haiti's
    ditches.
Hundreds of deferred dreams drowned
in Katrina's waters. . . "

My high school students stood on stage performing their collaborative poem at the Schomburg Center for Research in Black Culture in Harlem. How fitting that these budding protest poets would be given the opportunity to have their voices rise in the Langston Hughes Auditorium. DreamYard's annual spoken word poetry festival gave parents, teachers, youth, and even politicians a chance to witness New York City's teen poets speak their truth. I sat in the front row, beaming with pride, not only because their performance went off without a hitch, but also because I knew these students meant every word they were reciting. What started out as a compare-and-contrast assignment for a social issues unit turned into a piece of art. A declaration.

As a teaching artist in public schools, I am paired with classroom teachers to teach poetry and to give students an opportunity to experience their academic curriculum through the arts. At the beginning of the school year, I gave my students the ongoing, yearlong assignment to watch the news, to pay attention. We studied Gwendolyn Brooks, who wrote about Emmett Till, and Langston Hughes, whose poetry is a literary commentary on the Black experience in America. "Great poets listen to their world and speak back," I told my students.

Our poetry class started off with the sharing of works in progress and the reporting of current events students felt passionate about. At that point, headlines and news stories inspired students to write about human trafficking, Chris Brown and Rihanna's public display of domestic violence, and the HIV epidemic in the Bronx—where they live.

Just after winter break, on Jan. 12, 2010, five years after New Orleans' levees broke, Haiti's earth quaked.

How do race and class affect the aftermath and recovery from a natural disaster?

The next day, every student wanted to talk about it. But how do you talk about something so devastating, so heartbreaking, without repeating clichéd responses like "That's so sad" or "Can you believe what happened?"

I encouraged students to look at the situation with empathy, but also with a critical eye. Knowing many of them were working with their classroom teachers on sharpening their skills for writing compare-and-contrast essays, I asked them to apply what they were learning to our poetry class. I posed the question: How do race and class affect the aftermath and recovery from a natural disaster?

A Study in Contrasts

I gave students the task of investigating the similarities and differences among three natural disasters: Hurricane Katrina—New Orleans, 2005; the San Diego wildfires—California, 2007; and the 7.0 Port-au-Prince earthquake—Haiti, 2010.

Most of my high school students were in elementary or middle school when Katrina swept through New Orleans. They had faint memories of something bad happening in Louisiana, but had no emotional connec-

tion to it and knew very few facts about the aftermath of the storm. When I asked how many knew anything about the wildfires in California, no one raised a hand.

The following week, I started class differently. I passed out the lyrics to Jay-Z's rap "Minority Report," a four-minute history lesson about New Orleans. I decided to use Jay-Z's song to help students understand what took place in 2005. Using music in my classroom has given many students who resist writing—especially poetry—a way in. Printing out the lyrics for them helps me show the similarities between verses and stanzas, and students are able to point out literary devices that singers and rappers often use.

I played the song and instructed students to read along and underline lyrics that stood out to them because they liked the way Jay-Z said it, or because they agreed. "Circle phrases you don't understand," I added.

After students listened to the song, I led a brief discussion. "What is this song about? When did Katrina happen? How does Jay-Z feel about how things were handled in New Orleans?" Students volunteered to share what they underlined and circled.

Many students underlined the lyric "Wouldn't you loot, if you didn't have the loot?/Baby needed food and you stuck on the roof." Students also underlined phrases that referred to how poor the people in New Orleans were before the hurricane. Several students circled lines about the Superdome and the lack of water and supplies.

After discussing the song, I asked students to turn their handout over. On the other side, a worksheet had a three-column chart with the headers Before, During, and After at the top, and three rows labeled New Orleans, 2005—Hurricane Katrina; San Diego, 2007—Wildfires; and Haiti, 2010—Earthquake.

I showed students a slide show with images of all three places before, during, and after the tragedy. First, we watched the entire slide show without stopping it or talking. The second time through, I stopped the slide show and gave students time to fill out the worksheet. In the images of life before, I asked, "What do you see?" "What do you notice about the houses?" "How would you describe this community?"

When I showed the slides of San Diego, students blurted out, "I want to live there!" "That house is tight!" Words students wrote in the Before column for San Diego included fancy, wealthy, vacation, big.

When we looked at the slides of Haiti, one student pointed to the screen, which held an image of children so thin their bones could be seen, and asked, "Is that really how Haiti looked before the earthquake?"

The next slides showed the devastation that happens when storms come, fires spread, and buildings crumble. Words students wrote in the During column were solemn: death, destruction, demolished, memories vanished, helpless, fear, tragic. Whether the house had been flooded, sizzled to ash, or collapsed to dust, it was clear that these three places, which in the previous column had obvious disparities with regard to class, all suffered enormous grief and loss.

The next photographs showed what happened in the immediate aftermath of each natural disaster. "What do you see?" I asked again. For New Orleans, students noted: crowds, handwritten signs pleading for help and for water, sick elderly people, despair. For San Diego, students wrote: buffets, massages, sleeping on cots, pets playing with their owners. And for Haiti: people sleeping outside in the dark, wounded people, sadness, loss, dead bodies thrown on top of each other.

I gave students time to silently write a response to these images. "How do these images make you feel? What are your gut reactions to these images?" Students wrote for about three minutes and then we discussed their findings.

I asked students not to draw any conclusions yet, but rather to share with the class what they wrote on their chart. "Just tell us what you noticed," I said.

The first comment was about the loss. "I noticed that all three places had a lot of damage done to their homes."

Another student saw that the homes in San Diego had cars parked in the driveway and many of the homes in New Orleans didn't.

"I noticed that the people in New Orleans looked hot, frustrated, and stranded, and the people in San Diego looked relaxed and taken care of."

"The people in San Diego looked organized and calm, and the people in New Orleans and Haiti looked chaotic and a lot more stressed out."

Adding Research to Rap

To help students add facts to their observations, we read the article "Football Stadium Now a Shelter for Fire Evacuees," by the Associated Press, dated Oct. 23, 2007. I asked students to add pertinent informa-

> *"I noticed that the people in New Orleans looked hot, frustrated, and stranded, and the people in San Diego looked relaxed and taken care of."*

tion to their charts. "This article will give you facts to add to your feelings and observations," I explained. Occasionally, I stopped the class to see if anyone had a question or to make sure students understood the article. By the time I finished reading the second paragraph, students were gasping in disbelief. The article further explained what the images showed:

> *San Diego*—Like Hurricane Katrina evacuees two years earlier in New Orleans, thousands of people rousted by natural disaster have fled to an NFL stadium, waiting out the calamity outside San Diego and worrying about their homes. The similarities ended there, as an almost festive atmosphere reigned at Qualcomm Stadium. Bands belted out rock 'n' roll, lavish buffets served gourmet entrees, and massage therapists helped relieve the stress for those forced to flee their homes because of wildfires. . . .
>
> The New Orleans evacuees had dragged themselves through floodwaters to get to the Louisiana Superdome in 2005, and once there endured horrific conditions without food, sanitation, or law enforcement.

I also read them an article from the *New York Times*, "What Happens to a Race Deferred," by Jason DeParle, which I first discovered in Linda Christensen's essay "Hurricane Katrina: Reading Injustice, Celebrating Solidarity." After looking at a graph in the article titled "The Reach of Poverty in New Orleans," which details by race who had cars and who did not, students began to draw conclusions about how race and class play a role in natural disasters.

It was clear to students that there were many differences in the response, resources, and rebuilding of New Orleans and San Diego. I asked students, "Why do you think there is such disparity? Should anything have been done differently? If so, what? Why or why not?"

Students were full of answers and suggestions. "If the government knew the people of New Orleans didn't have much to begin with, they should have been more prepared to handle something like Hurricane Katrina," Urias answered.

Destiny pointed out that maybe by 2007, two years after Katrina, the government had learned a lesson and that's why Qualcomm Stadium had so many resources. "And besides," she added, "Hurricane Katrina affected everybody in New Orleans. But not everyone in San Diego had to leave their home, so more people were able to volunteer and help out."

Lydia saw her point, but was adamant that more could have been done for Louisiana. "But five days?" she yelled. "They had no water for five days!"

"How is it that we can get stuff to other countries overnight but can't help our own?" Vaughn asked. "I'm not saying California didn't deserve help, I just think that New Orleans deserved it, too."

After comparing the hurricane and the fires, we took a closer look at the earthquake. Students learned that Haiti is the poorest country in the Western Hemisphere, and they quickly drew the conclusion that if, five years later, New Orleans was still rebuilding, Haiti had a long road ahead. "I think it's good that everyone is donating money to them now, but where were all these donations before the earthquake?" Urias asked.

Instead of hiding their questions, fears, and frustrations, they did what the poets they studied have done: They sounded the alarm.

I didn't want to end the discussion, but I needed to bring our conversation to a close, so I could prepare students for their assignment and end class. I could

tell students had lingering questions and I wanted to give them a chance to ask them. I tore pieces of blank scrap paper and handed out colored strips to the students, asking them to write down any question or thoughts that they didn't get to share. They didn't have to put their name on the slip of paper. I explained that we might not be able to answer their question in class, but that they should search out the answer. The slips of paper included the following questions:

- What would happen if a tragedy took place in New York City? Would Times Square be restored before neighborhoods in the Bronx?
- Do the poor know how to save money? Do they have enough money to save for a "rainy day"?
- How does a homeowner choose an insurance policy?
- Are there places that are currently in great need but may never get help unless tragedy strikes them?
- Whose responsibility is it to help the poor?
- Will history books tell the truth about what happened in New Orleans?

Although not the purpose of our class, these questions could lead into units on a variety of issues in many different subjects, including math, economics, and history. Students were beginning to see that what happened in New Orleans and Haiti—and what happens in their neighborhood—is rooted in deep issues that span a variety of aspects of their lives.

'What Do You Have to Say?'

In our next class, students began their poems. I mentioned Jay-Z's song as an example of an artist who lent his pen to a cause. "Write your version of 'Minority Report.'"

"What do you have to say to New Orleans, San Diego, Haiti?" I asked them. "What do you want to say to America?"

I encouraged my students to incorporate phrases from the articles, the rap, their free-write, and their chart into their poems. "You've collected a lot of information and documented your feelings very well. Use the material you've gathered in your piece," I instructed. "If you don't know how to begin, state a fact from the article or a lyric from the song and start from there."

Students got right to work. And so did I.

Whenever possible, I model doing the assignment so that students see and hear a "real writer's" process, and so that I encounter possible frustrations and stumbling blocks before they do. I let them hear my first drafts, revise them, and read them to the class again as an example of how even adult writers revise and edit their work. I also want to show my students that I am willing to take the risks I daily ask them to take. To write their opinions; to express their anger, hurt, and joy; to shout out questions to a world that may not respond with the answer they hoped for is a brave thing. I encourage them to take those risks with me.

After everyone's poem was complete, I took lines from all of our poems and combined them to create a collaborative piece.

Destiny and Vaughn both wrote about the lack of resources in New Orleans:

2005.
New Orleans flooded. . .
they named it
Hurricane Katrina.
And Katrina means Pure.
But the Superdome
had no pure water. . .

New Orleans,
for five days
you drank your salty tears
and there were no medical supplies
for your heartache.

And the ignorant asked: Why didn't
you get out?
Not realizing the poor have no cars to
drive to hotels to wait out a storm. . .

Urias, Lily, and Jazmin created stanzas about the neglect of Haiti:

Haiti's earth quaked
five years after New Orleans' levees broke.

And we are the aftershock. Shocked
that it took a catastrophe to pay attention to
the poor.

Why is it that it takes tragedy to unify a world?

Haiti, we never remembered you. We knew
your people
stood in line for their only meal of the day—
beans and rice—
and we looked away.

Long before buildings barricaded your
children under tons of bricks
we knew you were the poorest country
in the Western Hemisphere.
And we looked away. . .

Denisse, who takes dance classes, volunteered to create an interpretive dance to go along with the poem. She rallied her peers together to rehearse outside of class. Observing them practice, I realized that, just a month before, all they could articulate about Haiti was that what happened was "sad," "a tragedy," "so unfortunate."

Now, they had facts and critical ideas to support

My students joined a new generation of poets committed to being recorders, responders, rebukers, rejoicers, and rebuilders.

them as they expressed their emotions. They took the skills they learned with their classroom teacher and applied them to their art. And instead of keeping silent, instead of hiding their questions, fears, and frustrations, they did what the poets they studied have done: They sounded the alarm. "Every time we say this poem, people will remember," Destiny told me. She understood that her words would not change what happened and her teenaged wallet might not be able to donate funds for recovery, but she could lend her pen.

Her voice.

There was a consensus in the group: "This is a tribute for people everywhere who are struggling. We have to make it special."

And they did.

And what happened on stage, in Langston's beloved Harlem, was more than a poetry recital. My students joined a new generation of poets committed to being recorders, responders, rebukers, rejoicers, and rebuilders.

What happened was the rising of voices:

Santa Ana winds come again.
Blow relief to the 9th Ward, to Haiti. . .
Let the fire of revival spread to Bourbon Street
    and Port-au-Prince. . .
Let our words be the rope you hang onto.
    May they pull you out of the rubble.
Syllable by syllable let each verb,
each noun
build a fortress on your insides. Strengthening
    the levees of your soul

so you do not break.
May you never break.

And if the history books forget to add
a footnote apologizing
for not being proactive but reactive. . .
take this account. Take this truth
and write it in stone. Carve an
evacuation plan
and post it in every poor city, every
desolate nation. . .

there is a way out. . .

tell every child that lives lacking: As long as
    you can speak you
can survive
because words are seeds and this oral
history will bring a harvest.
We plant your name in the ground
of hope,

Haiti.
New Orleans.
Ethiopia.
Flint, Michigan.
Bronx, New York.
You will not be forgotten. . . . You will rise. You
    will rise
because we will lift you up.

Renée Watson (reneewatson.net) is an author, performer, and educator. Her children's books have received several honors, including an NAACP Image Award nomination. She teaches poetry at DreamYard in New York City.

Resources

Associated Press. "Football Stadium Now a Shelter for Fire Evacuees." MSNBC.com, Oct. 23, 2007. (www.msnbc.msn.com/id/21435605/)

DeParle, Jason. "What Happens to a Race Deferred." *The New York Times*, Sept. 4, 2005. (www.nytimes.com/2005/09/04/weekinreview/04depa.html)

Jay-Z. "Minority Report." *Kingdom Come*. Roc-a-Fella Records, 2006.

Perspective Through Poetry
'Thirteen Ways of Looking at a Blackbird'

BY KELLY J. GOMES

SHAUN SLIFER

"It is a narrow mind which cannot look at a subject from various points of view."
—George Eliot

Wallace Stevens' "Thirteen Ways of Looking at a Blackbird," published in 1954, has become a valuable teaching tool in my classroom, as both a study of the author's craft and as a model for writing from multiple perspectives. When we used the poem as a model for investigating social issues, my creative writing classroom became an engaged community of writers who broadened their lenses and dove headlong and heart-forward into challenging topics.

Previously, I had used Stevens' piece as a model for different ways of seeing and observing with my creative writing class—a culturally, linguistically, and socioeconomically diverse group of juniors and seniors. In the original assignment, students noted the poem's craft and then chose an object to observe for several days in order to create a "13 Ways of Seeing" poem. This was a valuable tool for honing the ability to pay attention to details; however, one day I decided to expand this plan in order to dig deeper into multiple perspectives.

Although my school's population is one of the most diverse in the state, and we often affectionately refer to ourselves as a mini United Nations, we still individually suffer from the human predicament of limited worldviews to the point that we stop actively paying attention to the different experiences and perspectives around us. My hope was that by exploring multiple points of view on a topic, students would feel inspired to investigate societal problems. I repurposed Stevens' piece as a springboard for this endeavor.

We began with the original assignment in order to understand the poem's form before moving to weightier topics. To this end, we first observed the poem on the page. "Thirteen Ways of Looking at a Blackbird" is comprised of 13 numbered stanzas, each providing a differ-

Each stanza is a photograph that illuminates a particular perspective.

ent image of the blackbird and its landscape. Whenever we encounter a poem for the first time, we begin with a simple round of reading and observing. In this case, a different student read each stanza so that we could "feel" the changes in images as the voices changed. After 13 different student voices read the poem, students shared out lines and images they liked: "Among twenty snowy mountains,/The only moving thing/Was the eye of the blackbird." (1-3), and "It was evening all afternoon./It was snowing/And it was going to snow./ The blackbird sat/In the cedar-limbs" (49-53).

We then turned to the imagery within the form. I began with some of the lines students had chosen: "What do you see here: 'Among twenty snowy mountains,/The only moving thing/Was the eye of the blackbird?'"

"There's this background of still white mountaintops in a row. . ." one student offered.

"And there's the blackbird looking around. He's black against the white and his eyes are moving," finished another.

"Right. It's a picture by itself. Even if the rest of the poem didn't exist, that one image can stand by itself."

We continued. Some of the poem's images are obvious and others require a bit of work to understand, while a few are so distant to our experience that we work to visualize the stanzas the best we can. I admitted to them that I'm a bit confused by stanza VII even though I grew up near Haddam, Conn.:

VII
O thin men of Haddam,
Why do you imagine golden birds?
Do you not see how the blackbird

Walks around the feet
Of the women about you? (24-28)

I also admitted that some of the shifts in point of view caused me to re-read several times. And as always, I emphasized that reading and re-reading a piece, and speaking it out loud multiple times, are a normal and encouraged part of the process of understanding a poem.

Our purpose these first times through was not to understand every nuance of Stevens' poem, but to grasp the idea of situating a topic in 13 unique ways, and to discover how we could use perspective, image, and form to do this. In this way, at the same time that students deepened their knowledge of the author's craft in the original work, they also generated ideas about different ways of seeing objects in their various environments.

I wanted to get students headed toward social commentary. I asked, "What would it look like to see social problems and ideas in 13 different ways?"

Thirty-six heads turned toward me and paused. "Like what?" they asked.

"Well, what do you wish would change about the world?"

I gave them several minutes to brainstorm individually before we gathered a class list. I started the list with child abuse, and the class added racism, global warming, disease, homelessness, income inequality, war, gangs and much, much more. In fact, it was hard to stop the flow.

"Great. So, we're going to do an early brainstorm . . . just spilling on the page . . . choose one item on your list and consider it. For example, if my topic is war, what do 13 images of war look like? Or, can you think of 13 scenes of racism?" I suggested.

I continued by asking them to choose a topic that makes them "sit on the edge of their seats," and to list possibilities, like the ones shared out, before developing stanzas. I also encouraged them to pull in a topic of study from their other content classes by writing about war, global warming, redlining and gentrification, the Great Depression, civil rights, etc.

As students listed, I nudged them with reminders and ideas I wanted them to consider: "We'll work on one together in a minute, but for now, think about your topic . . . remember the shifts in point of view. Will you have 13 different people tell their story? How will you handle contrasting perspectives? How will you include perspectives other than your own?"

Now that they'd spent time generating ideas on a topic that mattered to them personally, we grouped back up for a whole-class model, and we worked together on brainstorming 13 images of poverty, a topic many of them are all too familiar with. "What are the possibilities for perspectives?" I prompted.

They volunteer: "Ohhhh, like you could have a millionaire complaining about taxes. Or the president."

"A kid without a home."

"A scene from a soup kitchen maybe."

"Maybe an immigrant who realizes it's not that easy here, or has to be a janitor instead of a doctor in this country."

"What about somebody who made it, but has a flashback to growing up without money or enough food?"

"Oh, and like in that poem you read us, a mother scraping together toys for her kids at Christmas."

"How about someone without papers who has to work for almost nothing?"

Students then returned to their chosen topics to add anything that was sparked by our whole-class list. As some students became uncomfortable writing in the perspective of a perpetrator, of someone "opposite" them, or of situations close to home, we discussed how writers often write about topics they haven't experienced themselves, and how this kind of brave, bold writing creates a space for personal growth. We discussed how even a writer who is familiar with poverty hasn't experienced all perspectives possible, so that writer has to stretch her imagination and research. I reminded them of the persona poems we had worked with, namely Patricia Smith's poems "Skinhead" and "Undertaker," and her book *Blood Dazzler*, in which she writes from the perspective of Hurricane Katrina. This stepping outside of ourselves is how we move beyond our individual experience to find greater understanding of someone else's perspective. And, as an audience, we have the responsibility to separate the author from the speaker of the poem.

This conversation was well received by the students and gave them permission to write and comment without the need for disclaimers or fears of association with their topics. I'd find them reminding each other in their writing groups, and sometimes with the whole

class, "It's not her, it's her character" or "He doesn't think that, he's just imagining that perspective." It also allowed them to own the parts that were their own if they chose to do so: "No, that didn't happen to me, but my neighbor told me a story like that once. But this part is me" or "I read this case study that talked about feeling like that after being attacked." And, of course, I'd remind the class when I felt like they were slipping back into assumptions, or when we needed to realign to our class norms, but as this was spring, we had established a good deal of trust in the classroom already.

Once students had a general idea of what they wanted to write about and how they wanted to write it, we spent a block period researching our topics. Because of the nature of some of the topics, this required a quick reminder about valid sources, and a healthy dose of adult oversight to ensure the students weren't encountering graphic images or paraphernalia. We agreed to never search images, and to be smart about our search, typing in "Sexual Assault Statistics and Case Studies" instead of "rape," or "Poverty Global Statistics and Research" rather than "starving children." Although challenging, I found this part of the process valuable, as it was the part of the lesson where kids found factual information to support their topics, such as how much the government spends on defense versus social support systems. This was also the part of the process where kids became incensed and inspired by what they discovered.

After our research, it was time for the next step, which was to take the form of Stevens' poem as permission to write "snapshots" of our topics, as if each stanza is a photograph that illuminates a particular perspective. I prompted them, "If you are still stuck on a topic, choose something from the class list," but most of them returned to their own chosen topic. We looked back at sections of Stevens' poem that we had talked about earlier, and reiterated how the stanzas were like photographs. "Remember the still mountains and the moving eye of the blackbird. That's a clear image and a picture by itself. So try to create separate scenes from your list. Don't even worry yet about what order they should be in, or how they fit together. You're writing images that *show* the idea, rather than just telling us directly."

We used our lists as fodder for these snapshots, and continued to discuss the idea of the image telling the story. A few of the more literal thinkers struggled a bit here, but were still able to write multiple, although less subtle, perspectives.

After some time drafting and sharing in small writing groups, John shared what he wrote about water:

A whirlpool swirling in a stream.
"I saw the same one there yesterday," he said.
"But the water that passes through it is entirely different,"
I reply, "How can you say it's the same whirlpool?"
~
Ubar, Southern Oman: The Lost City was swallowed into the earth due to groundwater pumping.
All over the World, water tables are being destroyed.
The land is desertifying,
While more children are dying from contaminated water than from wars.
Water, the source and sustenance for life, is slipping away from us.

John had managed to write philosophy and environmental justice into his poem. We applauded him for picking a topic that was less obvious but essential, and noted how he included researched facts in his poem.

Another student, Linh, a problem-solver in math and science, but a self-professed "literal thinker" in writing, wrote about hunger in juxtapositions of stark images:

My mother said I can't eat
because there isn't enough food for everybody,
so my little brothers and sisters get to eat first.
~
"Congrats, son,
Let's all go to the buffet for dinner.
You can stuff yourself after that sweet victory."
~
We need the money to protect this country;
there isn't enough in the budget to also feed everyone.
We are giving the people security.

Linh succeeded in providing multiple perspectives that included the individual and the government, and demonstrated curiosity about the possible causes and solutions for the issue.

It became evident that students carefully considered their topics and learned from the writing of others as well. There were many "I hadn't thought of that" comments, along with tears, hugs, applause, heavy pauses, weighty discussion, curious inquiries, and generous sharing of information on topics. And the students were so invested in their topics at the end of revising that we continued to explore and write about them in different forms.

I extended the activity into a mini unit, and we ventured on to writing persona poems by taking one of their 13 stanzas and expanding it. We also modified two- and three-voice poems for this purpose, and experimented with juxtaposing similar and opposing perspectives. The students were so prolific that we then made self-published zines for our classroom and the library. For many kids, these pieces were among the writings they were most proud of, and they submitted their "13 Ways" poems to the school literary magazine in such quantity that it defined the publication that year. We included a listing of hotline and outreach numbers in the front of the literary magazine, and some students even created public service announcements and distributed them to the student body. This, for me, was evidence that the students had built awareness of their topic at a deeper level, and they now were invested in sharing their learning with others.

In this way, we ventured from the blackbird to hunger, from "thin men of Haddam" to child abuse. We borrowed a structure to help us frame our understanding of social concerns, enlivening the text with modern connection and purpose, and empowering ourselves to investigate and talk back through writing. Students opened themselves to multiple perspectives and found their own voice amongst them. ✳

. . . .

Kelly J. Gomes teaches high school English in Portland, Ore., and is an MFA candidate at Pacific University. Her poetry has appeared in Rain City Review, The English Journal, *and in a chapbook,* Moving in Angles.

Resource

Stevens, Wallace. "Thirteen Ways of Looking at a Blackbird" in *The Collected Poems of Wallace Stevens*. New York: Alfred A. Knopf, 1954; reprinted by Random House, 1982.

CHAPTER FIVE

Turning Pain into Power

ERIK RUIN

hiraeth

by Renée Watson

Hiraeth: A longing for home; nostalgia, yearning, grief for the lost places of your past.

My roots are tangled in Marley's dreads.
I was nurtured in the womb of an oak tree.
Thunder and lightning and storm know me well.
I belong to the rosebush. Its thorn and petal, its leaf and stem.
I am not brownstone or skyscraper,
yellow taxi or suffocated sidewalk.
I am not made for squeezing in and out.
I want porch swing and backyard,
want Pacific Ocean around my corner, mountain at my back,
want Patois on tongue, drum in hips, coconut oil saturating hair.
Oh, Jamaica, can I call you home
even though I only know you through Grandma's hand-me-down tales?
Oh, Portland, you town of beauty, of ghosts,
where Tallahatchie waters flood into Columbia River
drowning Emmett and every boy and girl from Vanport.
Don't you know the past has a way of pricking memory,
like thorn to thumb, unexpectedly?

Turning Pain into Power

These days both students and teachers shoulder grief and fear: the deaths of young Black men, school shootings, record unemployment, gentrification, ongoing wars, climate chaos, and more. When students experience so much hardship and the future seems so bleak, their daily trek to school is itself a heroic act.

In order for our classrooms to be safe harbors of learning, we must make room for heartbreak and defiance in the curriculum. Poetry can crack a class open, create a community out of strangers, construct understanding across lines that divide. Poetry teaches students to use words instead of fists or drugs or other self-destructive behavior. Poetry can allow the pain to rise up and pour out. Through poetry, we can mourn our losses, expel our terror, tell our stories, and sing our joys. And we can confront those who have hurt us—as Renée Watson does in her poem "Black Like Me" when she challenges her middle school teacher to see her as "black and brilliant."

As the great poet Martín Espada reminds us, "Acts of resistance are documented, even where that resistance is nothing more than the assertion of human dignity." So when we read "Brown Dreams" by Paul Flores, which is a howl of despair—a public outcry against both war and immigration policies, we teach students to stand up, to rage, to speak and remember, to tell the story of those who have been silenced and to name the policies and the governments who took their voices (see p. 227).

In her book *What Is Found There: Notebooks on Poetry and Politics*, Adrienne Rich wrote, "You must write, and read, as if your life depended on it. That is not generally taught in school." The teachers and poets in this book understand that our students' lives depend on writing—to drive out the pain, to build solidarity with others, and to take action against injustice. As students use poetry to forgive—or not forgive, or to talk about their fears, they learn that they are not alone. When they write letter poems as Daniel Beaty does in "Knock Knock," they learn to gather up their emotions into words, to talk back to the pain, and give themselves direction for moving on. ✳

. . . .

Rich, Adrienne. What Is Found There: Notebooks on Poetry and Politics. *New York: W. W. Norton & Company, 2003.*

Forgiveness Poems
'An axe for the frozen sea within us'

BY LINDA CHRISTENSEN

BEC YOUNG

I was 13 when my father died. When I was in high school, my mother started dating other men. I resented this for many reasons. Partly, I suppose I wanted her to stay true to the memory of my father, whom I loved madly. But I also missed her; she was absent from my life during that time. My sisters and brother were grown, so our "family" consisted of Mom and me. She no longer cooked dinner. She drank more. She stayed out late. I was lonely and angry and hurt. Many years later, I realized that she was still a "young" woman in her mid-40s. She wasn't ready to be a widow for life, and there were few eligible prospects in our small town.

Teenagers often harbor resentment as well as love for their parents. Theirs is an age of rebellion and separation. During the last 40 years, I've listened as my students stormed in anger at their parents, but I've also witnessed their love and loyalty. As a daughter who has forgiven her mother, and as the mother of two daughters who I hope will forgive me all of my mistakes, I find the topic of forgiveness essential—and a recurring theme in literature and history.

As students grow into adulthood, they need to see their parents as people as well as family members. Sometimes understanding the cultural and social pressures that shaped their parents helps them begin to resolve some of the issues that divide them from the significant adults in their lives. For some students the pain is still too close and too fresh to forgive. Both responses are legitimate.

The forgiveness poem is a yearly staple in my classes. I use it when I teach Sherman Alexie's *Smoke Signals* in junior English, but it pairs well with many novels or historical periods. In *Smoke Signals*, Victor, the main character, struggles because his alcoholic father left the reservation, abandoning him and his mother. After his father's death, Victor discovers the reason his father left, as well as his father's guilt and pain.

At the end of the play, Alexie uses part of a Dick Lourie poem, "Forgiving Our Fathers," as Victor's friend Thomas mourns the death of Victor's father, Arnold, as well as his own:

> Do we forgive our fathers for leaving us too often or
> forever when we were little?
> Maybe for scaring us with unexpected rage
> or making us nervous because there seemed
> never to be any rage there at all
> Do we forgive our fathers for marrying
> or not marrying our mothers
> For divorcing or not divorcing our mothers?
> And shall we forgive them for their excesses
> of warmth or coldness?

Lourie's questions float through the class as we read the end of the play, just as Victor's father's ashes float on the Spokane River.

Beyond the curricular connections, I use this poetic prompt early in the year because it cracks my classes open. Instead of being cardboard characters—the basketball player, the dancer, the high achiever—students become real people whose veins pump equal parts hope and pain. As one of Bill Bigelow's and my former students said, "When you hear people's stories, you can't hate them anymore." Writing and sharing our lives builds a community in the classroom that allows students to risk more, to lose their fear of looking or sounding wrong.

We live in a society that is increasingly exploitative and unequal. As jobs fade into perpetual unem-

Writing and sharing our lives builds a community that allows students to risk more.

ployment, the loss of self-worth spins into alcohol, drug, and physical abuse. Families separate and fall apart under the pressure. Too often these issues are not addressed in school, and students take out their anger and grief on each other, creating disruptive and unproductive classrooms. The forgiveness poem gives students space to voice the ways these pressures have played out in their lives.

I begin by reading my poem about my mother to students. Sharing my stories helps build the bond between us. I make myself vulnerable when I'm asking them to be vulnerable.

> Dear Mom,
> I forgive you for all the nights
> you chose men over me,
> the nights you stayed out late.
> I forgive you for all the evenings
> I ate TV dinners,
> watching reruns of *Maverick*
> and roamed our lonely house,
> only my voice cracking the silence.
> I forgive you for all the days
> when your anger
> tumbled out
> coating me with curses.
> I forgive you, Mother,
> for I know your heart.
> I know your loneliness.

I know the tender ache
that wakes us, alone in the dark
when the foghorn reminds
me that Dad died
and all that is left
is emptiness.

Once I share my poem, we read Lucille Clifton's poem "forgiving my father." She berates her father for not giving her mother "what she was due." Her poem weaves in both understanding and anger:

but you were the son of a needy father,
the father of a needy son; you
gave her all you had
which was nothing.

We discuss the twin emotions that rise up from Clifton's poem and compare it to how Victor feels about his father.

Then we read two student poems: "Forgiving My Mother" by Tanya Park and "Forgiving My Father" by Justin Morris (see p. 188). After reading Tanya's poem, I ask students, "What do you notice about Tanya's poem? What's it about? Can you relate to it?" Students

Sharing my stories helps build the bond between us. I make myself vulnerable when I'm asking them to be vulnerable.

discuss the specific details—pushing her father away, the packing and unpacking. They don't think that having breakfast for dinner is something to be angry about. Then I encourage students to notice how the poem is put together. "How did she move her poem forward?" Students note the repeating lines, "For all the times . . . I forgive you." This repetition models an effective pattern that students sometimes bring into their poems.

We follow the same procedure for Justin's poem. Many students identify with his poem to his absent father. They quickly pick out details—not knowing what his father looks like, not having the same last name, no cards or presents for his birthday or Christmas.

Again, I ask them to notice the repetition in Justin's poem, "I'd like to forgive you, but. . ."

I tell students to take out a sheet of paper and write a list of people they would like to forgive—or not—including themselves. Then to select one of those people and think about specific reasons or events that need forgiving, like Tanya and Justin did. Students write ferociously. Very few get stuck on this assignment. Some use the repeating lines from the students' models, but others create their own. Most students write to their mother or father. One girl wrote to the man who murdered her cousin, one boy wrote to Hitler, but this is typically a poem between intimates—relatives and close friends.

Let me say that not all of my students have tragic lives, but some do, and this assignment allows them to speak bitterness about it. For others, the assignment lets them lay down some of the resentment they've been carrying. One student was placed in foster care after his grandparents were arrested for selling drugs. He wrote:

Hey, Mom, I forgive you
For all the times you didn't come home
For all the times you left us
At strangers' houses.
For all the times you left us
At our grandparents' house
For days on end and then forever.
Yes, Mom, I forgive you
For all the times you let
Dope come first.
For all the times that I found you
Passed out on the couch,
Thinking that you were dead,
I forgive you.
For all the times you let me down,
Mom, I forgive you.

Another student is high achieving, but he's pushed hard by his parents to achieve even more. His poem scorched the pages with his anger at being both yelled at and paraded by his mother:

I'd like to think you've learned
From the history textbook of your anger
Or maybe that a teacher would appear to help
you learn

And I'd like to think that your atomic bomb
Of rage had broken and wouldn't explode again.
But wishful thinking won't change your world.
I dream of a morning
When your werewolf screams of fury are nowhere
    to be heard
When your ceaseless gunfire won't rip me up
And I dream of a day when you don't thrust
    spears through the bars of my
cage of misery then show me off to admiring
    mothers like a trophy
But dreaming won't make a better morning.
I wish you wouldn't say, "I love you,"
Like you mean it.
Then tromp on me like I'm dirt
I wish I could forgive you,
But I can't, and for that I am sorry, Mother.

Absent fathers, like Justin's, are a common theme in the poems. This poem reflects a familiar refrain:

For all the times you came
In at 2 in the morning yelling
At my mom, I forgive you.
For the time you left for
11 years without telling me
I forgive you.

Many students demonstrate the conflict evident in Lucille Clifton's poem. They are angry, but also curious and willing to stretch out a hand:

If I could forgive you, Father, I would.
But who are you?
I don't have a clue.
You've got my inquiries stuck like a flame to a fuse.
Only you can extinguish them.
I never got a hug from Daddy.
You know what? It's fine.

We share the poems in class during a read-around, where each student shares their piece and others comment. Students are kind and thoughtful. Because of the painful content, we do not require everyone to share, but most do.

Franz Kafka wrote, "A book should serve as the axe for the frozen sea within us." For me, the forgiveness poem is that axe. This poem allows the class to address those who have harmed us so that we can move on, hold hands with others who have also been wronged, come to new insights about each other and our lives, understand that we are not alone in our pain. The assignment is not a command to forgive, but an invitation to understand—as Victor comes to understand his father's alcoholism and disappearance—an invitation to name our hurt and make sense of it. ✳

. . . .

Linda Christensen (lmc@lclark.edu) is director of the Oregon Writing Project at Lewis & Clark College in Portland, Ore. She is a Rethinking Schools editor and author of Reading, Writing, and Rising Up *and* Teaching for Joy and Justice.

Forgiving My Mother
by Tanya Park

For all the times you yelled
and all the times you screamed,
I forgive you.

For all the nights we had breakfast for dinner and
dinner for breakfast,
I forgive you.
For all the times I felt you
pushed
my daddy away,
I forgive you.
For all the times we ran away
and came back,
For all the times we packed
and unpacked,
for all the friends I've lost
and all the schools I've seen,
for all the times
I was the new kid on the scene,
I forgive you.

Forgiving My Father
by Justin Morris

I'd like to forgive you, Father,
but I don't know your heart.
Your face,
is it a mirror image of mine?
I'd like to forgive you, Father,
but I find your absence a fire
that your face might be able to extinguish.
I'd like to forgive you, Father,
but my last name isn't the same as yours
like it's supposed to be.
You rejected me, Dad,
but can I sympathize with your ignorance?
For all the birthdays
you didn't send me a card,
for the Christmases
when I'd wake up,
and you weren't sitting by the tree waiting for me,
I can't forgive you.
What about the summer nights
where prospects of you began to fade?
Fade like you did 17 years ago.
Out of my life.
I'd like to forgive you, Father,
but I don't know you.
And for that,
I hate you.

Forgiveness
by anonymous high school student

Hey, Mom, I forgive you
For all the times you didn't come home
For all the times you left us
At strangers' houses.

For all the times you left us
At our grandparents' house
For days.

Yes, Mom, I forgive you
For all the times you let
Dope come first.

For all the times that I found you
Passed out on the couch,
Thinking that you were dead
I forgive you
For bringing all those strange
People over.

For all the times you let me down,
Mom, I forgive you.

Dad, I Forgive You
by anonymous high school student

For all the times you came
In at 2 in the morning yelling
At my mom,
I forgive you.

For the time you left for
11 years without telling me
I forgive you.

For the times you don't come
See me and never call to say
I'm sorry
I forgive you.

For showing up in my life
Many years too late,
Dad, I forgive you.

Pain and Poetry
Facing our fears

BY TOM McKENNA

Apolice car races past our school. Its siren pierces the reverie my students have settled into during our writing class. A number of students push back from their computers and lift their hands in mock surrender. Their actions appear to be involuntary. One student remarks, "Hey everybody, our ride's here."

The students crack up. I crack up along with them. No more serious writing this morning. The police car has run off with my students' concentration and left me wondering about the negative experiences that underlie the laughter and poses of surrender.

I teach at a high school completion/GED program, the Portland YouthBuilders (PYB), in one of Portland, Ore.'s poorest neighborhoods. Many of my students have spent time in jail, two wear house arrest bracelets around their ankles, and few have had positive experiences with the police.

I decide that if I am going to help my students address some of the barriers that stand between them and the dreams for a better future that brought them to my classroom, I need to come up with effective strategies to help them heal from wounds masked by their laughter.

Even though I've been teaching for 38 years, this year is the first time I've ever taught a writing class. I have been with this particular group of students for about two months. I'm often scrambling to come up with lessons that really connect with these students, that are meaningful, that expand their skills, and that bring about transformative moments in the classroom.

My students' response to the police siren feels like a golden opportunity to lead them toward a deeper understanding of their lives and the world that has shaped them. What to do tomorrow? I wrestle with that question much of the rest of the day and evening.

How do I get to what lies at the base of their mock surrender? How do I connect with a core that allows them to safely find their way through the toxic worlds in which they live?

When I applied for the teaching position at PYB, I was asked to present a lesson plan to a group of staff members and students. I thought about using one of my "greatest hits" lessons from the past, but I wanted to do something fresh and honest, something new. I realized that I was beset with fears: fear I wouldn't get the job; fear I'd been away from the classroom for too long; and, despite the fact that I was teaching other teachers how to teach at local universities, fear I really didn't know what I was talking about anymore. So I decided to create a lesson built around one of my favorite poems: "Fear," by Raymond Carver.

Why not use that same lesson with my writing students to help them examine the roots of their fears? Carver's poem lends itself well to a class full of reluctant writers. "Fear" is a list poem. It follows an easily replicable structure and provides young people an opportunity to express and share feelings that often get in the way of their learning. Each line but one begins with the words "Fear of. . ."

Carver's 'Fear' Resonates with Students

I've found that teacher self-disclosure often gives students permission to write more honestly, freeing them from the fear of being judged. So I begin the lesson by telling the story of my group interview for the job at PYB. I tell my students all the things I feared as my interview approached. "I'm old," I explain, "set in my ways, and not a fan of rejection." At one point, I confess to them, I wondered if I should even go through with the interview. But, I tell my students, I decided to face those fears and address them head-on in the hope of freeing myself from their hold.

Then I hand out copies of Raymond Carver's poem. I ask the students to mark any lines that reach out and speak to them as I read the piece aloud: lines that grab them by their shirts and force a closer reading, lines that maybe even give expression to their own fears.

The first line of "Fear" hits home: "Fear of seeing a police car pull into the drive." I pause after reading the line and look up to see what my students are doing. Most are underlining the words, circling them, putting an exclamation point after the line, making some kind of mark that says, "Yes, this line resonates with me."

After reading the poem aloud, I ask students to share their favorite lines "popcorn style": "Just shout a line out when you feel so moved. Don't worry if two shout out simultaneously. Silences won't hurt us. Feel free to repeat lines for effect. Start whenever you want."

A chorus of student voices follows my instructions. Often I have to wait a bit for student voices to jump in. This time I don't.

"Fear of seeing a police car pull into the drive."
"Fear of death."
"Fear of the past rising up."
"Fear of waking up to find you gone."
"Fear of running out of money."
"Fear of having to identify the body of a dead friend."
"Fear of not loving and fear of not loving enough."

After a full five minutes, I bring the chorus to a stop and ask my students what they heard in each other's voices.

Jose says, "A lot of people don't like to see police cars."

I ask for a show of hands: "How many of you have had negative experiences with the police?" Every student raises a hand.

"Who would like to share one of your experiences?"

Ben shakes his head, looks down, and says, "Man, you don't even want to know."

Lisa talks about the number of times that she and her friends have been searched while sitting in the park close to their apartment complex. "They know we don't got nothing, but they do it anyway, every time they drive by."

Titus shares why he was late to school the day before. "I got stopped at the MAX [light rail train] stop. A TriMet cop asked to see my bus pass. I showed it to him with my student ID and he tells me I'm too old to have a student pass. I show him my student ID and he walks away, makes a call on his walkie-talkie, and before I know it there's two cop cars, I'm being searched, they bring out a drug dog who sniffs me and my backpack. They find nothing, take another look at my ID and say, 'OK, you're legal, you can go.' No 'Sorry,' nothing. And I'm an hour late to school."

I thank the students for their open and honest comments. "What else did we hear in each other's voices from the poem? Which other of Mr. Carver's fears hit home with us? What fears of your own did you become aware of?"

Students offer a variety of responses: fear of not being good enough, fear of the past catching up with them, fear of not being able to stay clean, fear of their infant children not respecting them and the choices they've made. The list goes on.

"We have lots to write about." I clap my hands and tell the students that we are going to write our own "Fear" poems.

Student Poems Break Down Barriers

I offer simple instructions. "Put down on paper what you were just saying aloud. Start each line with 'Fear of. . .' and use descriptive language to show your fears with your words. Look for detail like Raymond Carver did. Remember his first line that so many of you liked: 'Fear of seeing a police car pull into the drive.' Mr. Carver doesn't say 'fear of the police'; instead he uses one line to describe a scene so that when we read his words, we can say, 'He's afraid of cops.' Any questions?"

A rustle of notebooks opening is followed by requests for writing utensils, paper, and use of the computers. The students eventually get down to work after I remind them that this is quiet writing time—after 38 years, I can say "Quiet, please" quite well. I write with them. We manage to write quietly for about 20 minutes. I wait for all to finish off a final line and then ask students to share lines from their poems in the same manner as we spoke lines from Carver's original, "popcorn style." Not all choose to share, but a few students volunteer.

Deavon says: "Fear of everyone being right about me."

Chris says: "Fear of never seeing my brother again."

Uzi, in a voice one notch up from a whisper, says: "Fear of getting shot/Fear they'll get my family before they get me." A stunned silence hovers over Uzi's words. Before anyone can comment, our sharing time is cut short by the clock. It is time for lunch. God forbid I should run class time over into lunch. I collect the student papers and retreat to my office to read them.

As is often the case, I am humbled and deeply moved by the student work I get to read. I start with Uzi's piece. I want to know more from the tidbit he offered at the end of class:

Fear I'll get shot
Fear they'll get my family before they get me. . .
Fear my daughter won't know me
Fear she'll grow up to be like me. . .
Fear I'll go to hell

Lisa:

Fear I'm not good enough
Fear my past will catch up with me
Fear I won't stay clean
Fear I'll never find love

And Jose:

Fear my love only hurts those I love
Fear of being caught without my piece
Fear of being a father
Fear I'll never get the chance

I have to put the papers down for a minute to catch my breath and think about the worlds that my students take for granted as ordinary, everyday. I feel ill-equipped to deal with the honest writing "Fear" has wrought. I decide to start our next class by asking the students what they want to do with their "Fear" poems. Given the level of honesty expressed in their writing, I am surprised by what I hear in class the next day.

"We want to do a read-around," Deavon asserts. Everyone else agrees.

"OK." OK as in, *Are you sure you want to go that deep?* "Who wants to go first?"

Pierre raises his hand. "I will."

Pierre is one of the most challenging students at PYB. He has yet to write more than five or six lines in class. He is hanging on by a thread, having been sent home on a number of occasions by staff for refusing to work, for making threatening comments to others. He has spent time in jail. By his own admission, he is a fighter with anger management problems. He once was a championship wrestler from a famed program in Portland's African American community, but he also knows the violent side of making a living on the street. He is a new father trying hard to change his life for the better.

The class grows quiet. Pierre clears his throat and says, "OK, y'all, here we go," as if warning everyone to hang for a wild ride.

When he finishes, a pin-drop silence is followed by spontaneous applause.

I ask students to share with Pierre what they like about his piece.

"It was just so honest."

"I liked the line where you said, 'Fear of going back to drugs.' I feel the same way. I mean, what if I get out of here and there just ain't no job for me? I don't want to go back to slinging dope, but I got kids and a fella's got to do what a fella's got to do. I feel you, my brother." Pierre's classmate saunters over to him and gives him a hug with two taps on his back.

Another student turns to Pierre and says, "I know what you mean when you wrote about people taking kindness for a weakness. I feel that all the time, like I got to be tough all the time. I can't let my guard down or else somebody will get me."

Similar comments and gestures follow. Pierre breaks down some important barriers for the class. It is OK to show some vulnerability, to talk about fears, to share genuine emotion with classmates.

Ben goes next. Ben and Pierre first met when they were in jail together. They reconnected at PYB and share a mutual respect.

As Ben reads the final line in his poem, he is like a rap star after a show. He dances around the classroom basking in his classmates' accolades. "I'm bad. That's right." He either hugs or exchanges handshakes with everyone in the room before returning to his seat.

And then it is Deavon's turn. Her big blue eyes survey her poem quietly. Her right wrist, heavily adorned with bracelets, tries to steady the hand that holds her page. Alexxis, seated beside her, whispers some

words of support.

A palpable momentum surges around our reading circle. Reluctant students ask if they can be next to read. Classmates shout encouragement, as if those who read their pieces just got off Pierre's scary ride: "It's fun, you can do it."

Katie shares:

Fear of failing as a mother
Fear of losing my father to his good friend alcohol
Fear of trusting the wrong person again

And Mikey:

Fear of being arrested for mistaken ID
Fear of going to prison for life
Fear of being charged with a crime I didn't do

When class ends, I'm on cloud nine. I want to tell someone, anyone, what just happened. I go home after school and take my dog for a walk. He is more interested in the plethora of scents that inhabit the field where we walk than in my excited tales of the day. The day's joy is soon tempered by questions about what to do tomorrow. How do I follow what happened today? How can I build on the energy, authenticity, sense of community, and learning that we celebrated in today's writing class?

Students Reject a Dr. Phil Approach

I succumb to an Oprah moment and decide that I will have students take their "Fear" poems and turn them into affirmations. I'll have Pierre turn "Fear of people taking my kindness for weakness" into "My kindness is a strength." It seems like a good idea. I'll help students turn their pain into power.

I begin our next class by handing back the "Fear" poems and sharing my thoughts on the class. "I was really touched by your honesty and inspired by the

How do I connect with a core that allows my students to safely find their way through the toxic worlds in which they live?

places you got to in your writing. We all carry a lot of fear. Dealing with it is important because often fears get in the way of doing what we know is the right thing to do. So, today we are going to try to take our fears and turn them into positive statements, into affirmations."

I offer the example of Pierre's line about kindness being seen as weakness. I follow with a few more examples. Deavon is shaking her head.

"What?" I ask.

"Tom, you're scaring me. You're sounding a bit too much like Dr. Phil."

Chance, one of the most thoughtful students I have, emerges from his back-of-the-room slumber. "I see what you're trying to do, man, but you're missing something. Don't get me wrong, I'm not trying to be critical, man, but it's not that easy. It's not like we can just change our minds about the way our lives are and everything will get better. Shit happens to us, man. Look, I know all of us have made some bonehead choices along the way, I sure have, but we've also had a lot of stuff come down on us. I'm not trying to make excuses, but shit just happens to us. Do you guys agree, or am I crazy?"

Most students agree. Some have to digest Deavon's and Chance's words. Some aren't sure if it's OK to question a teacher like their classmates just did. Chance isn't crazy, but he does have those wild eyes, and swears he sees a conspiracy behind every bush (or Bush, as he likes to say).

We talk. Bottom line is that my lesson isn't going to work. The students aren't going to do it and, to be honest, I agree with Deavon and Chance.

The high of yesterday is threatened by the sobering reality of today. What happens now?

If I agree with Chance—that students have made some poor decisions, but those decisions have been made within a context defined by race, class, and cultural dynamics that disempower many of my students—then we need to explore the things that besiege them.

Search for a Collective Story

My initial goals for writing class were simple: motivate students to write, break down their resistance to writing, help them find their voices, use prompts that connect with their experience, and expose them to a variety of genres. In short: inspire them to write, to write more, and to write with passion and authenticity.

Now I'm asking students to use writing to heal open wounds. The first step of their healing is to identify their fears. Then I need to support my students as they explore the reality that their fears are not attributable simply to poor choices they have made.

The next step is for the students to locate their fears in the context of their considerable collective experience. Their fears, exacerbated by their sense of isolation and powerlessness, are not their fault. If writing can be used to explore and share individual fears, it can also be used to explore the social roots of my students' predicament. And, because we have the luxury of working together in a school with a deep commitment to social justice, my students can continue to build on their work in other classes.

The young people with whom I work have remarkable stories to tell. Their writing is not simply the stories of individuals who have made boneheaded decisions along a miserable path of failure; their writing is part of a collective story of survival in the face of daily crises, obstacles, and injustices. I continue to search for writing prompts that will push this exploration forward, and to work with colleagues to develop complementary activities throughout our curriculum.

It's another day, and we find ourselves settled in a writing reverie. Again, a police car screams by the front of our school. Again, students pull back from their computers, raise their hands in mock surrender, and we all crack up. This time our concentration is no longer handcuffed in the back of a speeding car. We get back to work.

Before class ends, I ask, "Is everyone finished writing?"

No, we're not finished. We're just getting started. ✳

. . . .

Tom McKenna teaches at Rosemary Anderson High School (POIC) in Portland, Ore.

Resource

Raymond Carver's poem "Fear" can be found online at writersalmanac.publicradio.org/index.php?date=2002/08/02.

FEAR
by Pierre Sails

Fear of GOD!!!
Fear of going back to prison
Fear of being a bad father
Fear of making amends
Fear of not making amends
Fear of my past taking over
Fear of being confused
Fear of death
Fear of guilt
Fear of people taking my kindness for weakness
Fear of growing up
Fear of not growing up
Fear of paying my own bills
Fear of being broke
Fear of going back to drugs
Fear of making the wrong choices
Fear of feeling it was the only choice I had
Fear of my daughter growing up
Fear of not giving my daughter what she needs
Fear of making mistakes and not learning from
    them!!!!!!!!!!!!
Fear of getting old
Fear of dying alone
Fear of being ME!

FEAR
by Ben Teasley

Fear of po-po. . .
Fear of going to sleep behind bars
Fear of never waking up
Fear of loving someone who don't love me
Fear of growing old alone
Fear of relapse
Fear of my daughters meeting men like me
Fear of happiness
Fear of a life that is not really mine
Fear of the man who will have the heart to take my life
Fear of the devil who will take my soul
Fear of not wanting to trust no one
Fear of not knowing
Fear of knowing too much
Fear of myself
Fear of the end when
I know this is just the beginning.

. . . .

FEAR
by Deavon Snoke

Fear of everyone being right about me
Fear of being right about myself. . .
Fear of relapse
Fear of recovery
Fear of figuring out who I am without drugs
Fear of my younger siblings finding out who I was. . .
Fear of anything I have to purchase in a park
Fear of an empty funeral home. . .
Fear of unfamiliar phone numbers
Fear of familiar phone numbers with unfamiliar voices
Fear of "sit down, we need to talk". . .
Fear of not proving everyone wrong
Fear of people knowing I'm afraid

Knock, Knock

Turning pain into power

BY LINDA CHRISTENSEN

SCOTT BAKAL

Too often today, schools are about standards and common curriculum: *Scarlet Letter* and *Huck Finn* first quarter, move on to *Great Gatsby*. . . . And too often, I get caught up in that land too. Then my heart gets cracked open by students, and I remember that first I must teach the child who is in the class. By structuring a curriculum that allows room for students' lives and by listening to their stories, I can locate the right book, the right poem that turns pain into power while I teach reading and writing. Unless I consciously build these opportunities into the curriculum, there is little hope of getting authenticity from students.

Daniel Beaty, poet and playwright, came to life for me one New Year's Eve when my husband, Bill, and I watched hour after hour of the HBO show *Def Poetry Jam*. I fell in love with many poets that night, but when I watched Beaty perform "Knock Knock," I knew I was witnessing a poet whose performance and words would inspire my students. I bought the *Def Poetry* DVD, transcribed the words, and carried Beaty with me to class. Partly autobiographical, the poem speaks directly to many of my students because of Beaty's drive-home message: In order to heal ourselves, our society, and our world, we must turn our pain into power.

When poetry, like Beaty's, touches students' lives in real ways, I am reminded of both the pain and the hope that schools harbor.

"Knock Knock" is constructed in three parts. Beaty begins with the story of the father's imprisonment, moves to a direct address to the father ("Papa, come home 'cause I miss you"), and ends in a letter that the poet writes to "heal" and "father" himself. The poem and Beaty's performance are so powerful that I didn't want to interrupt it with instruction or teacher talk before students watched it the first time. I wanted them to feel the poem. My only instruction was "As you watch the poem, notice what works for you or doesn't work. Just jot notes, so we can talk about it after we watch it a couple of times."

After students watched the poem twice, I asked them to take a few silent minutes to write their thoughts about the poem. "Look at the copy of the poem. What did you like or notice about the poem?" Students started off by talking about what they liked about the poem—from content to form. Greg said, "I like how the poem progresses from when he was young and dependent to the point when he got older and stronger." Jerome said, "He used repetition by repeating the words 'knock knock.' Nothing was sugarcoated. I also like that it tells a story of pain. The story wasn't a nice-feeling, sweet one talking about love or flowers and moonlight. I connected to the story." Theresa liked "how the end of the poem is like a letter from his father that he wrote himself." When Shontay said, "I loved the line, 'Knock, knock down the doors of racism and poverty that I could not,'" many students nodded in agreement. I have watched Beaty perform this poem many times, and I still get goose bumps and tears every time he hits that line. Demetrius spoke up, "This last part makes me think of how many positive things our generation can do. How much potential we have."

Harriet said, "You know, I really like the part during the letter where he says, 'We are our fathers' sons and daughters/But we are not their choices.' We aren't the reason they made bad choices. We aren't part of

their choices, and their decisions aren't our fault." I was stunned. I had taught this poem for several years with my classes at Grant High School, and I'd never thought about how children might feel like they might bear the burden of guilt for their parents' "choices." But Harriet's comment reminded me that as a child I shouldered a lot of fear about my future based on my family's history: Would I graduate from high school? Would I go to college when no one else in my family had? Would I get pregnant and be chained to a minimum wage job? Was my father's alcoholism a genetic stain that could explode my dreams and shackle me to relive my parents' story? Beaty's poem allowed those fears to surface in class.

Harriet's comment prompted me to share my fears when I was their age, and I asked, "What are your fears? What chains of the past do you drag around with you? What are you afraid of? What do you worry about?" Students wrote lists of their fears. Then we shared. Harriet said, "The women in my family have all

In order to heal ourselves, our society, and our world, we must turn our pain into power.

had children before they graduated from high school, and I'm going to break that cycle." When one student opens the door for an honest conversation, others follow, especially if I create the space by responding to the student's remark instead of rushing past it. So I said, "Yes, I was afraid of that too. Does anyone else have that fear?" A few other young women raised their hands.

Mark said, "My father went to jail, so I can relate to how he felt when his father never came home. A lot of Black men could relate to this poem. Like having to teach themselves things because of an absent father."

Larry said, "My dad went to school at Jefferson. He never graduated, and now he's in prison. I'm going to break that cycle." Another student added, "My mother went here too. She had a bad temper, and she got expelled for fighting. I don't want to get expelled for fighting." Other students shared their fears: Getting shot, becoming a drug addict, not graduating, losing a parent, not measuring up to their parents' expectations.

Writing the Poem

To move students to write the poem, I asked students to look at these three parts of the poem. "Read back over each part and write in the margin what the poet is writing about, how you connect to that part, and why you think it changes his writing style in each section." With a little nudging, students picked up on the story, the direct address, and the letter format of the poem. I didn't labor over this part of the lesson. I wanted to call attention to it, so students could build their poems in a similar style.

I gave them the following assignment: "Taking a page from Daniel Beaty, write a letter poem to yourself, giving yourself the advice you need to hear. Notice how Beaty begins with a story, then moves into the letter part of the poem that he writes to heal himself.

"Write a letter poem to yourself, giving yourself the advice you need to hear."

In his letter, he lists advice to himself: 'Shave in one direction, dribble the page with your brilliance.'"

"What advice do you need to hear? What do you need to do differently to succeed in school? In life? Beaty writes of the obstacles that need to be knocked down in his life: Racism, lack of opportunity. Are there obstacles in your life? Perhaps you have your school, friend, and home life together, then think of someone else who might need to hear a few words of advice."

"As an adult, there are things I wish my mother would have told me. This is not an indictment against her. Sometimes, children aren't ready to hear their parents. Also, we grow up in different times, different social periods."

Then I shared the beginnings of my poem and showed how I started with the apology, then moved from the negative to the positive in the second stanza. I also highlighted Beaty's lines to use as a frame for the poem:

Dear Linda,
I'm sorry for the nights I left you alone
after your father died.
I'm sorry for the solitary dinners

you ate those nights I chose a man over you.
For every lesson I failed to teach, hear these
   words:
Don't marry a man who drinks.
He'll spend money on booze
instead of the family.
If a man hits you once,
   he'll hit you again.
Pack your bags and leave.
Move on.
When school gets hard,
remember your brilliance.
Diamonds require hard work. . .

Although most students wrote to themselves, a few wrote poems to other people who they thought needed advice. Andrew wrote from his father's point of view: "As I sit in a tiny cell, it amazes me how the two of us can hardly ever speak or see each other in 16 years, and yet still go through so much together. Don't do the same idiotic decisions as me. Don't let the girls, gangs, and drugs ruin both of our lives. I apologize for choosing the streets over my own son."

Another student's father had died the night before our assignment. Lester wrote, "I'm sorry for leaving you five years ago without saying goodbye. . . . Son, do all you can to be better than me. Go to school and learn until your skull cracks. Grow up to be a wonderful father to your kids. Be there for them before they walk to the edge. . . . Son, I'm glad you're not here because I'm on a bed with wires attached to me and a machine that beeps every three seconds. I have to go because heaven is open, and I got to get in because this is the only way I can see you from a different angle."

Another student wrote a paragraph in response: "It's crazy how you love a man who was never there. I just learned not to care. When you say you're going to come to my games and you don't come, there's no disappointment. When you don't call on my birthday, there's no disappointment. Don't get me wrong, I love you, but you showed me everything I don't need to do. . . . Can you imagine the look on a little boy's face when the man he looks up to goes to the store for milk and never comes home. . . . Because of all those broken promises, I love you because you showed me how not to cry. I'm no longer weak."

Noah's poem below followed the format and

broke it at the same time. I love the way he played with the credit card commercial.

> Dear Father,
> Pay me!
> Pay me well and
> pay me now.
> Not with your hundreds of thousands
> of millions of dollars.
>
> Pay me some damn attention!
> My first bike: $87.00
> Varsity basketball: $175.00
> Having a care: Priceless.

Students need opportunities to hone their skills, to write essays, to practice becoming academics. They also need opportunities to write about the tough issues in their lives that rarely surface in schools. Beaty's work opened their veins, so they could write with the blood of their lives. ✳

. . . .

Linda Christensen (lmc@lclark.edu) is director of the Oregon Writing Project at Lewis & Clark College in Portland, Ore. She is a Rethinking Schools editor and author of Reading, Writing, and Rising Up *and* Teaching for Joy and Justice.

Resource

Beaty, Daniel. "Knock, Knock." Beaty's performance of "Knock Knock" is on his website: danielbeaty.com/wordpress/audios-videos/.

Knock Knock

by Daniel Beaty

As a boy I shared a game with my father.
Played it every morning 'til I was 3.
He would knock knock on my door,
and I'd pretend to be asleep
'til he got right next to the bed,
Then I would get up and jump into his arms.
"Good morning, Papa."
And my papa he would tell me that he loved me.
We shared a game.
Knock Knock

Until that day when the knock never came
and my mama takes me on a ride past cornfields
on this never-ending highway 'til we reach a place of
    high rusty gates.
A confused little boy,
I entered the building carried in my mama's arms.
Knock Knock

We reach a room of windows and brown faces
behind one of the windows sits my father.
I jump out of my mama's arms
and run joyously towards my papa
Only to be confronted by this window.
I knock knock trying to break through the glass,
trying to get to my father.
I knock knock as my mama pulls me away
before my papa even says a word.

And for years he has never said a word.
And so twenty-five years later, I write these words
for the little boy in me who still awaits his papa's
    knock.

Papa, come home 'cause I miss you.
I miss you waking me up in the morning and telling
    me you love me.
Papa, come home, 'cause there's things I don't know,
and I thought maybe you could teach me:
How to shave;
how to dribble a ball;
how to talk to a lady;
how to walk like a man.
Papa, come home because I decided a while back
I wanted to be just like you.

but I'm forgetting who you are.

And twenty-five years later a little boy cries,
and so I write these words and try to heal
and try to father myself
and I dream up a father who says the words my father
    did not.

Dear Son,
I'm sorry I never came home.
For every lesson I failed to teach, hear these words:
Shave in one direction in strong deliberate strokes to
    avoid irritation
Dribble the page with the brilliance of your ballpoint
    pen.
Walk like a god and your goddess will come to you.
No longer will I be there to knock on your door,
So you must learn to knock for yourself.
Knock knock down doors of racism and poverty that I
    could not.
Knock knock down doors of opportunity
for the lost brilliance of the black men who crowd
    these cells.
Knock knock with diligence for the sake of your
    children.
Knock knock for me for as long as you are free,
these prison gates cannot contain my spirit.
The best of me still lives in you.
Knock knock with the knowledge that you are my son,
but you are not my choices.
Yes, we are our fathers' sons and daughters,
But we are not their choices.
For despite their absences we are still here.
Still alive, still breathing
With the power to change this world,
One little boy and girl at a time.
Knock knock
Who's there?
We are.

Dear Father

by Noah Koné

Dear Father,

Pay me!
Pay me well and
pay me now.
Not with your hundreds of thousands
of millions of dollars.
Pay me some damn attention!

My first bike: $87.00
Varsity basketball: $175.00
Having a care: Priceless.

Charge to your card, a hug or even
a pat on the back.
Write me a check for some words of encouragement.
Send me a money order for the missed birthdays.
Your dollars will never be enough, but
Your time is priceless.
Your love is priceless.

Black Like Me

BY RENÉE WATSON

When I was in middle school, I was bused to the other side of town for my education. Portland Public Schools wanted to integrate middle schools in Southeast Portland. This meant that a handful of Black students—most of us from Northeast Portland who had attended elementary school together—boarded a yellow school bus before sunrise to ride across town. We sat at the back of the bus laughing at the boys stinging on each other with yo momma jokes. My best friend and I shared the headphones to her Walkman so that we both could sing along to Bell Biv DeVoe and Mariah Carey. For the 30-minute ride we were ourselves and there was no shame in the way we talked or related to each other. No one made a big deal about seeing my hair in braids one day and straightened the next. We bragged about how well our mommas cooked and shared our leftovers with each other at lunchtime, even though one day a white girl loudly whispered to her friend that "Black food smells bad."

We had pride and there was a care we took with each other. Though there were normal middle school cliques and dramas, there was also a strength and loyalty among us. On that bus, we were family. I felt like I belonged.

But when I got to school, I felt invisible. Which is ironic because I was a plump dark-skinned girl with hair that would kink and curl at one drop of rain.

I stood out.

So how is it that I felt no one saw me?

Being seen—truly seen—is to feel that all parts of who I am are recognized not as compartmentalized pieces of myself, but blended truths of my identity. So when my white friends told me they didn't see me as a Black girl that meant they didn't see me. When white teachers seemed shocked to hear me speak Black vernacular in the hallway with my friends when I "spoke so well in class," what they didn't understand is that code-switching came natural to me—I talked both ways and I wasn't trying to fit in with my friends or impress my teachers. I was being myself.

One day, on our way to a field trip to see the Oregon Symphony, a teacher tried to assure me that if I "gave the music a try" I might really find that I liked it. I told her that I loved classical music. That I loved jazz, too. Her smile told me that she thought this was a good thing. When she said, "Well, that's good because that rap stuff is not music," I told her that I loved hip-hop and R&B and gospel and country, too. My family was a musical family. We had a collection of records that included Tennessee Ernie Ford, Mahalia Jackson, Marvin Gaye, and the Jackson 5. My sister played in a jazz ensemble that traveled to Europe. My grandfather played the piano at church.

She didn't seem to value the variety of music I enjoyed. There was clearly one that was better than the others and I took this to mean that the Black parts of me were better off hidden. There was a shame that came with owning up to the parts of me that fit the stereotypes and assumptions of what people expected Black children to be like.

In middle school I learned that some adults saw me as an "exception to the rule." To be called confident for an overweight, dark-skinned Black girl was to say that overweight, dark-skinned black girls had low self-esteem. If I was smart for a Black girl that meant the rule was Black children weren't normally smart.

It was one thing to feel different, to be different. It was another thing to be judged on those differences. To realize that people had expectations of me because of what I looked like or the neighborhood I was from.

I often excused racist or insensitive remarks and actions, and instead blamed myself or thought that maybe I was taking it the wrong way.

But there was no excusing away what my 7th-grade science teacher said the day she passed out the tests we had taken a few days before. She walked to the front of the room and yelled, "I am so disappointed in all of you!" She paced the floor, walking between our desks. "None of you passed the test. You will be taking it again. Right. Now."

I looked down at my paper. Saw the capital A scribbled in red ink across the top of the page.

"I will give you a chance to look through your notes and then you will retake the test."

I looked back at my paper. "But I have an A," I said. First to myself and then out loud when I raised my hand and asked, "Do I have to retake the test?"

"Oh, that's right," my teacher said. "You got an A." She turned her back to me and addressed the rest of the class. "And this is why I am so disappointed in all of you. You let Renée Watson come all the way over here from Northeast Portland and get a better grade than you in science!"

I have often replayed that day in my mind. I have thought of new endings where I stand up for myself and walk out of class refusing to be humiliated. I have wondered what would have happened if she asked me to be a tutor for the other students in class. What if she taught me—and the rest of the class—about black scientists and their revolutionary discoveries? What if she had allowed space in her narrative for Black children from Northeast Portland to be capable of meeting high expectations, of achieving academic success?

What if she really saw me?

As an educator, I try to see my students. I encourage them to embrace all parts of their culture—where they come from, what they eat, the music they enjoy, the joyous and disastrous parts of their neighborhoods and families. I strive to learn their individual and collective histories. I share my stories with them, and we grow and heal together. We laugh at ourselves for sometimes being the stereotype. We proudly proclaim that we are more than the stereotype. We mourn and rejoice over our ancestors—their struggles and victories, their shortcomings and strengths. We commit to sharing our true selves. We commit to seeing each other. ✳

. . . .

Renée Watson (reneewatson.net) is an author, performer, and educator. Her children's books have received several honors, including an NAACP Image Award nomination. She teaches poetry at DreamYard in New York City.

black like me

by Renée Watson

black like me

and suddenly everyone would see

how black i am.

black like collard greens & salted meat simmering on
    a stove.
black like hot water cornbread & iron skillets, like
    juke joints & fish frys
black like soul train lines & the electric slide at
    weddings and birthdays
black like vaseline on ashy knees, like beads
    decorating braids
black like cotton fields & soul-cried spirituals.

my skin is black

like red kool-aid, red soda, the red blood
of the lynched and assassinated and the african man
those skinheads killed with a baseball bat when i was
    in the fifth grade.

i am as black as he was.
my science teacher knows this. she sees
my black and is blind to my brilliance.
can't believe i passed the test with an a
when all the white kids failed.

and when she says to the white students,
"you ought to be ashamed of yourselves. . ."
what she really wants to say is, "i can't believe this
    black girl is as smart as you."

all the white kids look at me
and this is when we learn that the color of our shells
come with expectations.

i stop being good
at science and math.

my english teacher gives me books and journals
and i read and write the world
as it is, as i want it to be.
i read past my black blues, discover that i am black
like benjamin banneker and george washington carver
black like margaret walker and fannie lou hamer

i am not just slave and despair.
i am struggle and triumph. i learn
to live my life in the searching, in the quest:

can i be black and brilliant?
can i be jazz and gospel, hip-hop and classical?
can i be christian and accepting?
can i be big and beautiful?

can i be black like me?
can anyone see me?

Keepers of the Second Throat

BY PATRICIA SMITH

MELANIE CERVANTES

Let me introduce you to my mother, Annie Pearl Smith of Aliceville, Ala. In the 1950s, along with thousands of other apprehensive but determined Southerners, their eyes locked on the second incarnation of the North Star, she packed up her whole life and headed for the city, with its tenements, its promise, its rows of factories like open mouths feeding on hope.

One day not too long ago, I called my mother, but she was too busy to talk to me. She seemed in a great hurry. When I asked her where she was going, she said, "I'm on my way to my English lesson."

My Mother Learns English

I.
Jittery emigrant at 64, my mother is learning English.
Pulling rubbery cinnamon-tinged hose to a roll beneath
her knees, sporting one swirling Baptist ski slope of a hat,
she rides the rattling elevated to a Windy City spire
and pulls back her gulp as the elevator hurtles heaven.
Then she's stiffly seated at a scarred oak table
across from a white, government-sanctioned savior
who has dedicated eight hours a week to straightening
afflicted black tongues. She guides my mother
patiently through lazy *ings* and *ers*, slowly scraping
her throat clean of the moist and raging infection
of Aliceville, Alabama. There are muttered apologies for
colored sounds. There is much beginning again.
I want to talk right before I die.
Want to stop saying 'ain't' and 'I done been'
like I ain't got no sense. I'm a grown woman.
I done lived too long to be stupid,
acting like I just got off the boat.
My mother
has never been
on a boat.
But 50 years ago, merely a million of her,
clutching strapped cases, *Jet*'s Emmett Till issue,
and thick-peppered chicken wings in waxed bags,
stepped off hot rumbling buses at Northern depots
in Detroit, in Philly, in the bricked cornfield of Chicago.
Brushing stubborn scarlet dust from their shoes,
they said *We North now*, slinging it in backdoor syllable,
as if those three words were vessels big enough
to hold country folks' overwrought ideas of light.

II.
Back then, my mother thought it a modern miracle,
this new living in a box stacked upon other boxes,
where every flat surface reeked of Lysol and effort
and chubby roaches, cross-eyed with Raid,
dragged themselves across freshly washed dishes
and dropped dizzy from the ceiling into our Murphy beds,
our washtubs, our open steaming pots of collards.
Of course, there was a factory just two bus rides close,
a job that didn't involve white babies or bluing laundry,
where she worked in tense line with other dreamers:
Repeatedly. Repeatedly. Repeatedly. Repeatedly,
all those oily hot-combed heads drooping, no talking
as scarred brown hands romanced machines, just

the sound of doin' it right, and Juicy Fruit crackling.
A mere mindset away, there had to be a corner tavern
where dead bluesmen begged second chances from the juke,
and where mama, perched man-wary on a stool by the door,
could look like a Christian who was just leaving.
And on Sunday, at Pilgrim Rest Missionary Baptist Church,
she would pull on the pure white gloves of service
and wail to the rafters when the Holy Ghost's hothand
grew itchy and insistent at the small of her back.
She was His child, finally loosed of that damnable Delta,
building herself anew in this land of sidewalks,
blue jukes, and sizzling fried perch in virgin white boxes.
See her: All nap burned from her crown, one gold tooth
winking, soft hair riding her lip, blouses starched hard,
Orlon sweaters with smatterings of stitched roses,
A-line skirts the color of unleashed winter.

III.
My mother's voice is like homemade cornbread,
slathered with butter, full of places for heat to hide.
When she is pissed, it punches straight out
and clears the room. When she is scared,
it turns practical, matter-of-fact, like when she called
to say
They found your daddy this morning,
somebody shot him, he dead.
He ain't come to work this morning, I knowed
something was wrong.
When mama talks, the Southern swing of it
is wild with unexpected blooms,
like the fields she never told me about in Alabama.
Her rap is peppered with *ain't gots* and *I done beens*
and *he be's* just like mine is when I'm color among color.
During worship, talk becomes song. Her voice collapses
and loses all acquaintance with key, so of course,
it's my mother's fractured alto wailing above everyone—
uncaged, unapologetic and creaking toward heaven.
Now she wants to sound proper when she gets there.
A woman got some sense and future need to upright herself,
talk English instead of talking wrong.
It's strange, the precise rote of Annie Pearl's new mouth.
She slips sometimes, but is proud when she remembers
to shun dirt-crafted contractions and double negatives.
Sometimes I wonder what happened to the warm expanse
of the red dust woman, who arrived with a little sin
and all the good wrong words. I dream her breathless,
maybe leaning forward in her seat on the Greyhound.
I ain't never seen, she begins, grinning through the grime
at Chicago, city of huge shoulders, thief of tongues.

Chicago Stole My Mother's Yesterdays

Chicago not only stole my mother's tongue, it also stole all her yesterdays. From the moment her battered shoes touched new ground, she wanted Alabama gone, she wanted nothing more than to scrub the Delta from her skin, rid her voice of that ridiculous twang, pretend and then adopt a city sophistication. She

How do we lose our own voices, how do we hand our stories over to other people to tell?

thought her *ain't gonnas* and *shoulda dids* and *ain'ts* and *been done hads* signaled ignorance, backwoods, branded her as one of those old-time Negroes. Even years later, after she had married my father, raised a daughter and had to know that her corner was not a promised land but no more than an obscenity of brick, she continued her relentless scrubbing. "I want to talk right before I die," she said, each of her words irreparably Alabama even after she paid an articulate white woman to please fix the mistake of her throat.

And how did my mother's insistence on a blank slate affect me? She slams shut when I ask about the faces in curled-corner Polaroids, when I urge her to tell me what kind of girl she was, when I am curious about her mother, father, grandparents, schooling, baptism, about the steamy hamlet of Aliceville, the stores, schoolhouse, was she fast, was she sullen, did she have the gold tooth then, did she sing? Before her confounding sense of shame, her "Don't know why you wanna know about that nasty ol' down South stuff no way," I was robbed of a history that should have been mine as well as hers.

My husband, on the other hand, has diligently traced his huge raucous family back to the early 1800s. He has remarkably preserved portraits, marriage licenses, death certificates, farm inventory, a rusted scale from his grandfather's store, even a yellowed handkerchief that has been passed gently from hand to hand for over 100 years. As we pore over the few faded and sun-stained photos my mother reluctantly parted with, I sound like an impossibility, an orphan with a living parent.

That is my mother, I say, pointing to a teenage stranger with an unmistakable gap-toothed grin. But in every picture she is surrounded by ghosts. I say, "I don't know who that is . . . I don't know who that is," because my mother claims not to remember. In one shot, a ghost turned out to be an aunt I didn't know my mother had.

Right now, if I close my eyes and concentrate, I can't hear my mother's voice. I hear something that sounds like her, but it's a tortured hybrid of the voice she had and the one she wanted so much to have. I've told her story time and time again, and I hear other 50-year-old children tell the same stories of their parents, who spent whole lives trying to reshape their throats, to talk *right* instead of talking *wrong*, ashamed of the sound they made in the world.

How do we lose our own voices? My mother spent her entire life telling me how wrong I was, how my nose was too broad, my hair too crinkled, my skin—Lord, I wish you could be light like cream, like your cousin Demetria. Don't tell anyone your stories, she said, your shameful stories of a mama from Alabama, a daddy from Arkansas, an apartment where roaches dropped from the ceiling into your bed and mice got trapped in the stove, a neighborhood burned down by its own folks right after the riots when that nice Dr. King got killed. Don't tell anyone your stories, stories you should keep to yourself, stories of how your mama and daddy both work in a candy factory, how your auntie lives in those projects, how the apartment we live in's been broken into three times. Don't tell how you live on the West Side, the side everybody tells you to stay away from, and how the school you go to is one of the worst schools in the whole city. And for goodness' sake girl, talk right. If you want to get out of here, ever, you got to talk like white people, and you got to talk about things white people want to hear.

In other words, I was to become a clean, colorless slate, scrubbed of my own history, a slate where people could write my life any way they wanted—any beginning, any middle, any outcome.

How do we lose our own voices, how do we hand our stories over to other people to tell?

The Second Throat

Follow me now to a 6th-grade classroom at Lillie C. Evans Elementary School in Dade County, Liberty City, Miami. For 10 years, I traveled from my home to teach for two weeks. I remember my first day, bounding into the classroom, full of enthusiasm: "I'm here to teach you poetry!" I faced a room of fallen faces: "That's good, but how can you make our lives better?"

I was shocked to learn that these 10- and 11-year-olds had already been told that their voices were not legitimate voices. Look where you live, they'd been told. Look who your mama is, how your daddy in jail. Look how you've lived your whole life in Miami and nobody's ever bothered to take you to see the ocean. Look at all those red marks on your papers, all those bad grades on your report card. Look at that house where you live, how there's no locks on the doors. Look how you've been written off already. In the morning, my kids would come in buzzing about the shots they heard the night before and if anybody knew what had happened, who'd gotten shot. They came in talking gang signs and beatdowns and who went crazy in church with the Holy Ghost and whose brother was locked up now. But when they sat down to write, it was as if they shed their skins and their stories. They'd sit looking blankly at me, their shoulders sagging from sudden shame and the weight of the world: "I can't spell good. I ain't got good handwriting. And Miss Smith, I ain't got nothing to write about."

I spent all my time introducing them to the idea of the second throat. First of all, all your stories are *yours*. I don't care that you've misspelled this word, that you're using double negatives, and I'll figure out that bad handwriting. What matters is the power that flows through you when you pick up a pen. And you can take any story, even stories that wear on your nerves and sag your shoulders, you can take those stories and you can turn them to triumph. You can pick up a pen and make your whole life make sense. The idea that you can take control of how events affect you—and that includes the mama on drugs, the locked-up brother—the idea that you can process that life through language and come out on the other side a better person, a smarter kid, one who doesn't get beat down by circumstance, but learns how to learn from it.

And they wait. They wait for you. They wait for me. The quiet bespectacled boy with his mind tangled in math is waiting for you. That girl who dressed two sizes too blue is waiting for you. The child who never lifts his eyes is really looking at you, through you, and she is waiting. That tall lanky boy who lives to make everyone laugh is waiting for you. That one white child in a sea of black is waiting for you. That one Black child in a sea of white is waiting for you. The one who takes the bus in from the suburbs is waiting for you. Not just the children with the hard, untellable stories, the stories they hold shamed and close to their chests, but any child with a yesterday is looking for a way to sing tomorrow. They wait for you to open another door beyond verb and adjective, punctuation and equation, beyond memorized fact and pop quiz and line and intersection and angle. They wait for you to open a door that leads to their own lives.

So there is hope. Every single time I walk into a classroom. I tell my story, the story of my parents in the South, the story of growing up in a place that was expected to defeat me. I celebrate every single word a child says, every movement of their pen on paper, and I'm mesmerized when those stories begin to emerge. I stop what I'm doing and I listen. We've got to teach that every utterance, every story is legitimate, that they exist to help you process your own life, to help you move your own life forward, not to complete anyone else's

We've got to teach that every utterance, every story is legitimate.

picture of you. Never relinquish control of your own life and the stories that have formed you. Write them down and read them to yourselves if no one else wants to hear. My mother used to say, "Ain't nobody trying to hear that nonsense." In the beginning, it doesn't matter if anyone wants to hear. What matters is what you have to say.

I've told you about my mother, about the tragedy of a voice lost, but now let me tell you about my daddy.

It Began with My Father

Grizzled and slight, flasher of a marquee gold tooth, Otis Douglas Smith was Arkansas grit suddenly sporting city clothes. Also part of the Great Migration of Blacks from the South to Northern cities in the early 1950s, he found himself not in the urban mecca he'd imagined, but in a cramped tenement apartment on Chicago's West Side. There he attempted to craft a life alongside the bag boys, day laborers, housekeepers, and cooks who dreamed the city's wide, unreachable dream.

Many of those urban refugees struggled to fit, but my father never really adopted the no-nonsense-now rhythm of the city. He never handed his story over. There was too much of the storyteller in him, too much unleashed Southern song still waiting for the open air.

From the earliest days I can recall, my place was on his lap, touching a hand to his stubbled cheek and listening to his growled narrative, mysterious whispers, and wide-open laughter.

Because of him, I grew to think of the world in

For every minute you stand before them, you are the beacon, the whole of possibility, the keeper of the second throat.

terms of the stories it could tell. From my father's moonlit tales of steaming Delta magic to the sweet slow songs of Smokey Robinson, I became addicted to unfolding drama, winding narrative threads, the lyricism of simple words. I believed that we all lived in the midst of an ongoing adventure that begged for voice. In my quest for that voice, I found poetry.

Poetry was the undercurrent of every story I heard and read. It was the essence, the bones, and the pulse. I could think of no better way to communicate than with a poem, where pretense is stripped away, leaving only what is beautiful and vital.

Poetry became the way I processed the world. In neon-washed bars, community centers, and bookstores, I breathed out necessary breath, taking the stage and sharing stanzas with strangers, anxious wordsmiths who were also bag boys, day laborers, housekeepers, and cooks. I loved the urgency of their voices and the way they sparked urgency in mine.

So, like you and you and you, I'm a storyteller—and so are your children. I've realized that we only get one life, and I've decided to own mine completely, to celebrate and mourn and lash out and question and believe and argue and explore and love and dismiss and fight on the page, at the front of a classroom, on the stage. No one, no one is authorized to tell that story but you. And if there is shame in that story, you own that shame and you turn it into lesson. If there

is darkness in your story, you write toward the light. If there are words you don't want anyone else to hear, you hold those words close. On the other hand, if there is joy threaded throughout that story, you sing it loud enough to rock the rafters. If there is triumph, and there will always be, in some measure, you pull everyone within the sound of your voice, within shouting distance of the page, into that circle of light.

A teacher standing at the front of a classroom is a little bit of religion. It doesn't matter if you are in Portland or Philadelphia or Kentucky or Indianapolis, whether you are overpaid or overlooked, whether your students soar thru their AP classes or stumble through single-syllable words, whether your school is five wings or five stories, it doesn't matter if the buildings are drab and fallen and surrounded by a dying neighborhood or glittering and expansive enough to brag its own ZIP code, it doesn't matter whether your students are colored like snow or sand or soil. For every minute you stand before them, *you* are the beacon, the whole of possibility, the keeper of the second throat. Like it or not, you are often the first chapter in the story they're writing with their lives. Their parents taught them to speak. Now you must teach them to speak aloud, to keep on speaking, to scream and to sing.

I am Patricia Ann Smith, the daughter of Annie Pearl Smith and Otis Douglas Smith. I am the story they wrote.

Stop. Say your name aloud.

Now find a way to tell your story. And find a way to introduce all those children who wait for you to that second throat. ✳

....

"Keepers of the Second Throat" was originally delivered as the keynote address at the Urban Sites Network Conference of the National Writing Project, Portland, Ore., April 2010.

Patricia Smith is the author of five volumes of poetry, including Blood Dazzler, *a finalist for the National Book Award, and* Teahouse of the Almighty. *Her most recent book is* Shoulda Been Jimi Savannah.

CHAPTER SIX

The Craft of Poetry

ROGER PEET

Ode to Writing

by Jessica Rawlins

I screamed
and scribbled
tore words from within
that were never meant to match.
I lived the story,
tortured the page
like life and death.
It was the fear that drove me
somewhere in my stomach
remembering the thought
of spilled words
numbers of them
that didn't make sense.
I yearned to be eloquent,
understood.
Somehow
the writing
bandaged the wounds,
made up for the words
not spoken
on the page.
I became powerful,
invincible,
knowing I could always be better
from the inside.
I spelled out a new name
making myself a face
with paper,
pen, and ink.

The Craft of Poetry

In the introduction to *A Poetry Handbook*, Mary Oliver wrote, "Everyone knows that poets are born and not made in school." We disagree. Over the years, we have witnessed students blossom as poets. We know that when we saturate children in the works of writers whose poetry helps them view the world in new ways, whose stanzas connect joy and grief with hope and justice, whose pieces provide inspiration for students' new poems to arise, that children can become poets in school and in the world.

Poet and teacher William Stafford offered an opposing perspective to Oliver's about the birth of poets. He wrote, "Everyone is born a poet—a person discovering the way words sound and work, caring and delighting in words. I just kept on doing what everyone starts out doing. The real question is: Why did other people stop?"

We believe that teachers must offer poetry not as a dried-up unit where students study other people's poetry every April, but as a living, breathing way to understand the world daily. We also believe that poetry is more than a series of skill lessons and exercises to be performed mechanically in class. Students need to care about their writing, and that means that all poetry begins first in a curriculum that matters, that encourages students to grapple with big issues in their families, neighborhoods, and world.

In earlier chapters in this book, we demonstrate an inquiry approach to teaching poetry, "raising the bones" of a poem through close examination of published and student authors. We look for repeating lines, strong verbs, storytelling, content—and then students push off those models to write their own poems. But there are times when we need to explicitly teach the craft of poetry writing. In the lessons in this chapter, we continue to immerse students in poetry, encouraging them to pay attention to how writers approach topics and apply poetic tools, then we isolate one or two craft lessons that we want them to learn: how to use strong verbs, lists, repeating lines, figurative language, and line breaks.

These craft lessons lay the foundation for our revision work, for giving birth to poets in our classrooms. ✳

Image Craft Lesson
Writing from photos and art

BY LINDA CHRISTENSEN

Felisbela 15annos

Felisbela lives in Monte Cafe. Her mother, Madeleina cooked Cachupa for the Cape Verde celebration at Monte Cafe.

SHADRA STRICKLAND

The image is the snapshot we retain years after an event, the one that stalks our dreams. It can be an actual photograph or it can be a rerun that our minds conjure up. But imagery in poetry is more than a mental photograph: It includes all five senses. We might remember making ice cream with a hand crank on the front porch every time we smell strawberries. A song on the radio or playing over the sound system in a luncheonette might take us back to a high school dance at the Lemon Tree. Smells and sounds can make a day in our childhood come back, every detail sharp and precise, as we hear a shallow creek running over the rocks, watch a newt pushing off the ledge, taste watermelon. Images are linked to memory. That's why they are powerful—and necessary in poetry.

Images are more than pretty words. I teach the craft of imagery in every poetry lesson. The "Where I'm From" poem, for example, saturates students in the imagery of their homes—from the kinds of magazines stacked next to the sofa, to the smell of lutefisk or rice and beans on the stove, to the repeated words of a mother or father on a road trip, "Do I need to stop this car?" Praise poems, odes, dialogue poems all steep students in images of people and places.

But I explicitly teach imagery through the use of photographs. One glorious day when I was a relatively new teacher, I invited William Stafford to come to my class, and he did. He asked students to write about a photograph, "a real one or one that you wish you had. Tell me what's in the photo." That simple direction created a tidal wave of poems from my students. I have used and tweaked his lesson over and over again for years.

The Personal Photo Poem

Sometimes student poetry suffers from the overuse of abstract nouns, like love and friendship. These poems wallow in clichés. I call these ghost poems. The photo poetry assignment helps students develop concrete images by clothing their ghosts as they describe details from the pictures. I use poems by former Jefferson High School students as mentor texts to help spark students' personal poems: Katrine Barber's "Photograph, 1969" and "Applegate Dam," and "Curly Bird" by Lila Johnson.

Katrine Barber's poem "Photograph, 1969" describes a photo of Katrine's mother when she is pregnant with Katrine (see p. 217). After I distributed her poem, I asked students, "What do you notice about the poem? What calls your attention?"

Lisa pointed out: "I like the line where she writes, 'lifting her hair/like a low whistle/off of her neck.'" This line has stayed with me since Katrine wrote it in 1987.

Jodelle remarked, "It's as if she's standing next to you, pointing to the photograph and telling you about it."

I said, "Tell me more about that. How does she make us see the picture in the poem, without us actually seeing the photo?"

Jodelle leaned over the page, dragging her finger across the lines, "See how she is lifting her hair, her fingers caught in the hair, the silver earrings. Then she shows us her father behind the lens, and her mother pregnant with Katrine."

"Those are the concrete details. We could draw the photo from her description. That's what I want you to do when you write your poems," I added.

"But my favorite part is at the end," Jodelle said. "She makes a statement about the photo. It's where

I teach the craft of imagery in every poetry lesson.

she moves beyond the details of the photo to show us something else about that moment." Jodelle's point is what Addonizio and Laux discuss in *The Poet's Companion: A Guide to the Pleasures of Writing Poetry*: "Images are seductive in themselves, but they're not merely scenery, or shouldn't be. An image, when it's doing its full work, can direct a reader toward some insight, bring a poem to an emotional pitch, embody an idea." And this is what Katrine does with the images in her poem. She describes the moment of the photo, but beyond the moment is the idea that everyone's life is about to change when Katrine is born.

We also examine Lila Johnson's "Curly Bird," which is both a still photograph and a video because of her word choice (see p. 218). Lila grounds the poem in strong images of Phillip—his smell, his body, his clothes:

Phillip had frog breath and
water-ballooned cheeks
he had a Pepsi-bloated belly,
greasy eyes
his jeans, a layer of faded blue skin
his cap, a growth, molded
on the frame of his skull—
L.A. Lakers, grimy purple and gold.

Then she puts the photo in motion with her "grasshopper light" run, her "saltwater sandal sprint." I want students to take away from our lesson that imagery creates the picture and sound in the reader's mind, and in order for the picture to be true to our memory, we need to carefully choose our sensory details.

While Katrine Barber's first poem is a single photo, her "Applegate Dam" is a larger montage of a memory, three scenes, perhaps sparked by a photograph or a memory (see p. 218). We discuss how she uses specific images that merge into similes: "It had rained for three days straight/leaving the tent roof/like the underbelly of a frog,/full and soft." But she also uses sound with the "humming" of the mosquitoes.

After examining student models, I return to the assignment William Stafford gave in my classroom three or more decades ago: "Think of a photo you have or one you wish you had. Create a poem that brings that photo to life in the same way Katrine and Lila did with their poems. Think about the five senses as you write. Evoke the memory, but also think about how to help the reader think about the impact of that moment."

Poems from History

Like most of my assignments, the photograph poem/imagery work is recursive; I return to the same concepts again and again throughout the year. In my Tulsa "Race Riot"/massacre and gentrification units, I show slides from the historical society or old newspapers, and students write poems from those photographs, creating an image or persona poem that helps tell the

I explicitly teach imagery through the use of photographs.

story of this moment in history. While we watch videos or examine photos, I tell students to "listen for language that you might use in your poem. Jot down the names of stores, buildings, parks, people, because these specific details will bring your poem to life." Christina wrote about a photograph from Tulsa, where one wall stood in the midst of burned-out homes:

Last One Standing
by Christina

I am the last one standing.
Nothing lives within me.

Nothing remains.
All around me are ashes of what used to be.
I am just a memory
of what this town was
before the riot,
before my family was taken
from the shelter of my walls.
I felt the others burning down
on my left and right.
I saw the glowing flames in the midst
of this dark night and the leftover embers
of the morning.
Bodies scattered about,
blood on my stoop.
I am the last one standing.
I am the remains of this race riot,
never written in a textbook,
but holding one of history's darkest truths.

I also teach this poetry lesson when I show artwork or take students to museums. In 1993, for example, Bill Bigelow and I were co-teaching a class, Literature and U.S. History, when Jacob Lawrence's Great Migration series came to the Portland Art Museum. This artwork depicts the movement of African Americans from the rural South to the urban North during and after World War I. His panels portray the story of people seeking a better life, escaping both violence and economic hardships. We told students, "Find a painting and sit in front of it. Describe what you see. What do you feel? What pieces from history do you recall as you gaze at the picture? Let the history of the moment seep into your words."

One of our students, Karellen Lloyd, wrote about panel number 15, which shows a woman with a red coat hunched under a bare branch with a noose hanging from it. "There were lynchings," the caption read. Karellen wrote:

Next to dark waters
she bends.
Her eyes drink in the empty noose
hanging from her favorite tree,
and she does not wander.
She waits.

Karellen's words capture the images of the painting: the dark water, the empty noose, the tree. They also capture the despair in the words "she bends" and "she waits." Karellen's poem, which describes Lawrence's painting, also directs the reader to understand the weight of pain that "bends" the woman in the painting.

Revision

My students used to laugh that I should have "get specific" written on my gravestone. But having read far too many poems, narratives, and essays that lack "evidence," I know that engraving the "get specific" mantra is important across the genres. When students work on revising their poems, I encourage them to highlight or underline their images in the same way we do in the "Elements of Poetry" handout (see p. 238). If they lack images, they lack poetry. William Stafford told my students, "All of those specific details buy you an abstraction in the end."

Whether we are working in literature or history, poetry and the practice of using specific images develop our students as writers. They put clothes on the ghosts of the student, literary, and historical past, burning images onto the page. If we want student writing to move out of the humdrum of the ordinary, we need to take time to pause, close our eyes, and remember the details that swim to the surface. ✳

. . . .

Linda Christensen (lmc@lclark.edu) is director of the Oregon Writing Project at Lewis & Clark College in Portland, Ore. She is a Rethinking Schools editor and author of Reading, Writing, and Rising Up *and* Teaching for Joy and Justice.

Photograph, 1969
by Katrine Barber

This is my mother
lifting her hair long
like a low whistle
off of her neck
These are her fingers
caught in the tangles
of brown and gold caught in
silver earrings
This is my father
reaching through the lens
to touch the edge
of a new family
to touch her opening belly
under her full dress

This is existing
before I exist

This is me growing up
against their lives
him watching for a sharp
breath from her
her looking out
onto the border of birth
this is bumping us into three.

Curly Bird
by Lila Johnson

Phillip had frog breath and
water-ballooned cheeks
he had a Pepsi-bloated belly,
greasy eyes
his jeans, a layer of faded blue skin
his cap, a growth, molded
on the frame of his skull—
L.A. Lakers, grimy purple and gold.
In the summer of
snail trails and scabbed knees
he chased me
on grated Nikes, puffed with heat
from one end of our block
to the next,
wild creature boy in love
with me.
Let's get married! he shrieked, a groom
not grown and
I ran
grasshopper light
three sidewalk squares at a time
a saltwater sandal sprint
I felt I could sprout moth wings
rise above his gummy-fingered grasp
flutter beyond his lips
puckered blue-green
a Kool-Aid tattoo
up, up
spiral away
until he realized
he would never hold me
the curly bird girl in the sun.

Applegate Dam
by Katrine Barber

It had rained for three days straight
leaving the tent roof like the
underbelly of a frog,
full and soft.
We hiked to the Applegate,
gathered BB-hard huckleberries,
swam among the pickerelweed
pregnant with another generation
of damselflies,
and prepared ourselves for a hot one
while old Hank kept cool
with his home brew.

When the mosquitoes started humming
Wilma would get out her
soft-as-leather cards and we'd play poker
    hearts
    gin rummy
and she'd clank her chips together, reminding
everyone that she had a good deal of the pot.

Now I see why her hands hurt—
she tried to rinse gold from the river bottom,
tried to crack the dam open
with a shovel and a couple of pans.
And Hank used his hands
to pick up Styrofoam along the highway,
to refund beer bottles in Jacksonville.

They held onto their claim and
waited for damselflies
while the river swallowed the canyon.

. . . .

Jacob Lawrence/Migration Series
by Karellen Lloyd

Next to dark waters
she bends.
Her eyes drink in the empty noose
hanging from her favorite tree,
and she does not wander.
She waits.

Verb Craft Lesson
The movement poem

BY LINDA CHRISTENSEN

KIERA AND URIAH / PHOTO AARON HEWITT

Book critic R. Z. Sheppard wrote, "Adjectives are the potbelly of poets." Verbs make poetry (and essays) strut and dance, or they make an audience snore. I tell my students to make the verb the workhorse of their sentences. Throughout the year, we examine verbs multiple times and multiple ways across genres. Study any great writer and you find strong verbs as a centerpiece of their work.

Unfortunately, too many of my students arrive believing that adjectives are the best way to "pretty up" a piece of writing—the more, the better. I find adjectives strewn like confetti sprinkles in their poetry and essays. I pry their fingers away from adjectives by introducing them to verbs.

To begin our work on verbs in poetry, we examine Quincy Troupe's "A Poem for Magic," a poem so lively we can hear and see the rhythm of the ball as Magic crosses the court, wipes the glass, and pauses before he dishes out the ball. I start with sports poems because verbs dominate the pieces. We listen to Troupe read the poem out loud, so students can hear how rapidly his poem moves, like a basketball up and down the court. He uses quick-paced language to simulate movement.

take it to the hoop, "magic" johnson,
take the ball dazzling down the open lane
herk & jerk & raise your six-feet, nine-inch frame
into the air sweating screams of your neon name
"magic" johnson, nicknamed "windex" way back
in high school
cause you wiped glass backboards
so clean, where you first juked and shook
wiled your way to glory
a new-style fusion of shake-&-bake
energy, using everything possible, you created
    your own
space to fly through—any moment now
we expect your wings to spread feathers for that
    spooky takeoff
of yours—then, shake & glide & ride up in space
till you hammer home a clothes-lining deuce off
    glass
now, come back down with a reverse hoodoo gem
off the spin & stick in sweet, popping nets clean
from twenty feet, right side. . .

Teaching Strategy

1. After we've listened to the poem, I ask students to appreciate Troupe's work: "What do you love about this poem? What works for you?" Students, especially basketball players, love the way Troupe catches the rhythm of a basketball game.

2. When we've discussed what we like about the poem, I hand each student two colors of highlighters. I ask them, "What is a verb? Give me some examples." I do this call out to establish a definition of verbs. Some students carry a backpack of failure when it comes to grammar terms. I don't want to add to that pack; I want to lift it off their shoulders by making them realize that they intuitively know what a verb is because they use them all day long. After it seems like they get the gist of a verb, I say, "Look at the first three lines of Troupe's poem. Tell me what verbs you see." After they call out the verbs in those lines, I tell them to highlight the verbs in the rest of the stanza. Of course, students frequently highlight adjectives and nouns as well as verbs; this is an opportunity to discuss the differences, in context.

3. Once students have highlighted verbs in the poem, I ask, "Which verbs made you 'see' Magic Johnson playing basketball?" Students read out herk and jerk, wiped, juked and shook, shake and glide, hammer. I tell them, "Notice how Quincy Troupe doesn't stick dull, old, stale combinations of verbs that one would expect in a poem about basketball; he shakes us with surprises and makes us see Magic Johnson on the court. Troupe saturates us in the language of the basketball court. Now go back to the poem and using your second highlighter color, I want you to color all of the basketball vocabulary he uses." Students note the lane, backboards, glass, and nets, which lead us to a discussion about nouns and the work they do in a sentence or poem. I ask students to keep Troupe's poem handy, so they can look back and see how Troupe handled verbs or line breaks.

4. I also bring in other sports poems: "Analysis of Baseball" by May Swenson, "Fast Break" by Edward Hirsch, and "The Base Stealer" by Robert Francis. (Most of these poems are available online.) In each of these poems, I push students to examine how the writers have slowed the motion of action so they can see the extension of an arm, the slide of a hand, the rotation of a ball. They use verbs to take the reader through each step, each movement as they record it in the poem. For example, in "Fast Break," Hirsch writes, "A hook shot kisses the rim and/hangs there, helplessly, but doesn't drop,/and for once our gangly starting center/boxes out his man and times his jump/ perfectly, gathering the orange leather/from the air like a cherished possession. . ." Again, the writing soars with tight language and crisp verbs.

5. Then I work with students to write their own movement poems—giving, as always, room for inspiration and surprise as well as riverbanks (parameters or gentle directions) to help the writing flow. Through this poem, I want students to bring their lives, their passions into the classroom, but I also want them to learn about the importance of verbs in writing.

   I say: "Make a list of people you know who are really good at something. Include yourself. If you are a pitcher, let us see how you throw the ball. If you dance, take us through a piece of choreography. List the person and their passion. For example, my nephew Lee is crazy about fishing. My mother was an artist in the garden. Think big. This doesn't have to be about sports. Naomi Shihab Nye wrote a poem about her father making Arabic coffee. Think of creating a poem about an organizer, a field worker, a cafeteria worker, a parent preparing dinner." Once students have created a list, I say, "Let's hear some of your thoughts. Anyone who's stuck, steal these ideas. Let these ideas jump-start yours."

6. Then we move to the next piece of the activity—focusing on the language of movement, especially verbs. We take one of the potential items on a student's list, and together we brainstorm a list of verbs. "Pete said fishing. Let's help him out. What verbs will move this poem?" Toss, spin, cast, reel, catch, release, flick, drift. "Great verbs. Sometimes writers use their imaginations and use verbs in unconventional ways to help us see more clearly. Quincy Troupe wrote that Magic Johnson wiped the backboard; he uses the verb 'hammer.' As you write your poems, think about visual verbs that might work in your poem."

   I take them back to Troupe's poem for one more lesson about verbs. I encourage them to use short, one-syllable words when they want to quicken the pace, like Quincy Troupe ("herk & jerk & raise") and to interrupt the pace of longer lines that weigh poetry down.

7. Then students generate a list of nouns that could be used: line, lure, dock, boat, bait, hook, fly, lunker, tube worms, bass, trout, steelhead. Once students have a list of verbs and nouns for their poem, I ask them to generate some insider knowledge. "What are the words that only the people who understand or play this sport or activity will know?" Wendell gave us his list for basketball: needle-rope pass, fake, blindside, take off, double-pump. Demetrius added the word "pill" instead of ball.

8. Before students slide into writing their own poems, we look over poems by former students as accessible models: "Bottom of the Ninth" by Scott Steele (see p. 222) and "Dragon Dance" by Loi Nguyen (see p. 64). Students write poems about basketball, baseball, and dance, as well as poems about people immersed in their art or craft.

Revision Activity

When we work on revision, I remind students to read their poems out loud and notice where the rhythm works and where it stalls, to find fresh verbs, to use their insider knowledge to make the poem light up. I also encourage students to highlight all "was," "were," and "are" in their poetry (as well as their narratives and essays), and see if they can create a more poetic sentence with an active verb. For example, "It was a hot day" might become "the day sweated." (See "Elements of Poetry," p. 238.)

   Craft lessons, like this verb work, help students

I pry students' fingers away from adjectives by introducing them to verbs.

learn the art of writing poetry, but these lessons also transfer into their essay writing. Explicitly teaching students the tools that make writing stronger invites them into the academic world by giving them access to both reading and writing in ways that are expected, but not often taught, in schools. ✳

....

Linda Christensen (lmc@lclark.edu) is director of the Oregon Writing Project at Lewis & Clark College in Portland, Ore. She is a Rethinking Schools editor and author of Reading, Writing, and Rising Up *and* Teaching for Joy and Justice.

Resource
Troupe, Quincy. "A Poem for Magic," in *Transcircularities*. Minneapolis: Coffee House Press, 2002. An audio file of Quincy Troupe reading this poem is available at www.poetshouse.org/watch-listen-and-discuss/listen/quincy-troupe-reads-poem-magic.

Bottom of the Ninth
by Scott Steele

Fingernails gliding smoothly
across seams,
rosin absorbing
sweat from palms,
dirt skyrocketing
from the intrusion
of cleats,
signals encoded
in fingers,
an imperceptible nod,
the slow and deliberate
bringing together of the hands.

A pause.

A furtive glance.
The knee ascends
then swing,
the arm plummets
then arcs upward,
the leg kicks,
the elbow
leads the wrist
expelling the ball
between the middle and fore
fingers.
The ball in
violent revolution
crosses the plate.
Strike out.

Athletes of God
by Uriah Boyd

When I'm dancing I feel at home.
The scent of stale sweat and rosin
fill my nostrils. I live for sweaty hugs
and the feeling
of not knowing whether
my face is drenched in perspiration
or tears.
I love the smell of Tiger Balm,
the sound of leather ballet slippers
on old, tired marley floors,
and the bars that hug the walls—
holding them up after years of being strong.
I love dancers;
the way we challenge the very laws
of physics every time our feet
lift off the floor.
I love mid-calf cotton blend socks,
oversized T-shirts that hang wearily
off the shoulder, and open-back leotards.
I love the language of dance;
how so much can be communicated
without the use of a single word.
I love my calloused heels and bruised toenails—
constant reminders that my body
is an instrument of divine arts.
I love the mountains and valleys
of defined muscles;
quadriceps tensed, toes pointed,
and poised to strike the air.
I carve my shape into the memory of the studio.
When I dance,
I don't need to think in words,
just pictures and sensations.
Dance is more than a verb.
It's a confidante,
a home,
a sanctuary.

The List and Repetition
Hooking the poem forward

BY LINDA CHRISTENSEN

ERIK RUIN

Many effective writers use lists and repetition as poetic devices in poetry, songs, novels, newspaper articles, speeches, prayers and sermons. I've even been known to throw down a list in an argument, dragging up every past wrong ever done to me. Lists create a rhythm in a poem. Patricia Smith, slam poet and writer extraordinaire, dazzles us with her lists in both poetry and prose. Her poem for her mother Annie Pearl Smith, "How Mamas Begin Sometimes" from her book *Shoulda Been Jimi Savannah*, shoots out a list from the opening lines:

> Raging tomgirl, blood streaking her thick ankles
> and bare feet, she is always running, screech raucous,
> careening, dare and games in her clothesline throat.

The lists in Smith's poem pitch the reader forward, running through her fast-paced lines, trying to keep up with Smith's tomgirl mother.

As a class, we examine writers' use of lists throughout the year. We look at the lists in Kelly Norman Ellis' "Raised by Women" poem, where she uses both lists

The list and the repeating line are as common in a language arts class as gospel music is in church.

and repetition to hook her poem forward (see p. 27). The list and the repeating line are as common in a language arts class as gospel music is in church. But sometimes, we have to step back in class and examine these daily language strategies more thoroughly.

In a lesson called "Eyewitness to History," for example, students read Patricia Smith's introduction to her poetry book *Close to Death* as a model for their own essay on a moment when they were an eyewitness to history—either a personal, local, national, or world event. In this poetic essay, Smith writes about the eruption in Chicago in 1968 after Martin Luther King Jr. was assassinated. We examine the way Smith uses phrase lists, sentence lists, and strong verbs as well as effective repetition:

> The next day, everything was gone. The world was a pile of rubble, whispering smoke, dotted in places by the bright color of a gym shoe, a discarded shirt, the severed head of a doll. The market where my mother haggled over the fatty cuts of meat was gone. The clothing store which once flashed cheap polyester promise from every window was gone. The shop where Motown's latest blared from every window was gone. Shards of glass sparkled on the concrete like unmined jewels. The air was so black that people on the street bumped into one another and the few buildings that were left could not be seen. Once they felt it was safe, white people—their eyes wide as saucers—drove their cars slowly through the streets of our neighborhood, gawking at the destruction like sightseers in a horrific theme park.

As students write their essays, they look back to Smith's introduction as a model, noting the repetition of the word "gone" as well as the incredible list: "The world was a pile of rubble, whispering smoke, dotted in places by the bright color of a gym shoe, a discarded shirt, the severed head of a doll." This list of images startles readers by making us pay attention to each image—from smoke to a headless doll.

I want students to understand that the lines between poetry, narrative, and essay are thin. Yes, they are different genres, but poetic language awakens readers through the details of the lists. When I engage in craft lessons in poetry, I want those lessons to carry those over to our work in essays, memoirs, and fiction.

Teaching Strategy

1. I begin this poetry craft lesson by saturating students in models of poetry that use lists. We read many of these poems in previous lessons. For this lesson, I focus their attention on the use of list and repetition—and always on the use of specific details.

   I use the poem "I Got the Blues," by former Jefferson student Aaron Wheeler-Kay, to get students in the listing mood (see p. 58). I like his piece because he keeps pushing the list.

   The reader can feel him changing as he explores words, like a blues riff, caught and held, then discarded as he finds a new word. In fact, Aaron choreographed a tap dance to punctuate his poem. When he recited the poem as he tapped, the jazz beats underlying the words and line breaks became even more evident.

   As we read Aaron's poem, I encourage students to look at how he uses the words "no" and "yes" to push his poem forward, an excuse to use a new simile to describe his eyes.

   > Blue eyes.
   > Yes, ma'am.
   > Blue.
   > Like the ocean—
   > No, blue like new jeans,
   > Stiff and comfy—
   > No, blue like hard times.
   > Yeah.

Blue like cold steel and oil.
Blue like the caress of jazz at a funeral.

2. I ask, "What do you notice about his repeating lines?" As students point out how he changes the phrase "blue like. . ." I tell them, "This is one way to keep the repetition fresh: Keep the initial words, but change the end of the line."

3. Then we read "Brown Dreams" by Paul Flores (see p. 227). This poem tells a story about immigrants who join the military in order to gain U.S. citizenship. We watch Flores perform his poem on HBO's *Def Poetry Jam*, then we read the poem out loud, and talk about the content of the poem. (See Resources.)

4. After we discuss the content of "Brown Dreams," I ask students to look at how Flores uses lists throughout his poem. He starts with a list of phrases beginning with the word "who": "Brown boy who wasn't even a citizen,/who had barely been a resident five years,/who didn't know much about education,/was now willing to die to become a student." Then he shifts to a list of similes in the final stanza of his poem:

> This is a brown dream,
> Brown as the bus riders union.
> Brown as gasoline.
> Brown as the Tigris-Euphrates
> The Mississippi, and the Rio Grande.
> Brown as coyotes,
> Brown as the blood-soaked sands of Iraq
> and on the ranches of Arizona border
>   vigilantes.
> Brown as Affirmative Action in the military
> but not the university.
> This is a brown dream.

I ask students to look at the similarities in the ways Aaron Wheeler-Kay and Paul Flores repeat and change their repeating lines. I want them to see how the repeating line "Blue like" in Aaron's poem and "Brown as" in Flores' poem provide a rhythm that keeps the poem on track.

5. "Now talk about the details of the poem. Why does Flores use these specific details? He could say 'brown as bears' or 'brown as my front yard in the summer.' Why these details?" I want students to see that Flores isn't just writing a poem about the color brown, he is making a statement about what happens to Latinx. Their poems can be about colors *and* about the world.

6. I also use a section of the slam poet Patricia Smith's poem "Left Memories," where she repeats the words "I can't" then moves into a tight list of who she is—a Black woman—by listing all of the things she can't stop doing, like "walk in a straight line without my hips wailing hallelujah."

> I can't
> stop listening to blues songs where some
>   checkertoothed growler
> informs me that my heart is worthless or
>   missing altogether.
> I can't unravel the mystery of me, and it's
>   growing late.
> I can't walk in a straight line without my hips
>   wailing hallelujah.
> I can't stop dancing like a colored girl with a
>   lit match at her backside.
> I can't believe that I will be 50 before I am 40
>   again.
> I can't find anyone to jump doubledutch with
>   me.
> I can't make my poems be happy. I have tried
>   neon ink,
> perfumed paper and writing naked under a
>   silver-spilling moon.
> I can't hold my mother close long enough for
>   her body to realize
> how completely it once harbored mine.

I have found Smith's repeating line "I can't" moves students into interesting places in their own lives. She is by turns poetic and searingly honest about her loneliness or relationship with her mother.

7. Depending on the time of year and the strength of student writing, I might saturate students with more poems. Deonica Johnson's poem "Where Poems Hide" is a play on a poem by poet Ruth For-

man. Her poem "Poetry Should Ride the Bus" from her book *We Are the Young Magicians* is a wonderful model for younger students. This playful poem encourages students to get imaginative with their lists about what poetry should do—ride the bus, play hopscotch, sit on the porch, and so on.

We also read "Silent Echo" by Meg Niemi. Her repeating line "I'll wonder where you are" evokes a farewell to her school. This is especially good at the end of the year.

8. After we have read both professional and student authors, I encourage students to think of a color or a word or a phrase as the springboard for their lists. "Remember how Aaron Wheeler-Kay used the word 'blues,' or Paul Flores used the word 'brown' then elaborated on the word. You might also try using a phrase like Patricia Smith's 'I can't.' Then extend your lists by thinking about the politics of color or the story behind the list. What else are you saying? Go beyond the typical, the usual."

    This is where we evoke both the poetic and political imagination. I encourage students to mix their lists to include the known—blue is for water—but also to extend the list to bring in the unusual, the unexpected—"brown as the bus riders union"—a reference to the inspirational Los Angeles organization formed to press for greater access to affordable transportation.

9. When I give this assignment, I tell students, "If you are listing why you love your grandmother's buttermilk biscuits, go for it. Add as many items as you can to the list: sights, smells, butter dripping over the edge, the way they feel in your mouth. This is a love poem to those biscuits. Make us all want them. You can weed later. Get it all down now."

Revision

When we work on revision, I remind students to find a place where they might include a list in their poem, to open up a stanza and stream some verbs or phrases to create a rhythm. (See "Elements of Poetry" on p. 238.) I also ask them to go back and see if their repeating line is too repetitious. Is there a way to tweak it slightly, like

Patricia Smith does? She uses the "I can't" but swings wide with the rest of the line. Can they use longer or shorter lines to vary the rhythm in the way that Paul Flores does in "Brown Dreams"?

Ultimately, my goal in these lessons is to give students a variety of ways to return to their poems (and prose), to wake up a sleepy line or startle us with their lists and repetition—to make us see the world anew. ✳

. . . .

Linda Christensen (lmc@lclark.edu) is director of the Oregon Writing Project at Lewis & Clark College in Portland, Ore. She is a Rethinking Schools editor and author of Reading, Writing, and Rising Up *and* Teaching for Joy and Justice.

Resources

Flores, Paul S. "Brown Dreams," 2006. www.youtube.com/watch?v=hhttoJwALoA

Smith, Patricia. *Close to Death: Poems*. Cambridge, MA: Zoland Books, 1998.

Smith, Patricia, "How Mamas Begin Sometimes." *Shoulda Been Jimi Savannah*. Minneapolis: Coffee House Press, 2012.

Smith, Patricia. "Left Memories," 2002. www.poetry.about.com/library/weekly/aa061202b.htm

Brown Dreams

by Paul S. Flores
(Inspired by Jorge Mariscal and Richard Rodriguez)

This is a true story
about a brown dream
sinking to the bottom of the Tigris-Euphrates

This is a brown dream.

It was Francisco's last night out with his friends.
Three of them on their way to see the latest sci-fi
    movie.
They were driving.
A stereo jocking the latest top 40 rapper,
because that was all he listened to.
But it didn't matter.

Music was only part of the setting
and not the motivation for late-night
brainstorms about how to make money,
or how to escape the feeling of being
left out of a dream so many painted
red, white, and blue.

But his dream was brown.
Brown as his skin.
Brown and impure.
Brown as Eve's apple after she took the first bite.
Brown as the everlasting blur of English, African, and
    Indian
moving through the forests of this continent
four hundred years ago
before it was known as destiny.
Before he had ever heard the word
"immigrant"
Beaner! Spic! Stupid! Dirty Mexican!
Before he had ever dreamt of assimilation.

He is 18 and Mexican.
He is in San Diego,
Topeka, Buffalo, San Antonio,
Oakland, California.
He wants a piece of the American Dream.

Francisco wanted a college degree.
He wanted to be a professional,
a stockbroker, or FBI agent,
because those were the jobs with the most power.
If he could have been a rock star or a super hero
there would have been no need to enlist.
But he had to be a U.S. citizen
if he was going to make a living like them.

The Army recruiter at his high school
told him that if he served in the military
he could automatically become a U.S. citizen.
After four years duty and an honorable discharge
there would be plenty of money left over
for him to continue his education
at a good institution.
Or he could take his technical skills
as a tank operator or small weapons expertise
and apply them to a civilian job.

It was exciting;
Brown boy who wasn't even a citizen,
who had barely been a resident five years,
who didn't know much about education,
was now willing to die to become a student.

One year later
he was working on a tank unit
fighting in Iraq.
Francisco heard it was the second time
the president had invaded this nation.
They were driving in the desert.
They were taking fire, swerving.
The tank lost control
and headed straight into the river.

As Francisco's lungs filled up with water
he remembered his last night out with his friends;
How his mother had wanted to cook dinner for him—
but he didn't want to spend another hour
in that cramped apartment
where she cooked for six of his brothers,
his two uncles and their compadres.
Instead, Francisco invited Jose and Diego
out to the movies
because that's what Americans did.

Now his soul is an ancestor in the Euphrates.
Chicano blood mixing with Arab soil,
returning to the Garden of Eden
by way of the U.S. Army,
same way it had come.

Only now, he would finally receive something
he had been promised:
An officially sealed envelope on top of Old Glory.
Citizenship had never been earned so graciously.
Even, if it comes posthumously—
Why don't they extend it to the victim's family?

The American Dream is dirty.
Why should Chicanos have to die
to earn the approval of this society?

This is a brown dream.
Brown as the bus riders union.
Brown as gasoline.
Brown as the Tigris-Euphrates
The Mississippi, and the Rio Grande.
Brown as coyotes.
Brown as the blood-soaked sands of Iraq
and on the ranches of Arizona border vigilantes.
Brown as Affirmative Action in the military
but not the university.
This is a brown dream.

. . . .

Flores, Paul S. "Brown Dreams," 2006.

I'd Miss the Rain
by Khalilah Joseph

I would miss the rain,
wandering down in sheets,
washing away the remnants of the day.
I would miss hearing the pitter-patter on my roof,
feeling the puddles splash under my feet.
I would miss the moisture
seeping through my coat,
chilling me.
I would miss searching for an umbrella,
or looking for a hood.
If I went away,
I would miss the rain.

. . . .

I Can't
by Ashley

I can't be the perfect daughter
I am a piece of charcoal
Waiting to be shaped into a diamond
Just like my mother

I can't stop looking towards the future
A life of more freedom
My empty quiet space
Not on parole, like my sister

I can't be optimistic
Everything I see is trailed by a dark shadow
My life is nothing but haunted memories
A past of old ghosts
A trap for the good hearted

I can't be something I am not
I am what I am
Not perfect or ideally thin
Not a rocket scientist or mechanic
Although nobody makes good brownies like I can.

Where Poems Hide
by Deonica Johnson

Poems can be found
under the bark dust of trees
and can be blown away in the wind
of a rainstorm.

Poems ride home on the bus
and keep you company
on that walk home.
Washing dishes,
vacuuming the carpet,
cleaning out the attic,
poems are everywhere.

I found a poem
beneath a blossoming rosebush
in the garden.

I've seen poems drizzle off plump lips
to say beautiful things.
I've seen poems dance with anger
and hide with fear
and laugh when nothing's funny.

Poems can be found
in the sweat of a basketball game,
in the buzz of bee delivering honey to the hive.

Poems can be found
when watching that favorite cartoon character,
even in that teacher that gives you the extra
push to continue.

I've found my poem, now where can you find yours?

Silent Echo
by Meg Niemi

I'll wonder where you are
when the curtain closes
and our footsteps
are only a whisper
on the checkered tile floor,
when our lockers are hollow
with an echo
of tardy bells,
a lost math assignment
and textbooks
unreturned.

I'll wonder where you are
when I'm called away to college
in some small autumn town.
I'll miss the click of heels beside me,
the low chuckle of your laugh.

When my teachers mispronounce my name
and my identity
is a social security number
on a computer readout,
I'll want your tap on my shoulder
so your smile will remind me
of the day we took the SATs
when all we really wanted to do
was drive to Cannon Beach
and wade in the November ocean.

Line Breaks Revision
Molding emphasis, appearance, and meaning

BY LINDA CHRISTENSEN

TARYN WRIGHT-RAMIREZ/PHOTO DOROTHY SEYMOUR

Over the years I have noticed that some of my classroom poets, who have had little exposure to poetry, write their initial poems as paragraphs instead of stanzas. Although there are no hard-and-fast rules about how to "break" a line in poetry or where to break a poem into stanzas, I want my students to understand when, why, and how poets make decisions about their writing. So we study the ways that multiple poets approach this piece of the art and craft of writing poetry.

In their wonderful book *The Poet's Companion: A Guide to the Pleasures of Writing Poetry*, poets Kim Addonizio and Dorianne Laux discuss the art of the line break in their chapter "The Music of the Line":

Denise Levertov says that the pause at the end of a line is equal to a half-comma. The reader's eye and ear, having taken in the words and rhythms of the line, get a brief respite before going on to the next. In other words, there's a momentary *silenc*e; and as musicians know, silence is an integral part of the music. A line break is not just a pause in the action of the poem; it's very much a part of it. In a piece of music, the silence is notated by a rest, which tells the performer how long the silence lasts. Think of line breaks as rests in the music of your poem, and stanza breaks as longer rests. . . . Poets need to tune their ears as finely as musicians; that's why reading poems aloud is a good idea, including your own poems as you write them.

To help students learn the "music of the line," we examine the line breaks of exemplary poets, turn prose into poetry, and play with our own line and stanza breaks.

Teaching Strategy

1. Poets use line breaks in a variety of ways. Some writers end-stop their poems, meaning they stop at the end of a sentence line; others straddle or "enjamb" the line, meaning the sentence carries over from one line to the next. To begin our work on line breaks, I read the paragraph from "The Music of the Line" to students. I tell them, "Think about this: Your poem is like a piece of music. You are the conductor of that music. Imagine the baton in your hand. When you break a line, you are telling your readers to pause. Sometimes you pause because you want a moment of silence, sometimes you pause because you want to emphasize a word or phrase, and sometimes you pause to surprise your reader."

2. We read Patricia Smith's poem "My Mother Learns English" out loud (see p. 206). Before we read, I ask students to think about where she uses breath to straddle a line, showing the reader when to pause.

> When Mama talks, the Southern swing of it
>   is wild with unexpected blooms,
> like the fields she never told me about in
>   Alabama.
> Her rap is peppered with *ain't gots* and *I done*
>   *beens*
> and *he be's* just like mine is when I'm color
>   among color.
> During worship, when talk becomes song, her
>   voice collapses
> and loses all acquaintance with key, so of
>   course,
> it's my mother's fractured alto wailing above
>   everyone—

uncaged, unapologetic and creaking toward heaven.

After reading the poem, I ask students, "Why do you think she paused there? How would the poem sound different if we paused in a different spot?" We try out a few variations before moving onto the next poem.

3. Kelly Norman Ellis breaks her lines by phrases in her poem "Raised by Women" (see p. 27). (Students can listen to Ellis read her poem: www.vimeo.com/62904155.) Before we read, I ask students to think about the differences between Smith's and Ellis' line breaks, to notice the length of the line and how those differences affect our reading:

> I was raised by
> Chitterling eating
> Vegetarian cooking
> Cornbread so good you want to lay
> down and die baking
> "Go on baby, get yo'self a plate"
> Kind of Women.

Each stanza in this poem becomes one sentence, filled with descriptive lists, so when Ellis raises her baton for the reader, there is only a slight pause, the "half-comma" that Denise Levertov mentions above. I want students to see how Ellis' lines are short and fast, allowing the reader to pause slightly at the end of each line, but also how when she reads the poem out loud, she draws out the dialogue, "Go on baby, get yo'self a plate."

4. For our final example in this lesson, we look at how William Stafford breaks the lines in his poem "You Reading This, Be Ready" (see p. 2). As we study Stafford's poem, students notice that he breaks his first lines at the end of a question. Then in his final two lines, he bends the sentence into the second line.

> Starting here, what do you want to remember?
> How sunlight creeps along a shining floor?
> What scent of old wood hovers, what softened sound from outside fills the air?

5. Once we have listened to the music in Smith's, El-lis', and Stafford's stanzas, I distribute the hand-out "Craft Lesson: Patricia Smith Line Breaks" (see p. 234). First, we read the paragraphs from Smith's introduction to her book *Close to Death* out loud. Then I ask students to help me break the first paragraph into a stanza as a model for working on their own poems. I put the paragraph on the document camera and say, "Where should I put the first slash mark to indicate a line break? Read it out loud and see where you pause."

6. We play with this as a class. One class made these notations:

> In 1968, Martin Luther King was murdered
> and the West Side of Chicago exploded.
> Black folks
> —my friend Deborah,
> my cousin Alfonso,
> the taxi drivers,
> the busboys,
> the postmen,
> the nurses,
> the hustlers,
> the teachers,
> the church deacons
> and the pump jockeys—
> spilled into the streets,
> sparked by a rage
> that would not be harnessed.

Although not everyone agreed, students thought the list was fast and the opening lines should be slower. They discussed the idea of isolating the word "exploded" on its own line, but decided to leave it in the longer line. For this exercise, it is important for students to explain why they made the choice of longer or shorter line breaks, so they can articulate that although there is no right or wrong way to cut a line, their choices do affect the reader, and they've thought about those reasons.

7. Once we've rehearsed line breaks together, students turn one or two of Smith's other paragraphs into poetic lines. This exercise serves multiple purposes. Certainly, I want students to think about where to break their lines, but I also want them to notice how strong essays use poetic language. (Also, this introduction is an incredibly powerful piece of writing about an important moment in history. I use it multiple times throughout the school year. Initially, I use it as a model for an essay where students write about a time they were eyewitnesses to history.)

8. I tell students, "Pull out a few of your poems. Do the line lengths seem the same in each one? If you have a pattern, see if you can break it. Try rewriting one of your poems by changing where you break the lines. Maybe vary the lengths. Maybe try a single word or phrase on a line."

9. Then we move on to stanzas. "What about your stanzas? Are they always one long block or do they vary?" See what happens if you use a single word or line stanza. What if you broke up a long block into several shorter stanzas? You can always go back to the original, but for this exercise, play around."

Learning about line and stanza breaks brings students inside the craft of writing poetry. And it doesn't happen with one lesson, which is why we return to the "Elements of Poetry" (see p. 238) each time we work on revisions. As we read model poems, line breaks are one part of our "noticing."

Although poetry lessons are not going to start the revolution, they do give students knowledge about how writers work. For those of us who stood outside the doors of the academy, feeling slightly vulnerable and ill at ease in the presence of a learned institution, knowing how things work builds a growing sense of ownership over our writing, the beginnings of a belief that we belong inside those walls, too. ✳

....

Linda Christensen (lmc@lclark.edu) is director of the Oregon Writing Project at Lewis & Clark College in Portland, Ore. She is a Rethinking Schools editor and author of Reading, Writing, and Rising Up *and* Teaching for Joy and Justice.

Craft Lesson
Patricia Smith line breaks

Read the paragraphs from Patricia Smith's introduction to her book Close to Death *out loud. Listen for where you will put the line breaks. Put a slash mark (/) where you want the line to break, where you want readers to pause or to take a breath, or to surprise them. Look back to her poem "My Mother Learns English" as a reference. Choose one or two paragraphs and create stanzas for a poem.*

In 1968, Martin Luther King was murdered and the West Side of Chicago exploded. Black folks—my friend Deborah, my cousin Alfonso, the taxi drivers, the busboys, the postmen, the nurses, the hustlers, the teachers, the church deacons and the pump jockeys—spilled into the streets, sparked by a rage that would not be harnessed. Fire was a most visible fury, and it didn't take long for the world to burn. The air grew bitter with smoke that simply refused to move. The electricity had failed in my overcrowded apartment building, and tenants cowered in the gloomy halls, frightened of the erupting chaos. The bright dot of a lit cigarette would swell, someone would begin a hymn low in the throat. I was 13, the daughter of a no-nonsense, hat-wearing, God-fearing, church-going woman, so I was not allowed outside. No way.

I stood at the living room window with my trembling mother while neighbors pushed entire racks of clothing down the street, balanced cases of J&B on their shoulders, scooted past on stolen 10-speeds. Blood spurted from wounds that the wounded didn't seem to notice. Fire from the burning buildings reached for the shirt cuffs and pant legs of daring looters. The air, now a visible thing, crept through the gaps in the window frame, bit into my eyes and tore at the lining of my throat. Even the trees on my street burned, matchsticks with their heads aflame.

Lying on a pallet on the floor that night, I watched flames lick at the sky. Bullets whizzed past my window as mothers screamed for their wayward or wounded children. "But how could the sky burn?" I kept asking my mother, who was planning to sit up all night, her back against the door. "How could the sky burn?"

Remixing Revision
Using music to motivate poetry revision

BY RENÉE WATSON

"But Miss, you said it was good!"

"I like it the way it is."

These were common statements my students made whenever I asked them to revise. Even students who love to write sometimes shrink away from editing their poetry.

I decided to try a new approach with revision as we prepared for our BronxWrites poetry slam, where I work as a teaching artist. When the time came for students to revise a poem of their choice, I introduced the notion of remaking, revising, and editing. I started the revision lesson by telling students, "Write about a time you took one thing and made it into something else." I gave one example: "Maybe you took a pair of pants and made it into something else."

After a few minutes I asked students to share what they wrote. Nissa wrote about taking leftovers and making them into lunch for the next day. "Instead of eating the chicken like we did for dinner with rice and beans, I made a sandwich." Jasmine wrote about taking the strap from a purse she loved and using it as a headband.

I listed their "revisions" on the board as students talked. "You all have experience remaking and remixing something," I told them.

"Now I want you to think about remaking, remixing, and revising by listening to two songs. I'm going to play two versions of 'Killing Me Softly.' Write down some of the differences you notice." I played the song "Killing Me Softly" by Roberta Flack. A few students moaned at my music choice. Some recognized the song, and I wasn't sure if it was a compliment when a student said, "My mom likes this song."

I let Roberta's voice fill the room. The slow tempo brought calm and students silently wrote their observations. Midway through the song, I changed to the Fugees' version of "Killing Me Softly," which features Lauryn Hill's melodic singing alongside Wyclef Jean's voice on top of a beat that makes heads bob. Students immediately reacted to the switch of songs, some of them sang along, some of them just moved to the music.

"What did you notice about the first song I played for you?"

"A woman was singing," Remy said.

"It was kind of slow but not that slow," Kewayne said.

I asked them to talk about the second version.

"It was hip-hop," a student answered.

"The second was faster and it has more instruments."

Then, I asked the class to compare the songs. "What are the similarities? What are the differences?"

Students noticed that both songs shared the same lyrics but because of the beat and music of the second song, they created different moods. I listed their ideas on the board. They noticed that there was only one voice in the first version and two in the second. When I asked which song they liked best, most students liked the remake better. I wanted to show them an example of how artists change things up while leaving some pieces intact, how just by changing one element of a piece of art, you can change the mood. I asked the class, "Do you think Lauryn Hill and Wyclef hated Roberta Flack's song?"

"No!"

"Well, then why did they change it? If they liked it why not just leave it alone?"

Students guessed that maybe they wanted to pay tribute to Roberta Flack, or maybe they wanted to experiment with it and see what could happen if they changed the beat. We talked about other songs they knew where the artist remixed their own song. I loved that students used the word experiment, so I used that

language when introducing revision to them. "Today, you are going to choose one of your poems and experiment with it. You're an expert on your life, and you have the literary tools we've been exploring and your classmates' feedback to help you tell your own story, in your own words."

Revising for Sensory Details

After our revision discussion, we focused on sensory details because that was one of the literary devices students learned and practiced in the previous unit. We reviewed examples of sensory detail, then we looked at a sample of what a poem might look like before sensory detail was added.

I took out the sensory details from a stanza in Willie Perdomo's poem, "Where I'm From" and wrote it on the dry-erase board:

Before revision:
Where I'm from I can smell breakfast being made
    in the morning.
Where I'm from I can hear dogs barking at night.

Then, I showed them his real poem:

After revision:
Where I'm from, Puerto Rico stays on our minds when the fresh breeze of *café con leche y pan con mantequilla* comes through our half-open windows and under our doors while the sun starts to rise.

Where I'm from, babies fall asleep to the bark of a German shepherd named Tarzan. We hear his wandering footsteps under a midnight sun.

It was obvious to the class which version was stronger, but I wanted to make sure they understood why. "How do sensory details enhance a poem?"

"They bring it to life?" Kewayne said.

"What do you mean by that?"

"Well, it's not general. I can actually see and hear the things that he hears and sees by the way he describes them."

"Exactly. I want the details of *your* life. We may all eat breakfast in the morning but do we all eat the same thing? At night Willie heard a barking dog. What do you hear? If you just write, 'I hear noise at night,' that doesn't paint a clear picture of your world."

I distributed colored pencils and asked students to go through their poems and color the moments where they used sensory detail. "Look over the places you highlighted. If you identify sensory details in certain lines, you might remake those images to make them stronger. If you have areas in the poem where there's no color, then you'll know where to focus when you revise." We ended class with students sharing the before and after stanzas of their own poems with a partner.

Earlier in the year I modeled giving feedback and the students developed a shared language around how to give appropriate critique: Point out what's working in the poem first, be specific in both praise and questions. Students had already demonstrated they could verbally comment on their classmates' drafts. This time I wanted them to take the time to write down feedback suggestions before sharing them with their partner.

Each student had a handout of how to respond to their partner's poem: "To enhance your poem, I suggest you add, change, or delete the following." There was space on the sheet for students to write why they suggested the revision. The last prompt asked the reader to ask a question of the writer of the poem.

Students worked in pairs, taking turns reading their pieces out loud to each other, writing down comments and questions, and then sharing feedback with their partners.

Students took editing each other's work seriously. Perhaps because they knew they'd be receiving feedback, too. Students were able to practice what they learned earlier in the year and use the vocabulary we focused on. One student wrote, "I think you should add a metaphor or simile in your second stanza." Another student asked, "How did you choose the title of your poem?"

A few students didn't feel they needed to change anything. I could see their poems were strong and had a hard time finding something to critique, too. But I pushed them to experiment. "What if your last line became your first line? Have you thought about a title that intrigues the reader? Is there a phrase you want to repeat throughout the poem?" I assured them that they didn't have to stick with the remake poem if at the end, their heart really was with the first poem. In all cases but one, students who changed something—even if it was a small edit—chose to slam the revised poem.

For our last day of revision, we focused on line breaks and stanzas. "One thing to pay attention to is how your poem looks on the page. If someone else is reading your poem out loud, where should they take a pause? What lines should be said fast or with heavy emotion? How you break the line will determine how the poem is read. Is there one word that should be on its own line for special emphasis?" I asked. I told students to make a deliberate decision. "As long as you can justify why you broke the line or didn't, I'm fine. It's not about doing it the way I want you to; it's about you making an intentional choice. Writers make choices about how words go together. You're in control."

We had been analyzing and discussing professional and student poets' line break choices throughout the year. We looked back at a handout that included Gwendolyn Brooks' poem "We Real Cool" as an example: "We real cool. We/Left school. We/. . ." We read the poem, noticed where we took breaths, and talked about the poem's visual appearance on the page.

As they reflected on the revision process, students shared something they learned, something they struggled with, and something they were proud of.

Several students expressed pride in helping someone become a better writer. Students wrote that they felt more confident using literary devices and many were proud of their revised poem. A few students struggled with being nervous about giving feedback and others mentioned that they learned "remixing poems can be fun."

I learned teaching revision could be fun. I learned to relinquish my power and trust that students could coach each other. I was reminded that lessons on revision don't have to be about a red pen marking up page after page. Lessons on revision can leave young writers feeling more powerful and more hopeful. ✷

. . . .

Renée Watson (reneewatson.net) is an author, performer, and educator. Her children's books have received several honors, including an NAACP Image Award nomination. She teaches poetry at DreamYard in New York City.

Resource

Perdomo, Willie. "Where I'm From," in *Where a Nickel Costs a Dime*. New York: W. W. Norton & Company, 1996.

Elements of Poetry

As you revise your poem, think about the following elements of poetry.

1. **Concrete Images:** Poets express strong emotions (love, anger, sadness) or tell us about big ideas (poverty, war, hunger, friendship). These are "ghost words." To give the ghosts some clothes, poets must include concrete images—things you can taste, touch, see, hear, smell. Concrete images are specific: They name the street, the kinds of trees; they bring us voices; they make us touch the wet back of a seal or the bumpy skin of a lizard.

    Stanley Kunitz wrote about a whale stranded in Wellfleet Harbor. His use of specific words and similes to evoke sounds brings the whale's voice to the reader: "You have your language too,/an eerie medley of <u>clicks</u>/and <u>hoots</u> and <u>trills</u>,/<u>location-notes</u> and <u>love calls</u>,/<u>whistles</u> and <u>grunts</u>. Occasionally,/it's like <u>furniture</u> <u>being smashed</u>,/or the <u>creaking of a mossy</u> <u>door</u>,/sounds that all melt into a liquid. . ."

    Katrine Barber brings her "Applegate Dam" poem to life with specific details that call up images for the reader: "When the <u>mosquitoes</u> started <u>humming</u>/Wilma would get out her/<u>soft-as-leather cards</u> and we'd <u>play poker</u>/<u>hearts</u>/<u>gin rummy</u>/and she'd <u>clank</u> her chips together, reminding/everyone that she had a good deal of the pot."

2. **Figurative Language:** Metaphors, similes, and personification surprise the reader by making us view the world in a fresh way.

    In her poem "Left Memories," Patricia Smith uses personification to give her hips a life of their own: "I can't walk in a straight line without <u>my hips wailing hallelujah. . .</u>"

    Paul Flores uses a series of similes to bring the situation of Latinx in the armed services to life: "This is a brown dream,/Brown as the bus riders union,/Brown as gasoline,/Brown as the Tigris-Euphrates/The Mississippi, and the Rio Grande,/Brown as coyotes. . ."

3. **Active Verbs:** Verbs are the workhorse of the poem. Strong verbs create visual images for the reader. Eliminate as many *is, was, were* from your piece as possible. Also, consider replacing verbs like *could, would, should.* When possible, use verbs in unusual ways that wake the reader: Instead of "It was a hot night," write "The night sweated."

    In "Oranges," Gary Soto immerses readers in the sounds and sights of a foggy night: "A few cars <u>hissing</u> past,/Fog <u>hanging</u> like old/Coats between the trees."

    Patricia Smith surprises the reader with sassy verbs in "Hip-Hop Ghazal": "As the jukebox <u>teases</u>, watch my sistas <u>throat</u> the heartbreak,/<u>inhaling</u> bassline, <u>cracking</u> backbone and <u>singing</u> thru hips."

4. **Line Breaks:** Poets use line breaks in a variety of ways. Some writers end-stop their poems, meaning they stop at the end of a sentence line; others straddle or "enjamb" the line, meaning the sentence moves from one line to the next.

    In her poem "Raised by Women," Kelly Norman Ellis breaks her lines by phrases. Her lines are short and fast, allowing the reader to pause at the end of each line:

    > I was raised by
    > Chitterling eating
    > Vegetarian cooking
    > Cornbread so good you want to lay
    > down and die baking
    > "Go on baby, get yo'self a plate"
    > Kind of Women.

    Mary Oliver, in "The Summer Day," uses complete questions and longer lines, building on a phrase "This grasshopper, I mean—" to expand the image.

    > Who made the world?
    > Who made the swan, and the black bear?
    > Who made the grasshopper?
    > This grasshopper, I mean—
    > the one who has flung herself out of the grass,
    > the one who is eating sugar out of my hand,
    > who is moving her jaws back and forth instead of up and down—
    > who is gazing around with her enormous and complicated eyes.

5. **Explode a detail:** Take one image and keep moving in on it, adding more and more detail. Think of a pen as a camera that zooms in gathering details. Jefferson student Mira Shimabukuro wrote, "I learned how to start with a detail and get smaller:"

    > One thin-necked vase
    > Pinwheel full. . .
    >
    > A photo, half hidden moon
    > Rising in the half pane. . .

6. **Punctuating Poetry:** William Stafford says make it easy on your reader. I usually use standard punctuation. Some writers capitalize all first lines; others, like Lucille Clifton, do not capitalize anything. Many follow traditional capitalization.

The Read-Around
Raising writers

BY LINDA CHRISTENSEN

FAVIANA RODRIGUEZ

The read-around is the class-room equivalent to quilt making or barn raising. It is the public space—the *zócalo* or town square—of my room. During our read-around, we socialize together and create community, but we also teach and learn from each other. If I had to choose one strategy as the centerpiece of my teaching, it would be the read-around. It provides both the writing text for my classroom and the social text where our lives intersect and we deepen our connections and understandings across lines of race, class, gender, sexual orientation, and age.

Starting with What Works

At the beginning of the year, from the first day of class, I require that all students read their poetry out loud to the class. Some students are eager; their hands are always in the air. Other students are too cool; this is why I count sharing work as part of the grade. They can maintain their smooth facade and act like they are just reading for the credit. Sometimes students want to share, but they need to be coaxed. I use National Writing Project teacher Keith Caldwell's technique of teasing students into reading, "Who's dying to share, but doesn't want to raise their hand?"

Before we start our read-around, I distribute stacks of "compliment sheets"—paper strips—to each student. I initiate the read-around by saying, "I am always a little bit worried when I share my writing. What if I don't sound smart? What if my piece isn't as good as other people's? In order to keep me writing and the rest of the class writing, we have to focus on what is good in a piece. Your piece will not sound like someone else's. It will sound like you. And that's great. You won't recognize your brilliance because it just sounds like you. We will recognize it for you."

I tell students, "You are going to write a compliment to each student in the class about that student's piece. No one is allowed to make critical comments about a poem or paper. We focus on the positive—on what works. As each person reads, you will take notes and give positive feedback to the writer. We also applaud each writer for having the courage to read in front of the class."

In order for this to work, I discuss how generic comments like "Good poem" or "I like your imagery" aren't specific enough to help anyone know what s/he did right. Instead, I say, "List the words or phrases, images or verbs that make the poem come alive. That's what we mean by 'tell the writer what is working.'" Students respond to the content of the piece¬—what they like about the topic of the poem. They also respond to the style, the way the poem is written. "What line, what phrase did you like? Do you like the imagery, the repetition?" Instead of working on a deficit model—what's wrong with this piece—we work on a positive model: What's right? What can we learn from this poem? This writer? As Pete noted in his class evaluation:

The way you have us make comments (what did you like about the piece of writing) has helped me deal with people. My skin is thick enough to take a lot of abuse just because I've always had a fairly high opinion of some of the things I can do. I didn't realize a lot of other people don't have that advantage. After a while I found out positive critique helped me more than negative, too.

The Read-Around as Writing Text

During the read-around, students provide accessible models of writing for each other. When I encourage

We deepen our connections and understandings across lines of race, class, gender, sexual orientation, and age.

them to listen for what "works" in their peers' pieces, to take notes on what they like, I am also encouraging them to use those techniques in their own writing. After students have shared their observations, I might point out particular writing strategies that I want them to incorporate into their writing. I might note how Aaron used a list in his poem or how Brandon opened his poem with a repeating, but changing line. I might ask Alisha to re-read a stanza of her poem so that we can notice her powerful verbs. I do this consistently in each read-around to bring students' attention to the writers' tools. In her portfolio evaluation Heather wrote about what she learned from her classmates:

When I listen to other people's writing, I hear things I love or wish I'd written myself. Most of the time that's where I get my inspiration. Sometimes I catch myself saying, "I wish I could write like so-and-so." Then I think, "What was it about his/her piece that I liked?" When I figure that out, I'm that much closer to being a better writer. I use their papers as examples. I steal their kernels of ideas and try to incorporate them into my own writing. For example, I love how Ki uses her personal history in her writing, so I try that out for myself. I like Lisa's use of unusual metaphors, so I try as hard as I can to steer clear of the generic type I've been known to use in the past.

Because students learn to listen closely to each other's poems for both ideas and literary tools, they can identify those strategies and use them in their own writing.

Students in every class I've taught have made it clear that the read-around was the best part of my teaching. Adam wrote:

> There is so much to learn about good writing. I know that a lot of what shaped my writing was not the diagramming sentences or finding the

"What was it about that piece that made me get all goose-bumpy?"

subject and verb that we learned in grade school, but the desire to learn more about what I'm hearing around me. Just hearing the work of good writers makes an incredible difference. When I find something I really like, I ask myself, "What was it about that piece that made me get all goose-bumpy?" That's why I think it is really important to have those read-arounds in class. Not only does the author get to hear comments about his/her work, but the rest of the class gets a chance to hear some pretty amazing stuff. Like when we heard Nicole's home language paper, I don't think there was anyone who wasn't touched by it. At some point everyone had felt like that, and her paper was able to capture those feelings and describe them perfectly. At the same time, everyone thought, "How can I write like that?" We all learned from the paper. Now, this is only one example, but almost every day we share, something like this happens.

Pulling in Reluctant Writers

Not all students arrive on the due date with a paper in hand. To be sure, some students haven't taken the time to do the work, but others can't find a way to enter the work; they either don't know where to start or they feel incapable of beginning. Even my pep talks about "bending the assignment to find your passion" or "just write for 30 minutes; I'll accept whatever you come up with as a first draft" don't entice these students. That's why I'm not a stickler about deadlines.

During read-arounds the students who wrote papers will spawn ideas for those who either couldn't write or who haven't learned homework patterns yet. Listening to how Amanda, Alyss, or Deanna approached the assignment helps teach reluctant writers a way to enter the writing. Sometimes students write a weak "just get it done" paper, then hear a student piece that sends them back home to write with more passion.

There are advantages for both the strong and the weak writer in this process. While the struggling writer gets an opportunity to hear drafts and figure out a writing strategy, the strong writer gets feedback: What worked? Was there a spot where listeners got confused? In reading their papers aloud, writers often notice the places where the language limps and needs tightening. They notice repetitions that need to be deleted.

The Town Square

The read-around is also the place we share our lives. As students listen to each other's poems they try to feel what it's like to be in someone else's skin. Jessica Rawlins wrote:

> Never before have I sat in a circle and expressed my opinion about rape, internment, and injustice with my peers and listened while they agreed or disagreed. Never has the teacher said, 'I didn't know that. . . . Tell me how you feel.' Talking about our lives was a rare treat in most classes and it only happened on holidays and special free days. In here it was part of the lesson. We educated each other through our writing. We brought the beauty out of our skin and onto plain paper.

While the read-around provides the writing text and it helps us share crucial stories from our lives, it can also miss some important teachable moments. For this reason, Bill Bigelow and I developed what we called the "collective text," so we could step back from the writing and figure out what our individual poems/stories said about ourselves and our society (see p. 87).

For example, when students in my junior class at Grant High School wrote their "Raised by Women" poems, we stepped back and examined the poetry for common threads. I said, "Look back over your notes from our read-around. What do the poems have in common? What can we learn about our class from listening to these poems? Write a paragraph about what you learned." Students discovered that most of them were raised by their mothers, that their fathers were absent.

We don't write a collective text after every poem, but when we do, the poems help students understand some fundamental truths about contemporary society.

Creating a Safe Space for Sharing

Some students love to share their writing. Reading aloud in class is a conversation, gossip session, a chance to socialize in a teacher-approved way. Unfortunately, too many students arrive with bruises from the red pen, so when we begin the year, it's necessary to build their confidence:

1. I seat the students in a circle—or the nearest approximation. This way they can see each other and be seen as they read. The attention is focused on the reader.

2. I distribute as many blank strips of papers as there are students in the class. I ask students to write a compliment to each classmate as s/he reads, again we focus on the positive and the specific.

3. I ask students to write each reader's name on the paper. So if Vonda volunteers to read her paper first, everyone in the class writes Vonda's name on their strip. (This is also a way for students to learn their classmates' names.)

4. I tell students they must respond with a positive comment to each writer. I emphasize that when they listen and "steal" what works in their classmates' writing, they will improve their own. I write a list of ways to respond on the board:

Respond to the writer's style of writing. What do you like about how the piece was written? Do you like the rhyme? The repeating lines? The humor? (Later, these points can change, particularly if I am focusing on a specific skill—verbs, lists, repeating lines, etc.)

Respond to the writer's content. What did the writer say that you liked? Did you like the way Ayanna used a story about her mother to point out how gender roles have changed?

Respond by sharing a memory that surfaced for you. Did you have a similar experience? Did this remind you of something from your life?

As the writer reads, write down lines, ideas, words, or phrases that you like. Remember: You must compliment the writer.

5. As students write each compliment, I tell them to sign their slips so the writer knows who praised them.

6. I ask for a few volunteers to share their praise with the writer. This is slow at first, so I also model it. This is an opportunity to teach the craft of writing poetry.

7. I tell students to look at the writer and give that person the compliment. Usually, students look at me as they talk about what they liked about their classmate's piece. I tell the writer to call on students who have raised their hands. I establish early on that all dialogue in the class does not funnel through the teacher.

8. After everyone has read, I ask students to hand out their compliment strips to each other. (This is usually chaotic, but it's another way for students to identify who's who in the class and to connect with each other.)

9. After the first few read-arounds, I drop the strips of paper and rely on oral feedback. But I find that some classes need to take notes for the collective

text as a way of keeping on task—so they don't write love letters or complete a math assignment during the read-around.

When It Doesn't Work

Some classes move into read-arounds like my black Lab to water. Others are more reluctant. There are awkward silences after I say, "What do you like about that piece?" Sometimes students come in carrying past histories with each other that make them fearful about sharing. One year Bill and I taught a very difficult class. They not only had a history; they had a present. A few students made fun of classmates and held us all hostages to their anger. We read more pieces anonymously that year. We brought in graduates from previous years to model appropriate behavior. Bill and I sat

We focus on the positive and the specific.

next to the troublemakers and attempted to "control" their negative comments by placing our bodies in their path.

Classes usually warm up during the first quarter. The strategy takes time, persistence, and energy, but it's worth it. As Jenni Brock wrote in her class evaluation, "The read-arounds are totally awesome stud vicious. They really helped the class to become closer. They teach us so much about each other." And I would add—about writing. ✳

. . . .

Linda Christensen (lmc@lclark.edu) is director of the Oregon Writing Project at Lewis & Clark College in Portland, Ore. She is a Rethinking Schools editor and author of Reading, Writing, and Rising Up *and* Teaching for Joy and Justice.

An Autobiographical Resource List

BY LINDA CHRISTENSEN

Let me begin by admitting, I am not a poetry expert. I can say truthfully that my greatest assets are my willingness to seek out poetry, literature, and history that will engage students and my willingness to fail in little and big ways in that endeavor. So this is not an exhaustive list of the great poets and great anthologies all teachers must buy and use. Instead, it is a list of some poets who inspired my students and who I believe will inspire other students. In this afterword, I offer some thoughts on poetry resources I've found helpful in shaping my curriculum.

Books

It is impossible to recommend all of the great poetry books on my shelf, so I will begin with a few from contributors to this book.

I first heard Patricia Smith when she kicked off a National Coalition of Education Activists conference with "The Undertaker," a poem from her book *Close to Death*. I wept by the end of the poem. Smith wrote from the persona of an undertaker, discussing the death of a young Black man. Smith's poetry—whether she's writing about her mother, her father, Hurricane Katrina, a skinhead—is visceral. She leaves chisel marks on the reader/listener, imprinting pain and laughter, marking us with every one of her poems. When I'm starting a new unit, I pore through her books for poems to include: *Blood Dazzler*; *Teahouse of the Almighty*; *Life According to Motown*; *Big Towns, Big Talk*; and her newest book, *Shoulda Been Jimi Savannah*. Smith is the master of persona poetry. When the Oregon Writing Project hosted the National Writing Project's Urban Sites conference, we invited Patricia to give the keynote. The article "Keepers of the Second Throat," included in this book, is from that keynote so powerful that the hotel bartender stopped serving wine, the waiters and waitresses folded their arms and trays and leaned against the walls, and the teachers in the room grew still.

William Stafford had a profound effect on my teaching, both through his poetry and his stance as a teacher. *Ask Me: 100 Essential Poems of William Stafford*, edited by his son Kim, is an essential part of any classroom. Stafford was a conscientious objector during WWII, a lifelong pacifist, and an interpreter of the daily moral choices we face. As a teacher, he led by listening intently to his students, teaching me to step back and make room for the students to share.

I found George Ella Lyon's "Where I'm From" in a book I bought at my first poetry slam: *The United States of Poetry*. The book is a feast for poetry teachers. In addition to Lyon's poem, it includes Ruth Forman's "Stoplight Politics," Amiri Baraka's "The X Is Black," Leonard Cohen's "Democracy," and Wanda Coleman's "Poem," about the politics of money. This is a book as well as a DVD set of the poets reciting their poems. Their website speaks truth: "Here, the disparate and unheard languages of our country—pidgin, Spanish, hip-hop, Creole, Tagalog, and American Sign Language—speak out for themselves, weave together the accents and dialects of our nation."

Kelly Norman Ellis' "Raised by Women" is published in her book *Tougaloo Blues*, but I first encountered her work in a wonderful video called *Coal Black Voices*. The poems in *Coal Black Voices* evoke delicious details from students' lives and a rhythm so alive, I want to dance when I hear them; it's a valuable educational resource for engaging students in African American experience and literary traditions. *Coal Black Voices* shares images, poetry, and storytelling by Affrilachian poets Kelly Norman Ellis, Frank X Walker, Nikky Finney, and several others. The poets draw on traditions such as the Harlem Renaissance, the Black Arts Movement, and experiences of the African Diaspora. The poetry of the Affrilachian poets celebrates their African heritage and rural roots while encompassing themes of racism and Black identity. In this documentary, they give voice to the pleasures of family, land, good food, artistic community, music, and transformation.

Sandra Cisneros called Martín Espada "the Pablo Neruda of North American authors." I first met Espada in the pages of *The Progressive* magazine, where he is a frequent contributor. I read his letter to Nike refusing to write a poem for a Nike ad because of its exploitative labor practices. Then I bought as many of his books as I could find. I love the anthology he edited, **Poetry Like Bread: Poets of the Political Imagination**. In fact, when I was a literacy leader for Portland Public Schools, I purchased copies of the book for every high school library. His poems "Jorge the Church Janitor Finally Quits" and "Federico's Ghost" are both housed in this anthology. The book features other political poets like Devorah Major, Luis Rodriguez, Margaret Randall, and Jimmy Santiago Baca. Many of the poems are printed in both English and Spanish. His other books, **Imagine the Angels of Bread**, **The Republic of Poetry**, **Rebellion Is the Circle of a Lover's Hands**, **A Mayan Astronomer in Hell's Kitchen**, and **City of the Coughing and Dead Radiators** are frequent visitors to my classroom. "The Poetics of Commerce: The Nike Poetry Slam" can be found in **Zapata's Disciple**, Espada's book of essays.

The indispensable anthology **In Search of Color Everywhere**, edited by E. Ethelbert Miller, hosts Margaret Walker's poem "For My People." I have had to buy and replace this collection often because it is so popular with teachers and students. It includes poetry from the Harlem Renaissance as well as contemporary poets—from James Weldon Johnson to Kevin Young and Rita Dove to Lucille Clifton. I love the way the chapters are arranged by themes, like "Freedom," "Celebration of Blackness," "Love," "Family Gatherings," "Healing," and "Rituals: Music, Dance, and Sports." I used pieces of this anthology in my Harlem Renaissance unit, to help frame August Wilson's play *Fences*, during my praise poem and ode units, as well as the verb craft lesson that features Quincy Troupe's "A Poem for Magic."

The Big Aiiieeeee!: An Anthology of Asian Writers is edited by Shawn Wong, Jeffery Paul Chan, Frank Chin, and Lawson Fusao Inada. Over the years, I have used many pieces from their collections in my Japa-nese American internment unit, immigration units, language units as well as my yearlong unit about being displaced from home. Inada's book **Legends from Camp** is one of our core texts when we study the internment. But I also teach his poem "Rayford's Song" when we examine the hidden curriculum in education.

Yusef Komunyakaa's **Dien Cai Dau**, a book of poetry about his experiences as a journalist in Vietnam, helped students grapple with the human impact of the war. When I taught Tim O'Brien's novel *The Things They Carried*, Komunyakaa's book became a companion text. **Of Quiet Courage** is an anthology of poems from Vietnam, whose poetry invites students to see the war from the standpoint of the Vietnamese.

I use Elizabeth Woody's poetry during both my exploration of Native American literature and history and as models in my Writing for Publication class. Her books **Hand into Stone** and **Seven Hands, Seven Hearts** are treasures, calling up Celilo Falls and the struggle of Indigenous people in the Northwest, past and ongoing.

Teachers & Writers Collaborative is a wonderful resource for books about writing. Located in New York City, TWC provides workshops as well as books and a magazine. One of my favorite anthologies is **Luna, Luna: Creative Writing Ideas from Spanish, Latin American, & Latino Literature**, edited by Julio Marzán. The literary models are drawn from both Spain and the Americas, and range from such early 20th-century masters like Federico García Lorca and Pablo Neruda to contemporary writers like Sandra Cisneros. Among the distinguished contributors are Julia Alvarez, Martín Espada, and Naomi Shihab Nye. I also enjoyed **Sing the Sun Up: Creative Writing Ideas from African American Literature**. Among the authors discussed are James Baldwin, Gwendolyn Brooks, Countee Cullen, Rita Dove, Zora Neale Hurston, and Jean Toomer.

Marge Piercy has been a steady, significant influence on my own poetry as well as the poetry of my students. Her **Early Ripening: American Women's Poetry Now** anthology is a who's who of women poets: Wendy Rose, Adrienne Rich, Sharon Olds, May Sarton, May Swenson, Nellie Wong, Diane Wakoski, and many more. Piercy's book **My Mother's Body** has nourished and comforted and inspired my work as both a teacher and a poet.

Wendy Rose's poetry has been a mainstay in my Literature and U.S. History as well as my Writing for

Publication class. Her book *The Halfbreed Chronicles and Other Poems* is filled with poetic gems that raise up both historical and contemporary issues in the Native community. I use her poem "Loo-Wit," the name the Cowlitz people called Mount St. Helens, during my naming unit. I also teach her poem "Truganinny," about the indignities of stuffing and mounting Indigenous people and placing them in museums as artifacts.

Two of my favorite and most often referred to books of poetry are *The Collected Poems of Lucille Clifton 1965-2010* and *The Collected Poems of Langston Hughes*. Clifton and Hughes have a poem to match any curriculum unit—love, war, family, union work. They are constant companions in my teaching.

Copper Canyon Press is a nonprofit publisher dedicated to poetry. I love getting their catalogue, which features a new poet, seducing me to buy my next book. Most recently, I purchased *When My Brother Was an Aztec*, by Natalie Diaz. Her poetry is a searing portrayal of a sister struggling with her brother's meth addiction; her imagery illuminates a world set against tribal life: "Tonight the city is glimmered./What's left of an August monsoon/is heat and wet. Beyond the open window,/the streetlamp is a honey-skirted hive I could split/with my hand, my palm a pool of light."

As every teacher knows, our curriculum is more than poetry. Our lessons on poetry link the larger world. For that reason, I want to highlight the Rethinking Schools books that align with the vision of curriculum we have articulated in this book: *A People's Curriculum for the Earth*, *The Line Between Us: Teaching About the Border and Mexican Immigration*, *Rethinking Columbus*, *A People's History for the Classroom*, *Rethinking Popular Culture and Media*, *Rethinking Multicultural Education*, and *Teaching About the Wars*. And, at the risk of sounding like an advertisement, my two books *Reading, Writing, and Rising Up* and *Teaching for Joy and Justice* show how to blend poetry, story, and personal narrative with social analysis; and how to ground this work in the power of students' own lives. The **Zinn Education Project** website offers in-depth background lessons organized by historical periods and themes, providing the historical background too often left out of textbooks.

From the Inside Out: Letters to Young Men and Other Writings—Poetry and Prose from Prison is a stunning anthology recording life inside of prison. As Mike Rose wrote, "These men write to make amends and maintain connection, to pass on lessons learned, to bear witness to a new life." I pull this slender volume out to share with students who need it, but the letters also pair up with Daniel Beaty's poem "Knock Knock."

This Same Sky: A Collection of Poems from Around the World was compiled by the poet Naomi Shihab Nye. The anthology is organized by themes and brings poets from Norway, Uruguay, Palestine, Kuwait, El Salvador, and more into the classroom. I consider it a passport to primary source documents of poets across the globe.

Books on the Craft of Teaching Poetry

We reference Adrienne Rich's *What Is Found There: Notebooks on Poetry and Politics* throughout our book. Rich blends social commentary and analysis with craft lessons on poetry. Although I don't use her books in class, they fill me with insights and understandings that I bring to the classroom.

The Poet's Companion: A Guide to the Pleasures of Writing Poetry by Kim Addonizio and Dorianne Laux was my own constant companion when I was a fledgling poet. They offer great writing strategies for upcoming poets.

Poets on Poetry is a series of 111 titles published by University of Michigan Press. I have not read them all, but two of William Stafford's books in the series have perched by my bed for many years since I first devoured them in 1980 at the Oregon Writing Project: *Writing the Australian Crawl: Views on the Writer's Vocation* and *You Must Revise Your Life*. I also read and learned from Marvin Bell's *Old Snow Just Melting* and Tess Gallagher's *A Concert of Tenses: Essays on Poetry*. If you want to immerse yourself in the craft of poetry, I highly recommend this series.

'Def Poetry Jam'

One New Year's Eve, Bill Bigelow, my husband, and I came across *Def Poetry Jam*. We binge-watched for hours that night. On that stage I first heard Suheir Hammad, Daniel Beaty's great "Knock Knock," Paul Flores' "Brown Dreams," and Amalia Ortiz's "Women of Juárez." Later I bought my first DVD of the program. Over the years, I acquired—and used—all six in my classroom. This amazing program brings poetry to its feet, mixing new poets with poetic giants, like Amiri Baraka, Nikki Giovani, Quincy Troupe, and Sonia Sanchez.

Poetry Websites

Although I love to browse the poetry section at Powell's to find new poets and new anthologies, I have found the following websites to be important resources.

www.poetry.about.com
This site contains news articles, poems, books reviews, links to contemporary and classical poems, poetry writing, publishing, bios, interviews, and multilingual poems. This is the website for poets and valuable for teacher/poets, too.

www.pbs.org/wnet/foolingwithwords/index.html
This is the "Fooling with Words" website with Bill Moyers. It contains poetry by Lucille Clifton, Sharon Olds, Marge Piercy, Paul Muldoon, Kurtis Lamkin, and more. There are videos of the poets reciting their poems and lesson plans to go with the poetry. An excellent site.

www.writersalmanac.org
The Writer's Almanac, a daily program of poetry and history hosted by Garrison Keillor, can be heard each day on public radio stations throughout the country. This site has archives of the poems from 2001.

www.poets.org
The Academy of American Poets posts a collection of more than 500 poet biographies, 1,400 poems, and 100 audio clips. Through its informative and entertaining daily entries, the National Poetry Almanac provides a starting place to learn more about poetry. The website can be browsed by poems; forms, like blues or epistle; areas of life, like war or work; and "schools and movements," like the beat poets or the Harlem Renaissance. Each takes you to a biographical page as well as to selected poems.

www.poems.com
This site features a poet a day and has archives of great poets and their poems. It also features a book a day. It's a wonderful way to start one's day.

www.loc.gov/poetry/180
This is Billy Collins' poem a day website for high school students. It has a list of fine poets and poems. I use a number of poems from this site.

voices.cla.umn.edu/
This is a website devoted to women writers of color. It has biographies and reviews of each author's books—a great resource. The site can be searched by keywords that connect you to these women writers. The downside is that there aren't poems.

www.favoritepoem.org
Robert Pinsky's Favorite Poem Project includes lesson plans and videos of poems being read. The project celebrates documenting and encouraging poetry's role in Americans' lives. Robert Pinsky, the 39th poet laureate of the United States, founded the Favorite Poem Project shortly after the Library of Congress appointed him to the post in 1997.

A poetry curriculum that prompts students to celebrate their lives, question the world, and create poems about the big and small ways that people have been marginalized needs both imagination and community. At a time when those in authority want to slice student voice from the curriculum, those of us in the classroom need to wed our classroom scholarship with social action, taking courage from poets like Martín Espada, Adrienne Rich, Paul Flores, Patricia Smith, and others who have harnessed their poetic imagination with defiant hope. ✳

....

Linda Christensen (lmc@lclark.edu) is director of the Oregon Writing Project at Lewis & Clark College in Portland, Ore. She is a Rethinking Schools editor and author of Reading, Writing, and Rising Up *and* Teaching for Joy and Justice.

About the Editors

Linda Christensen taught high school language arts and worked as a language arts curriculum specialist for almost 40 years. She is currently the director of the Oregon Writing Project at Lewis & Clark College. She is the author of *Teaching for Joy & Justice: Re-Imagining the Language Arts Classroom* and *Reading, Writing, and Rising Up: Teaching About Social Justice and the Power of the Written Word*, and co-editor of *Rethinking School Reform: Views from the Classroom*, *The New Teacher Book: Finding Purpose, Balance and Hope During Your First Years in the Classroom*, and *Rethinking Elementary Education*. She lives in Portland with her husband, Bill Bigelow.

Dyan Watson is an assistant professor of education at the Lewis & Clark Graduate School of Education, and an editor for Rethinking Schools. She is the author of "Letter from a Black Mom to her Son," "What Do You Mean When You Say Urban?" "'Urban, but Not Too Urban': Unpacking Teachers' Desires to Teach Urban Students," and "Norming Suburban: How Teachers Talk About Race Without Using Race Words." Watson studies how teachers semantically encode race and how race intersects with teaching. Previously, she was a high school social studies teacher. She lives in Portland with her sons Caleb and Nehemiah.

Index

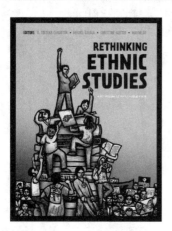
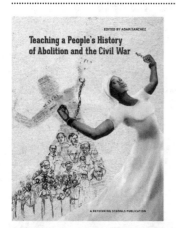

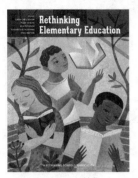
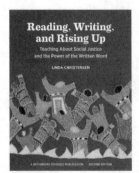

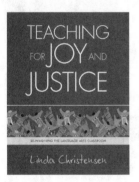

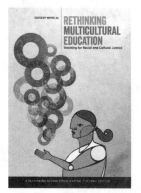

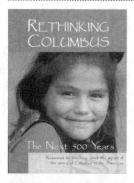

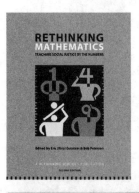